December 2018

The Bridegroom from Baghdad

To my dear, loved Anna,

With so much love & fond memories of our walks, talks, & laughter!

With much love,

Shan

# The Bridegroom from Baghdad

∾

## Shar Mitchell

ONE VOICE PRESS · ESSEX, MARYLAND

Published by One Voice Press, LLC
Essex, Maryland
www.onevoicepress.com

ISBN: 978-1-940135-82-3
ISBN epub: 978-1-940135-83-0
ISBN Kindle: 978-1-940135-84-7

First Edition: October 2018
10 9 8 7 6 5 4 3 2 1

In loving tribute to my beloved husband, Redwan (Ridvan) Moqbel and our long-suffering family in Iraq.

*"Lord, make firm their feet on Thy straight path, make wide for them the needle's eye, and cause them, dressed in royal robes, to walk in glory for ever and ever."[1]* —'Abdu'l-Bahá

1     'Abdu'l-Bahá, Bahá'í Prayers (Wilmette, Illinois: Bahá'í Publishing Trust, 1991), 268.

# Table of Contents

# Prologue

*I'm going to tell you a story I once heard, I couldn't tell you where or when, about the kindness and compassion of a man who encounters a robber. That story moved me deeply and ultimately led me to meet and marry that man's son – my bridegroom from Baghdad.* —Shar Mitchell

## —Vessal Lane off Moniriye Street, Tehran, Iran 1931

Kaykhosrow Moqbel, 26, yawns and lays down his book. For a moment he closes his eyes and stretches before rising. He pads to the bathroom in well-worn slippers, the backs folded under his heels. He studies his eyes intently in the mirror as he washes his hands and then slowly washes his face. He drags a comb through his straight black hair.

His ablutions thus performed, Kaykhosrow enters his bedroom, crosses over to a cupboard in the far corner and picks up a folded bundle of crimson material from a shelf. He runs his well-shaped fingers thoughtfully across the slippery fabric. He smiles wistfully at this tangible reminder of his late mother's love. Then he lays the cherry coloured prayer mat, with burgeoning yellow and orange flowering vines winding their leafy way around its borders, carefully on the floor. He frowns at the sight of two sections his knees have worn beyond repair.

Seated cross-legged on the mat, Kaykhosrow straightens his broad shoulders. He picks up a notebook and chants several handwritten prayers in Arabic and Persian. Then he sets the book aside and chants healing prayers for his three-year-old nephew, Farahmand. The house feels empty without him. Earlier that day, Kaykhosrow's older brother, Faraydoon, and his wife, left for the mountains of Davamand north of Tehran in the hope that Farahmand

9

would more readily recover from whooping cough there. *Poor little guy* thinks Kaykhosrow.

Then he rises, folds his prayer rug and returns it to its place. He changes into pale blue and white striped pajamas. As he settles his lengthy frame on his bed he sighs. *All I want from life is to be of service to others,* he thinks. He reflects on his day in search of moments when he might have fallen short, but drops into a deep sleep before completing his inventory.

Soon after midnight, a noise disturbs Kaykhosrow's sleep. His eyes fly open as a sudden current of terror shoots through his frame setting every hair on his body on end. He sits bolt upright and strains to listen. A distinct clink of glass from down the hall causes his heart to pound in his ears. *Calm down; breathe slowly,* he tells himself. Without a sound, he creeps out of bed, rifles around on a chair for his trousers and pulls them on over his pajamas. Then, barefoot, he creeps silently down the hall. When he reaches the living room he stands absolutely still. Directly in front of him a burly man is bent over a large tablecloth spread on the floor and is placing a crystal vase alongside other valuables. With his back to Kaykhosrow, the robber rises from his squat, walks over to a large wooden cabinet, opens it, and continues to forage.

Ever so quietly, Kaykhosrow enters the room, picks up a bowl from a nearby table and places it on the cloth. Suddenly aware he is not alone, the burglar spins around and in a loud whisper says, "What are you doing? I got here first! Get out of here!"

"No, no, you don't understand," Kaykhosrow says, pointing to the laden tablecloth." "These are my things. I live here." Fear registers in the crook's eyes. He makes ready to bolt.

"No, no, don't go!" Kaykhosrow cries stretching his arms to block the doorway. "Take whatever you want. I'm not concerned about these things; I'm more concerned about you. You must need them badly to have resorted to stealing."

The crook's chin begins to quiver. "Honestly sir, I'm not a thief," he stammers. "It's just that I've fallen on hard times and I'm desperate. I'm so sorry."

"It's alright, but it makes me sad to see you in this state. Believe me, this is no way to solve your problems." The would-be robber hangs his head in shame.

"Look," Kaykhosrow says, "it's late. I'm tired and you must be too. If what you say is true, why don't you sleep on this couch and I'll sleep on the other. In the morning we'll talk. Maybe I can help you sort out your difficulties." Speechless, the burglar merely nods in agreement as he looks over at the couch he's just been assigned. With that, Kaykhosrow lies down and immediately falls asleep.

Dumbfounded by the response from his victim, and now host, the robber stares at the ceiling for a long time. *I could have been a murderer*, he thinks.

∽

At 5:30 the next morning Kaykhosrow quietly slips off to a nearby market. He is careful not to disturb his guest who is fast asleep, one arm resting across his eyes. Despite Kaykhosrow's fears that the man may have fled by the time he returns from the market, Kaykhosrow is delighted to find him sitting on the couch, a sheepish expression on his face.

Kaykhosrow greets him warmly. Over a breakfast of sweet tea, flatbread, cheese and fresh apricot jam they discuss the man's difficulties. After his last sip of tea Kaykhosrow turns and retrieves another package he brought from the market. "Here," he says as he hands a parcel to the man.

"What's this?" the man asks wide-eyed.

"What do you think about selling these vegetables at the market?" Kaykhosrow asks. "There's a small cart outside you can use to display them if you like. With the money you earn today you'll be able to buy more vegetables to sell tomorrow. If you're honest and provide good quality products over time your business will grow."

"But how can I accept these things when you've already given me so much?" the man asks shaking his head in disbelief.

"You can pay me back gradually when you've earned enough money to meet your family's needs," says Kaykhosrow. "I'm not concerned how long it takes. I just want to see you on your feet and beginning to reap the rewards of honest work."

"Thank you," the man stammers as he prepares to leave.

"Please drop by my shop and let me know how you're doing. It's called *The International*. Do you know it?" The man nods.

With that Kaykhosrow escorts his guest outside and bids him farewell. Once back inside he leans against the closed door. A slow smile appears on his face.

Each day on his way home from work, for as long as Kaykhosrow remains in Tehran, the would-be burglar visits his shop.

"Hey boss," he calls as he enters the store grinning, "I'm here."

Profoundly aware that Kaykhosrow's courage and love transformed him, the man begins to prod Kaykhosrow for the source of his beliefs. Eventually, he adopts them as his own. His business prospers and until his dying day he never stops singing Kaykhosrow's praises.[2]

### —Central Train Station, Tehran, Iran 1943

A crowd of about 150 people gather around Kaykhosrow at the train station platform. By far the majority are youth from his well-established Friday Bahá'í youth classes. Many appear sad. One seems heart-broken.

Kaykhosrow's brother, Faraydoon and Faraydoon's son, Farahmand, now a teenager, stand back from the crowd waiting their turn to bid Kaykhosrow farewell.

"See that man over there crying and hugging your uncle?" Faraydoon asks. Farahmand surveys the crowd and easily picks out the weeping man.

"I see him," Farahmand responds.

"That's the robber," his father replies.

---

2        Redwan first learned of this story from an "In Memoriam" written by his father's close friend, A.Q. Faizi, published in *Bahá'í World*, vol. 15, 1968-1973, p. 445.

# Into the Fire

Twenty-four-year old Redwan Moqbel sits in an airport waiting room. He is staring at a wall, a magazine open on his lap. He reflects over the past year, a year that though challenging in many unexpected ways, has been the best year of his life. Now, with his Master's Degree in Medical Parasitology from the London School of Hygiene and Tropical Medicine completed, and the promise of a full scholarship to do his PhD in the Department of Helminthology, he couldn't be more pleased.

The bonus of returning to Iraq to attend his sister Sharaf's wedding is that he can tell his mother in person about his bright future and his new girlfriend, Ann Macleod. He is excited to let his mother know that she'll no longer have to sacrifice her meagre pension for his stipend. She'll be thrilled to learn that he is going to become a doctor, albeit a medical research doctor and not a physician as he'd hoped. He shudders as he relives the moment when a fellow student threatened him with a switchblade during his university entrance exams. That incident botched any chance of getting into medical school. His reverie is interrupted by the boarding call for his Iraqi Airways flight to Baghdad.

Once in the air, a flood of memories from life inside Iraq's repressive regime engulf him. Although Iraq was more secular than religious, the government demanded its citizens pledge allegiance to the Ba'ath Party. Redwan found himself on the wrong side of the law. The teachings of his religion, the Bahá'í Faith, eschew party politics because of their divisive nature. Regret and foreboding about his decision to return to Iraq wash over him. He tries to console himself imagining the wonderful time he'll spend with his family

13

before returning to England to settle into life as an expat. When he disembarks at Baghdad International Airport he can't help but recall the five bloody coups d'état he'd witnessed since 1958.

Redwan allows himself to enjoy life in the embrace of his loving family who are delighted to see him. In no time he is absorbed in the wedding preparations but the day before the wedding he can no longer bear the anxiety of delaying the steps he must take to ensure his departure. He sets out for the Ministry of Higher Education to have his University of London admission documents certified so he can leave Iraq in two weeks. He assumes it will be a straightforward task.

Inside the Ministry, he hands over his passport and watches the clerk flip through it. "Where's your Security clearance stamp from when you left in 1971? I don't see it."

"I don't think I had one."

"What? You can't leave the country without one. That's illegal!"

"I didn't know," Redwan exclaims, "What am I supposed to do now?"

"You'll have to go to the passport office to get an application to submit to the Security Police for a permit to leave."

Redwan sets off immediately for the passport office aware of the potentially devastating consequences that may await him. En route, he passes the Bahá'í National headquarters confiscated two years earlier by the Iraqi government after its crackdown on the Bahá'í Faith. *How odd that those two buildings should be so close together*, he thinks.

Redwan joins a line up at the passport office. Eventually a clerk dispatches him to the Security Police Office to retrieve his file. He obtains it easily but is shocked by its size. *I'm only 24. How could my file be so big?* he wonders. A hand-written note stapled to a corner of the folder reads, "Sir, should this person be allowed to travel outside Iraq since he is a Bahá'í?"

Though tempted, Redwan can't bring himself to rip off the note and thereby commit a criminal offence. He dutifully returns to the passport office where he hands his file to the same clerk who sent him to fetch it.

"You'll have to go back to the Security Police Office again and get your passport verified and obtain the requisite exit stamp," the clerk says.

"But I'm a Bahá'í!" Redwan blurts out. "Will that interfere with getting a visa?"

"Probably," the clerk replies nonchalantly.

The next day Redwan's mother, Hajer, conscious of her son's anxiety, puts him to work on wedding preparations. That night, dressed in a brown and yellow plaid shirt and grey suit, and trying to bury his feelings, Redwan greets the fifty to sixty guests, mostly relatives, that begin to arrive. After the guests have settled in the packed living room, the happy couple, Sharaf and Aqeel enter. On cue, Redwan starts up the record player and plays Cliff Richard's hit song, "Congratulations." He had brought it with him from England for the occasion. In a simple ceremony the couple exchange the Bahá'í wedding vow, "We will all, verily, abide by the Will of God." Then, coin by coin, Aqeel places Sharaf's dowry, today's equivalent of nine dollars, into her hands in a symbolic gesture of respect. Afterwards the wedding party dines on "bo'ragg," bread stuffed with meat. Later, Sharaf and Aqeel depart by train for their honeymoon in Mosul in northern Iraq.

The following day, Redwan, file in hand, incriminating note still attached, reluctantly returns to the Security Police Office. As he waits in line he rehearses his plea, then hands the file to the officer. "I must get permission to return to England to finish my education," he says. "I've been accepted into a PhD program with a full scholarship and I'm committed to being there."

The officer ignores Redwan as he thumbs through his file. Finally he looks up, a deadpan expression on his face. "Well," he says, "I'm afraid that'll be impossible."

"Impossible?" Redwan cries. "Why? What have I done? I was studying there last year and I worked hard and did well. And I came back. I want to get my PhD to better equip me to serve my country. Why can't I return there?"

"Look, you might have been there last year, but you shouldn't have been! Looks like you left illegally. Now you'd better accept that you aren't going anywhere, especially England. Now move along."

Speechless, Redwan stares as the man turns away from him and slams the window wicket in his face. Redwan stumbles out the door, his hopes dashed.

∽

Over the next two weeks, despite consuming anxiety and a sense of impending doom, Redwan visits with friends and shares stories about his experiences in the UK and mainland Europe. At home, he paces in the front garden praying silently for a door to open by which he can squeeze out of Iraq. He has already refused to join the Ba'ath Party and is terrified he might "disappear," be imprisoned, or barred from employment. Sensing worsening conditions for Bahá'ís in Iraq, Hajer insists Redwan leave by any means. Their discussions focus almost entirely on his escape.

Redwan's despair continues to deepen until his brother Sarmad's best friend makes an astonishing offer: his uncle works at Security Police Headquarters and is willing to try to retrieve Redwan's passport and obtain the required stamp. This man understands that, as a Bahá'í, Redwan is a victim of religious persecution. But his offer comes with a condition: should he succeed in his mission, Redwan must leave Iraq within 24 hours. There's another catch: Redwan can't purchase a plane ticket without a valid passport.

For the ten days, Redwan remains entirely preoccupied. He tries to will the phone to ring. Finally, the call comes; mission accomplished. Sarmad immediately sets off to retrieve his brother's passport and then to drive Redwan to Lufthansa Airlines ticket office. (Redwan had already ruled out Iraqi Airways for fear it would increase his chances of getting caught.) Much to his relief, he secures one of the last seats on a flight leaving for London via Vienna and Frankfurt the next morning at 7 a.m. His spirits soar as he allows himself to imagine returning to England.

∽

## —Baghdad, November 30, 1972

In a darkened bedroom, lit only by a reading lamp, Redwan, brow furrowed in concentration, bends over an open suitcase and meticulously folds and stacks his clothes in the weathered case. Hajer watches in silence.

Redwan looks up as Sarmad enters the room and playfully attempts to punch Redwan on the shoulder. "Hey! Wait a minute you little brat!" Redwan cries. "I'll teach you to…"

Hajer breaks in sternly, "Hush, keep it down and stay away from the windows, Sarmad! And don't turn that light on!"

"Okay, okay, I'm almost finished," Redwan says to his mom.

"Where's the document?" she asks.

Redwan points to the centre of his case to a neat pile of folded cotton dress shirts. "Here in the middle. It will protect me."

His mother nods silently, "Inshah Allah," she says quietly. "Now get some sleep. We have to leave for the airport at 4:30. Your sister and Aqeel will be up soon to make our breakfast."

"The last meal," offers Sarmad as he pats his brother on the back.

Hajer tenderly places her arms on Redwan's shoulders, pulls him into a hug and then kisses his eyelids as was her habit with her children whenever she caught sight of the first sliver of the new moon. Teary-eyed, she turns and leaves the room. She knows she may never see her son again.

Outside Baghdad International Airport, Sarmad pulls the car up to the curb and parks. Redwan climbs out of the back. Sharaf follows. She places her hand on his shoulder. He turns around with an inquiring look and puts his arms around her.

"I know I'm not going to see you for a long time, Redwan, and I don't like that." Tears stream down her face as she hugs him.

"Don't cry, Sharaf, it probably won't be that long," Redwan offers without conviction.

"Maybe the longer the better," Sarmad jokes before adding, "Just kidding."

Redwan smiles and shakes his head at his brother, "Guess you were just born to be a pest." Hajer smiles at her sons. Redwan places his arm around her shoulders as they walk towards the airport.

Once they locate the check-in counter Redwan says, "I think it best if you go now. I'd better do this alone." The family nod in agreement. Redwan whispers into Sarmad's ear as he hugs him, "Take care of Mom."

Sarmad's eyes tear up. "I promise." Sarmad collects himself and adds mockingly, "And you have fun studying worms!"

Redwan turns to shake hands with Aqeel who pulls him into an embrace. "You know I'll do whatever I can to support your mom and brother and, of course, Sharaf."

"I know you will and I'm so grateful."

Sharaf, still teary eyed says, "I'll miss you so much, and so will we all, but don't worry about us. We're strong." Redwan nods in agreement.

Hajer studies Redwan as if trying to engrave his face in her memory. "Redwan, I want you to promise me that you'll always do the right thing."

"I promise, Mom."

Mother and son embrace. Redwan watches his family pass through the exit doors. Then he turns around and slowly makes his way to the check-in counter. He feels his heart quicken and his stomach cramp. Checking in goes off without a hitch but, as he heads towards the security counter, he is overcome with nervousness. He discreetly drags his sweaty palms down his pant legs and instructs himself to breathe in and breathe out.

"Next," shouts the officer behind the counter as he stretches out his hand for Redwan's passport. The officer studies it carefully. "There's something familiar about your name," he comments.

Redwan's stomach sinks as the officer's gaze settles on him. "Thank you," is all he can think to say. Inwardly he is dying. *Oh, please, please God, let me out of this country. I'll do anything to get out of here. I need to return to England. I should never have come back for Sharaf's wedding. I made a huge mistake. Please help me out of this country.* But he stands there, breathing in and out and trying to look calm and nonchalant.

The officer turns to his desk and picks up a document with what appears to be an extensive list of names. He studies it intently. "Well," he says finally, shaking his head, "I must be mistaken." He hands Redwan his passport. "Take your suitcase over there for inspection," he says, pointing to another line-up.

When it is his turn, Redwan hoists his suitcase onto the counter and pops open the locks. The inspecting officer regards the contents with obvious surprise and whistles under his breath. "Wow! Do you always pack so neatly?"

Redwan giggles nervously and prays silently. *Oh God, please don't let him find that document. If they discover I'm taking information about the persecution of the Bahá'ís out of the country they'll kill me for sure and maybe the rest of the Bahá'ís too.*

The officer picks up the pile of clothing on the left side of his case and places it gently on the counter top, still clucking in amazement at Redwan's packing job. He gingerly thumbs through it, taking pains not to disturb its perfection, and replaces the clothing in the suitcase. His hands hover momentarily over the middle section of clothes, where Redwan hid the document, as if undecided, and then settle on the pile on the right. The officer does a rapid and non-exhaustive investigation of those clothes. "Well, I guess that's it then," he says as he snaps the lid shut.

Redwan, shaken and still terrified that the first officer will find his name on the "no fly" list, tries to navigate his jelly-like legs to carry him down the long hallway to the transit lounge. Once there, he eases his body into the first available chair and tries to shrink into invisibility.

Minutes later, he cringes at the unmistakable sound of approaching military boots. A soldier rounds the corner and shouts out, "Redwan Moqbel! Is there a Redwan Moqbel here?"

Redwan manages to pull himself up out of the chair. "That's me," he stammers.

"Follow me!" commands the officer as he spins around and strides quickly back down the hall.

With resignation Redwan follows the soldier. *One glorious year in England and my life is over, he thinks. Kaput, done with. Why did I chance returning to*

*Iraq?* he wonders for the millionth time. He sees the Security Police sign ahead and braces for the customary slap across the face he associates with the first act of interrogation.

Near the office door, the soldier turns to Redwan and says quietly, "Your uncle and your cousin came to see you off. I didn't want to embarrass you by announcing that in the waiting room."

Incredulous, Redwan utters a quiet thank you. The soldier conducts him to the atrium where his Uncle Munir and cousin, Ikbal stand waiting. Their faces light up as they rush forward to greet him. "We brought you some candy, dear Redwan," Ikbal says tenderly as she presents him with a beautifully wrapped box. Noticeably shaken, Redwan falls into their embrace.

"When I see you next, Ikbal, you'll be a famous surgeon," he says with a smile.

"Not at all," she says blushing. "I'm so proud of you, Redwan."

"And your dad would have been too," Uncle Munir offers. "Take good care of yourself and remember to stay in close touch with your mom. She really missed you last year."

Afraid to utter a word least he totally break down, Redwan nods and chokes back his tears. He adores his cousin and his uncle Munir. His uncle had counseled him to choose a career path with the "noble goal" of being of benefit to humanity.

Redwan bows silently to his relatives, then backs up a few steps, smiles, waves and returns to the departure lounge. En route, he spots the soldier and hands him the candy. "This is for you, sir, a small thank you for your kindness."

Once seated in a window seat near the rear of the airplane Redwan studies the airport terminal, intently half expecting to see the first officer rushing towards the plane to apprehend him. After what feels like an eternity, the plane lifts off. For the first half hour in flight he continues to worry that the control tower will order the pilots to return to Baghdad. Gradually he relaxes and falls into a deep sleep.

Redwan wakes up with a start just as the plane is about to land. He looks out the window and is confused not to see Heathrow's familiar surroundings. Then he remembers the two-hour stopover in Vienna before another in Frankfurt.

Shaking off his slumber and unfolding his cramped body, Redwan follows the other passengers out of the plane and onto the runway. The moment his feet touch the ground armed soldiers close in around him.

"You!" one of them shouts. "Hand over your passport and ticket!"

"Why?" Redwan stammers. "I haven't done anything wrong!"

"Are you quite sure of that?" shouts another soldier, his menacing face inches from Redwan's.

Two of the men grab Redwan on each side and march him over the tarmac, into the airport, and down a dark hall where they frisk him, before shoving him into a small cubicle, and locking the door. Redwan sinks to the floor in a sweating, fretting mass. *The Iraqis instructed the Austrians to detain me,* he thinks.

Redwan's distress deepens further with each repeated departure announcement. He struggles not to cry. Just after the final boarding call he hears the sound of boots rushing towards him and braces for the next assault. The door opens abruptly. One of the men that initially pitched him into this room, thrusts Redwan's ticket and passport into his hands. "Here," he says, "You look like one of the Black September terrorists behind the Munich Massacre but you're not. Sorry about that. If you run you might still be able to catch your flight."

Redwan sprints off and just manages to make it to the gate before it closes. It is some time before his trembling stops. During the Frankfurt stopover he declines to de-board. Hours later, as the plane moves towards the brilliant pink and orange setting sun, Redwan catches sight of his beloved England and weeps with relief. Once through customs, he is delighted to see Ann Macleod waiting for him.

# *An Unlikely Seeker*

## —Stansted Airport, England, August 30, 1971

I can picture myself as a 22-year-old unfulfilled seeker about to return to Canada. Dressed in my handmade long purple and white printed caftan, I am climbing airplane stairs on the runway. My long layered light brown hair moves gently in the breeze. I pause on the top step and turn towards the sun for one long last moment.

*Wait!* I want to tell my younger self. *Stay in England for two more weeks. Someone who holds the key to your search is packing his bags in Baghdad at this very moment.* But alas, there is no voice to speak and no ear to hear. I disappear into the womb of the plane.

But I wasn't leaving Europe empty-handed. In the seven months since I'd set sail on the Italian ocean liner, Cristoforo Colombo, from New York, I'd travelled through North Africa and Europe and garnered inner riches to add to what I'd accumulated since the age of twelve when I began my search for truth.

Back then I was walking to my friend Beverly's house on Beaverbrook Street in Winnipeg. I'd left my backyard, crossed the lane behind Westworth United Church, rounded the corner and was heading west on Grosvenor Avenue.

The summer sun beat down on my tanned bare arms. Relaxed and content, my mind was a perfect blank of undisturbed peace. Suddenly an extraordinarily large thought barged in: *What would happen if Christ were to return? I slowed my pace to better contemplate that thought. Impatient excitement built inside me. Oh yes, I'd love to meet Him!* But, how would I recognize Him? What if He didn't look like the longhaired, ivory complexioned version of Him that

22

hung on the wall in the music room at Westworth United Church? Skepticism dampened my hopeful enthusiasm. After all, what were the chances that He would return while I was alive? And who was I anyway? Just a regular kid. How would I ever meet Him? And what if He didn't come until I was an adult? Would I be too preoccupied to notice? That concern was worth contemplating because adults, judging from my parents, always seemed to have lots to deal with. Certainly I gave them plenty to worry about.

I began to rock my mother's world on December 30, 1948, the evening before I was born. While snow fell and brutally cold winds howled, she went into labour, alone in a small Edmonton inner city apartment with paper thin walls. At the time, my father was busy partying on a plane heading home from a Weston's Biscuits sales meeting in Toronto.

His pre-New Year celebration started during a stopover in Winnipeg where he joined his wartime Winnipeg Rifles' buddies at Rod Beattie's house on Lanark Street. On the last leg of his journey home, Dad found the flight attendants (then stewardesses) and pilots such "good sports" that he invited them over for a drink. My mother, wearing her raccoon coat and counting her contractions, met the partygoers at the apartment door. At her insistence, Dad drove her around the corner to the Royal Alexandra Hospital, dropped her off and returned to the party to wait for the phone call. My dad describes that era in his life as "carefree." Not so for my mother. She was a nurse, but until she gave birth to me she later admitted she had no idea what her maternity patients endured or what caring for a colicky infant entailed.

I was born sometime in the wee hours of December 31. My dad was delighted to be able to claim me on his income tax for a full year. It had been a win-win situation for him. But, while my mother recovered from childbirth, I'm not sure she ever recovered from the injustice of that New Year's Eve. He got to party: she got the pain.

When I was two, my parents moved back to Winnipeg, from whence they came. For a short time, we lived with my maternal grandmother, Jessie Knight. Among other outstanding qualities, she was known for her ability to play the piano at parties with her nose. Just before the historic flood of 1950 we moved into a new bungalow. (It cost a whopping $8,900 and took my parents 25 years to pay off.) Our house was on Lanark Street in a semi-circle of fifteen houses. The houses faced onto a park the equivalent of five properties wide and five properties long. We referred to our park and loop of houses as a bay. The Beattie family (my dad's army buddy) lived on the straight of the street, kitty corner to us.

Our family expanded to include a black Lab Dad named Archie, and two brothers, whom I initially tormented and then pretty much ignored until I left home at the age of seventeen.

For some reason, everyone but Dad had a nickname. My brother Gerald was "Sam," after "Sam, Sam the Garbage Man." Don was "Pookie," compliments of Sam and me. Mine was "Toodie," an appellation I deeply loathed. It evolved, my mother says, from the cartoon tugboat "Little Toot" because of a certain and abundant propensity I had as an infant. The effort it took to finally shake off that name supplied me with my first lesson in applied determination.

My mother's nickname was "Slim." Through 58 years of marriage, 57 of which I've been alive and listening, I never once heard my father refer to her by her real name, Donna. My dad recently informed me that he decided to call her Slim "by way of encouragement" after meeting his future and rather hefty mother-in-law. His strategy worked. Shapely, 5'6", with green eyes, high cheekbones and thick, wavy black hair and a figure to die for, my mother was what my dad referred to as "a knockout."

Just before my startling thought about Christ returning, I'd watched the movie *A Nun's Story*. Perhaps that movie sparked the notion of Christ's return. Certainly, Audrey Hepburn's stature and beauty entranced me. For a time, I fantasized about becoming a nun. However, I wasn't Catholic and since boys were becoming increasingly interesting to me, I wasn't up to pursuing the life of an ascetic, so the fantasy soon vanished. Left in its wake was a vague longing for faith of some sort. That feeling was further fuelled by a book of my dad's that I found on our limited bookshelf, *The Power of Positive Thinking* by Norman Vincent Peale. I was enthralled by the near-death experiences he recounted that alluded to an existence beyond this world. This was of great comfort to me because I was concerned about a boy in my class who had a heart condition. I was probably too shy to tell him the good news that even if he died he'd live on in another form.

At the age of fourteen, I enrolled in confirmation classes at Westworth United Church, the church my mother attended with some frequency. Her childhood was hell because she was born out of wedlock in 1921 in an era when that was considered scandalous. She confided in me one day that she didn't know how she could have survived her early years without faith in God. But her faith lagged in later life perhaps around the same time her church going crashed to a halt after a surprise visit from a church elder. He stopped by our house to drop off communion cards. By then I was 22 and travelling through Europe. The elder queried my fifteen-year-old brother Don, who happened to answer the door, as to why none of the Mitchells had been attending church. Don explained that I'd joined another religion and that he'd been looking around as well. My mother appeared just in time to hear the elder huffing about his disappointment in our family. That did it for her. She never went back to that church or any other for that matter. By this time, my brother Gerry had moved to Australia. His churchgoing ended with his confirmation as had mine.

My dad never did go to church. On Sunday mornings, in fair enough weather, he preferred to dig in our garden. We are talking Winnipeg here, notorious for its extremely cold winters and boiling hot, mosquito-rich summers. Our yard happened to face the back of the church and the intersection of three alleys. An assortment of neighbours and strangers regularly cut through our yard. This meant that there were four routes by which churchgoers could take notice of my dad's Sunday activities. It occurred to me one day that others might be judging him for not going to church. I asked my mom why he didn't go.

"Your father experienced dreadful things during the war," she said, "things so horrible that he has never even talked about them. He found it difficult to believe in a God that would allow such atrocities. I think that experience badly shook his faith."

When I asked my dad he said, "I never discuss war or religion, but if you must know, when I married your mother, I gave up going to the Anglican Church because she went to the United Church. I went once or twice but I didn't care for it." Perhaps that explains why my parents never bothered to have me baptized until I was old enough to wonder why I was lined up with a number of crying babies.

Though my father professed no religion, he was big on virtue. He constantly drilled his pet maxims into us,

It's put and take. By this he meant you have to give of yourself before you can take.

It's better to give than to receive.

You get what you give.

There's no policy like honesty.

A man is only as good as his word.

In our household, and certainly in those of my parents' friends, mostly war buddies and their wives, religion was very much a case of to each his or her own. Consequently, when after my confirmation classes I didn't feel moved to make that commitment, I was free not to.

After I turned fifteen I decided to repeat those classes. In 1964, on the appointed day, and then sixteen years old, I stood waiting in a long line of would-be confirmees facing the altar. I wore a sleeveless, off-white bouclé dress that I won when crowned "Princess" during a modeling course at the Hudson's Bay department store where I worked part-time.

Recently, I rediscovered a group photograph taken that confirmation day. To my astonishment, standing in the row behind me is my brother, fourteen-year-old Gerry. I'd completely forgotten he was a part of that confirmation process, which isn't surprising, given my self-absorption.

The minister lived across the bay from us and was the father of a classmate. When my turn came to be confirmed he placed his hand gently on my head and whispered, "What took you so long?" Though he meant well, I immediately knew that I'd made the wrong decision. I'd be a fraud if I continued to go to church because as hard as I tried to attain it, I simply lacked faith.

While attending Kelvin High School in South Central Winnipeg, I checked out a local Anglican Church, partly out of curiosity about my dad's earlier leanings. Compared to the United Church, the pomp and ceremony of its services appealed to me. I also liked the minister's son. I briefly considered becoming an Anglican but their confirmation classes conflicted with my basketball practices and, since that boy never showed any interest in me, I let that one go too.

In September 1967, fresh out of high school, I enrolled in nursing at the Misericordia Hospital in Winnipeg. There was never any discussion about my going to university; no one in my immediate family ever had. Frankly, I'm not sure if I'd ever even seen a university, let alone understood what went on there. Perhaps Miss Hawkley, my Grade 8 English teacher, who doubled as a guidance counsellor, had succeeded in penetrating something into my brain after all when she told me I wasn't "university material."

Earlier that year, my dad sat me down in the living room facing him. "Sharon," he said, for that was my given name, "it is time for you to decide what you are going to be when you finish high school. Now, the way I look at it, you're just going to get married and have kids anyway, so you might as well be a nurse or a secretary. There's no point in thinking about anything else." At the time, Dad considered mothers who worked outside the home to be "show-offs."

A secretary? I thought. I don't want to be a secretary! But a nurse, hmm, maybe that's a good idea. Mom was a nurse. She always knows what to do when we're sick. Besides, I'll get to move out of the house, learn a trade and make money to travel. I re-emerged from my reverie to see my dad staring at me. "Okay," I said, "I'll be a nurse."

"Great!" he said. End of discussion.

Because I was preoccupied with boys and my appearance, and because being "cool" meant everything to me, it hadn't occurred to me to put much effort into schoolwork. Certainly, little I learned in school engaged me or seemed relevant, apart from an independent school project on bacteria that I did in Grade 4. Between the covers of a copy of the *Golden Book Encyclopedia for Children*, which my mom bought at the corner Safeway, I discovered the hidden realms of spheres, rods and spirochete microorganisms.

Grades good enough to get into nursing school could have become an issue, which was why I applied to the Misericordia Hospital School of Nursing. Their entry standards were lower than those of the other alternative I considered, the Winnipeg General Hospital (now The Health Sciences Centre). That was my mother's alma mater and where she gave the valedictorian speech at her graduation ceremony in 1946. I think that was the highlight of her life; perhaps she finally felt validated as a human being given her rough start in life.

Everything was all lined up for me to begin nursing. My tuition fee of just over $2,000 would be covered by the Baby Bonus or Family Allowance cheques issued to parents post WWll to help cover costs of child rearing. My parents put this money aside for each of us kids even when those funds would have come in handy for them.

I planned to earn spending money from my summer job at Paulin Chambers Company Limited. I was glad the factory was located deep within the bowels of Winnipeg's inner city. I would have been mortified if anyone I knew saw me in my very "uncool" attire: a hairnet with a narrow white, wavy Paulin's label on its headband, a white uniform, an apron, and cheap white oxfords. And if that get-up wasn't enough, suffering the job was worse. It entailed shoving handfuls of cookies into sharp corrugated cardboard forms that barreled past at breakneck speed. I sliced my fingers repeatedly on the cardboard. Soon I learned to tape them for protection. When I complained about my working conditions, my dad scoffed at me. "That's nothing! You should try working in a needle factory." That still gives me pause for thought.

One day, the supervisor called me off the assembly line to take a phone call. It was my dad. His fury made the heat of that factory with its horrid smell of burning sugar seem pleasant. He and my mother had opened a letter from Kelvin High School to discover that I had failed three final grade 12 exams. My father, a decorated lieutenant in the Second World War, commanded me home.

I arrived home on the bus already feeling like a beaten dog. My dad sat me down for one of his lectures. "You sit there! I am completely disgusted with your performance. There is no excuse for it. You were just wasting your time all year fooling around with boys..." On and on he went, while I did my best to sing "Mary Had A Little Lamb" as loud as I could inside my head to drown him out. I tuned in again in time for his summation comments.

"You're going to go to summer school, then come straight home, and study for six hours every day. And you're going to like it!" Dad thundered. "And you are going to pass those exams in August!"

I didn't return to the factory, immediately enrolled in summer school, and for the first time in my life, I studied. I remember working at a table on our patio outside our back door. The big surprise was that I loved it. I actually loved studying. Who would have thought?

Later, sufficiently cooled down and pleased to see me slaving away over my books, my dad explained that I couldn't afford to start a failing streak and that if I did, it would be difficult to break.

I passed all of my exams and have always been grateful that Dad hauled me out of that cookie factory by the scruff of the neck and forced me to apply myself.

Though I had never given the slightest thought to my intellectual development, I had moments of concern about the lack of purpose in my life and, I suppose, an unacknowledged yearning for faith. I needed to know why I was alive. It occurred to me that mental institutions were filled with people who, like me, couldn't cope without an answer to that question.

One day during my final year of high school, while cleaning out my messy bedroom closet, I came across a scrap of paper I'd forgotten I'd saved. On it was a quotation from Albert Einstein that resonated with me about the purpose of life being to give to others. Aha! I thought, that's at least part of the answer.

Later, this verse from "Desiderata" became my mantra and the source of my own validation:

You are a child of the universe,
no less than the trees and the stars;
you have a right to be here.
And whether or not it is clear to you,
no doubt the universe is unfolding as it should.[1]

In retrospect, it would have been extremely good for my self-esteem, not to mention my knowledge deficit, to have attended university with my peers. In my second year of nursing, a visiting psychologist, Dr. Mitchell, asked me why I hadn't gone to university. In fact, she said, "Why are you punishing yourself by not going to university?" I was stunned but greatly encouraged by her comment. Obviously, she disagreed with my junior high guidance teacher's considered opinion.

But even if university had been an option, I was restless. Perhaps I sensed that I was the kind of person who "feels" her way through life. My interests lay primarily in people.

In February 1970, after graduating from nursing, I took a job in Lynn Lake at the Sherritt Gordon Mines Hospital. The isolation pay I earned in that remote, northwestern Manitoba town meant I could set out to explore the world sooner. I couldn't wait to exit Canada.

In Lynn Lake I made fast friends with Lynette Jacques, a spirited young woman from Calgary who also worked for the mine. She lived in a bungalow next door that looked exactly like the nurses' residence where I lived, only her house had stairs. Ours opened to a five-foot drop. We had to use the side door entrance.

Lynette was a committed Christian. She sympathized with my struggle to find faith and invited me to meet her minister, whom she held in high esteem. So, one still and frigid winter evening we set out on foot for his home. The minister was engaging, kind and gracious. He did his best to answer my questions about how I could acquire faith, but all to no avail; I abandoned my efforts that night. It wasn't that I didn't believe in Christ, I just didn't think

---

1    Max Ehrmann, "Desiderata," 1952.

His teachings were relevant to me so many hundreds of years after He walked this earth. I also had trouble lining up what I knew about His teachings and His life with the hypocrisy and man-made rules I'd witnessed at church, such nonsense as having to wear a hat and gloves, according to my mother, and not taking off my coat lest someone think I was showing off my dress.

Meanwhile, back at the hospital in Lynn Lake, my nerves and new skills were put to the test, especially as charge nurse on evening and night shifts. Learning how to deliver babies, and deal with serious mine accidents, terrified me. But, for all the stress there was an upside. Most of my patients were Swampy Cree Aboriginals. Never in my white, urban experience had I encountered people who endured such adversity. It was the bread of their daily lives, yet they acquiesced to it with patience and fortitude.

Take Alex, an eight-year-old boy admitted to our hospital with serious burns from a house fire that killed his mother and burned down their house. At the same time a white boy from Lynn Lake was admitted with burns to his backside. That boy whined and cried and demanded and ate candy constantly. By contrast, the indigenous boy suffered with dignity and patience as did his father and sister who were also admitted with burns. I admired this family as well as the other Cree I met. Their spirituality, though I couldn't have named it as such back then, moved me deeply.

∽

In January 1972, thanks to the added isolation pay, a perk that came with working in a remote northern community, I set sail from New York on the Cristoforo Colombo, which was headed for Spain. With me was Susan, (not her real name), a young woman I met through a mutual acquaintance just before I left Lynn Lake. She was looking for a travelling companion and my own intended travelling partner, a former fellow student nurse, had opted to marry instead.

North Americans my age, who would later be termed the "Me Generation," were deeply disturbed by anti-peace choices "the establishment" was making on our behalf. Among other things, we wanted the war in Vietnam to end and nuclear weapon proliferation to stop. Like me, young hippie types set out in hordes to explore the world in search of socially progressive ways of being.

I always fancied I would have been a sailor had I been a boy, but I changed my mind after that stormy January Atlantic journey. On a foolish whim one dark night, I snuck out onto the upper deck of the ship and was immediately buffeted against the outer railing by force of the roiling waves and wind. I had to fight to pull myself hand-over-fist along the guardrail to keep from being blown overboard. This is it, I thought. I'm going to be tossed into the Atlantic and no one will ever know what happened to me. Relief barely describes how I felt when I finally pried open a door to the stairwell and slipped into safety.

We disembarked in Malaga on Spain's southern coast. While observing the sand at low tide I heard an inner voice say, *you could call yourself Mud and no one would know the difference.* With that I lopped the "on" off Sharon and became Shar pronounced Share. There, I thought, now I am free of parental restrictions and can get on with finding myself. Personal autonomy was paramount to me.

The chill in the air encouraged Susan and me to head south to Morocco. The port of Gibraltar was closed due to a strike, so we hitchhiked to Alicante and found our way to the appropriate pier where we waited for hours for our passage across the strait to the north coast of Morocco. Eventually, we began talking to two young men, who were waiting for the same ship, and who happened to be Canadians.

Once on board, men dressed in long robes provided a foretaste of the country to which we were headed. Upon disembarking in Ceuta, a most bizarre, Fellini-like world pushed in on us. Images from the coloured pictures in the white leather Bible my Auntie Mar and Uncle Bill gave me at my ill-fated confirmation ceremony appeared before my eyes. Men dressed in long woolen jalabas pulled camels down stony roads. Children tugged on our clothes and pleaded to be of service for a fee. In passing, a fellow North American, who was leaving Morocco, handed us a clear pink plastic bag filled with opium pods. I can't remember what we did with it but I know we didn't smoke it.

Overwhelmed by this onslaught, I was grateful that I was not alone. The four of us decided to make a hasty exit from that port town. After a short night in inexpensive lodgings, we boarded a bus headed for Fez. I sat beside one of the young men, who was from Calgary. Some hours into our journey I said, "When I first saw you I was shocked at how much you looked like my friend, Loretta Jacques' brother, Lance." If there had been room on that jam-packed bus for my new friend to topple into the aisle he would have. "Lance," he gasped, "is my best friend."

Morocco's stunning and diverse terrain, from deserts to snow-capped mountains, even a village that looked like it had been lifted directly out of Switzerland, passed by the bus windows. My high school French proved adequate to converse with the locals because French is that country's second language and Moroccans speak it more slowly than they do Arabic.

In Marrakech, Susan and I settled into a youth hostel constructed of cement where the rooms faced in toward an open courtyard. I still recall my struggle to muster the courage to step into the ice cold shower.

A visit to the market was like entering another world. The place teemed with Moroccans against a backdrop of exotic scents and enticing textures of earthy reds, browns and yellows. I was desperate for a jalaba, a long flowing robe that Moroccan men wore over their clothes like a coat but I was foiled by my repeated, dismal efforts to bargain for one. I could almost feel its warmth on those cold winter nights and early mornings. But I refused to pay more than my traveling companions had paid and never did get one. I was unaware of market entertainment protocol, so it came as quite a shock to me when I was forced to either pay or, in one case, to outrun a small wiry man I had been watching coax a snake out of a large wicker basket.

Then there was my hashish scare. One of the "bread ladies" at the market ran a little side business. Everyone knew who she was. One day I smoked what was evidently some very strong hashish, after which I lay on my cot in the youth shelter. The hostel owner came around to check those of us who were similarly laid out. As he lifted the covers to look at our faces, he shook his head and muttered knowingly, "Hashish."

As hard as I struggled, I couldn't move beyond that altered state in which everything appeared fractionated. I was terrified I would never be able to think again. Eventually, the drug wore off and I was relieved I could string my thoughts together once more.

One evening, we heard a commotion behind the hostel. Our kindly host explained that a Muslim man had just returned from a pilgrimage to Mecca and that his family and friends were gathering to celebrate with him. We watched as this man, called a "Haji," was carried along on a large wooden pallet, accompanied by a small parade of noisy musicians and happily shouting onlookers.

Though it was February and beginning to warm up, it was still brisk in the mornings. Susan and I decided to fly to the Canary Islands where, we correctly surmised, it would be warmer. A number of fellow travellers (we called ourselves freaks) told us that the Canary Islands weren't to be missed. So we booked our tickets and flew into Las Palmas on the Island of Tenerife.

Fortune soon smiled on us as we hitchhiked along the coast. The owner of a brand new seaside resort picked us up and invited us to stay there free of charge. Evidently construction delays meant that he had missed out on the tourist season.

We reveled in that flat-roofed, pristine white apartment with its spacious balcony overlooking the sea, lapping up onto a beach of black silt sand. We had our own kitchen and cooked for ourselves and each day a friendly maid showed up to clean our glorious abode. My introduction to yogurt, canned artichokes and mineral water came from a local store there.

Eventually, we wearied of our leisure and travelled south to a commune where a motley collection of about twenty people languished on a beach in a drug-altered state. Much more intriguing was the vibrant community life at the informal nightly events in the local village square, where townspeople gathered to sing and dance. We got into a discussion one such night with the local restaurant owner about the invasion of hippies and their squatter camp. The whole scene deeply dismayed him. We weren't too impressed either. We shared a shed-like structure with a young blonde couple. Each night began with a noisy sexual encounter on the other side of the thin tin wall that separated us followed by the most shocking snoring, from both of them, that I'd ever heard. The combined racket soon motivated Susan and me to move on.

As fascinating as I'd found that side trip to the Canary Islands, my return to Morocco would soon provide me with a life-changing perspective, seeing a concrete example of faith in action, the Muslim faith. We sailed overnight from the Canary Islands to the Spanish Sahara (then a Spanish colony), with an international assortment of seventeen young passengers. En route, a Danish traveller handed out little white pills. As a nurse I knew better than to accept one but I swallowed it anyway. Fortunately I enjoyed a lovely sleep, rocking gently back and forth in a white cloth hammock.

The next morning, as we approached the shores of the Spanish Sahara in the blazing sunlight, an amphibious craft met our ship. We transferred onto this smaller boat. One of my fellow travellers, an American who called himself Charlie Brown, had no arms or legs. His pill-sharing Danish friend rode a bike and had been pulling Charlie in his wheelchair around the world. Etched in my memory is the sight of Charlie Brown in his wheel chair being hoisted by a lift, swung out over the ocean and lowered into the amphibious taxi.

Once on shore, the amphibious craft birthed wheels that rolled us over the desert and deposited us beside a bus set to carry us north to the Moroccan border. The bus broke down mid journey and the driver shooed us off. He said we would have to wait for a truck caravan the following week. A lone small hut, and a few scattered shelters made of old tires and tin, broke the vast desert horizon. Though not terribly concerned (perhaps the after effect of that pill), I pondered how we would manage since the small red vinyl bag I carried held only a change of clothes and the novel I was devouring at the time.

By Western standards, those Berber nomads had nothing of value, unless you counted a few ornery camels. With a rusty tin can attached to a long dirty string, they hauled murky water out of a small but cavernous hole in the desert. Yet, despite their material lack (and as I later came to believe, because of it) they shared everything they had with us, their uninvited guests.

By some good fortune the police chief invited me to stay in his hut. There, along with a few others, I slept on the floor protected from the cold desert nights by heavy blankets compliments of our host.

On the appointed day, about a week later, a fleet of fully loaded red flatbed trucks arrived. One of the drivers offered me a seat in the front with him and his buddy. I turned them down, in favour of the adventure of riding on top of the cargo, in the company of several goats and three Moroccan youths, who proceeded to get drunk as we crossed the desert. When not distracted by these boys, who kept trying to shove each other off the moving truck, I read from Khalil Gibran's book, *The Prophet.*[2] In it, Gibran describes a dog that buries a bone, but later can't find it. To me, the dog symbolized my culture. It was probably the first time I understood, that I actually came from a culture, a culture that like the dog, busies itself amassing and hoarding wealth. Moroccan hospitality stood in sharp contrast.

Observing the piety of these rural Muslims rendered another insight. Five times a day they abandoned whatever they were doing, prostrated themselves on their hands and knees, and prayed. Their sincere devotion and generosity convinced me that Muhammad, like Christ, must have been a Prophet from God because these Muslims behaved like the best Christians I'd ever known. It puzzled me that I had heard nothing about Muhammad at church or in school.

The truck caravan took us to Tiznit, where Susan and I found a room to rent in something that approximated a barn. Susan, who was blonde and blue-eyed, had a fling with the local police chief, a stunning-looking man. He arranged a dinner invitation for us. What a feast it was. We sat on the floor around the perimeter of a large patterned carpet. The women of the household placed huge earthen dishes laden with aromatic food in the middle of the rug in front of us. I soon learned the eating etiquette. With my right hand, never my left, which is reserved for bathroom duties, I used flat bread to scoop up the most delicious food my 22-year-old palate had ever tasted. This fabulous

---

2    Kahlil Gibran, *The Prophet* (Alfred A. Knopf, 1923).

journey to taste bud heaven included couscous, fruit and meat combinations, such as apricots and prunes cooked with lamb and lemon-drenched herbed fish.

Later that night a group of veiled Muslim women had great fun dressing me up in a floor length, pale turquoise, robe-like outfit with a veil. These people and their culture enchanted us, Susan, so much so that she stayed on with the police chief after I left. Many months later when I was in England, she somehow got word to me that she had become pregnant and had survived an abortion in Morocco. I can only imagine the nightmare she must have endured. I lost contact with her after that.

From there I found my way to a Moroccan beach that was a focal gathering point for travellers like me. On the first night, I slept on the top of a hill overlooking the ocean. In the morning someone pointed out tarantula tracks in the sand around the imprint of my head. The next night, I graduated to considerably more comfortable accommodations in a yellow and white Volkswagen camper, compliments of a Californian freak. Though a good deal older than most of us, he made friends through his generosity.

While in Morocco I learned that our outspoken and dapper Canadian Prime Minister, Pierre-Elliott Trudeau, was to marry Margaret Sinclair, a British Columbian woman young enough to be his daughter. Someone had a tabloid picture of them. I studied that photograph in search of clues about the mystery of their obvious mismatch. The tradeoff, I surmised, had to be his intelligence, money and power versus her youthful beauty and spirit.

It took some time to adjust to the sight of everyone wandering naked around the beach, everyone except the Moroccan men, who lay prone on a nearby sandy hill where they spied on us for hours on end.

For entertainment, hashish abounded. People got stoned in the morning and then sat around for the rest of the day. Pierre, a wild-looking Quebecois with a mass of mangy-matted, dark brown curly hair, had obviously lost his mind. I wondered if his family knew where he was and in what condition.

A dark-haired American woman commented, "Isn't it great that all the grime under your toenails gets washed out in the ocean." I looked down at my feet. Mine were clean. *I wonder how hers got so dirty*, I thought. About six months later, I happened to run into this same girl in Hyde Park in London, England. She told me that she and her friends had contracted scabies in Morocco and had a difficult time getting rid of it. I thought back to the filthy beds I had slept in, like the one in Tiznit where we amused ourselves counting the fleas hopping around on the sodden-looking mattress, and I realized how fortunate I was to not have been troubled by anything worse than constipation.

As if on cue, each night at sunset pink flamingoes would congregate on the bleached white Moroccan shoreline creating the most stunning silhouette against the turquoise ocean and the crimson streaked sky. But the beauty wasn't enough to sustain me. Soon this apathetic crowd painfully bored me. I decided to return to Spain with Terry, a young Berkeley student I'd befriended. Two of her friends from California lived on the island of Ibiza, so we made that our destination. We arrived on the eve of Good Friday. Our first stop was a bakery with a spectacular array of ornately decorated Easter sweets. The next day we followed crowds that ultimately led us to a commemorative procession that included a beleaguered Christ who dragged a huge wooden cross along cobblestone roads followed by hundreds of somber Spaniards.

I explored France, Switzerland, Germany, Holland and England for the next several months. Last stop: Wales. That particular jaunt marked another defining moment for me. I recall sitting with a former fellow student nurse, Bea Mudge, on a gigantic boulder overlooking the sea. The bleakness of that setting appealed to me. Bea had lived in Newfoundland because her dad, an RCMP (Royal Canadian Mounted Police) officer, had been stationed there. Something prompted me to ask her if the Welsh terrain resembled Newfoundland. She said it did. Then and there, I decided to abandon my search for truth in Europe and move to Newfoundland. I remember hoping I would discover what I had come to think of as "what it's all about" in Newfoundland. Somehow I had concluded that meant love and unity. I wasn't looking to religion for answers any more but I never forgot my Muslim Berber nomad hosts' demonstration of faith.

# Palms Down in Iraq

*"Man is even as steel, the essence of which is hidden; through admonition and explanation, good counsel and education, that essence will be brought to light..."*[1]

Upon his return to England, Redwan moved out of the university residence into an apartment in North West London. Within a month of his dodgy exit from Baghdad, Saddam Hussein's uncle, President Ahmad Hasan Al-Bakr, arrested a number of Bahá'ís whom he considered leaders. Redwan's mother, Hajer, and cousin, Ikbal, were among them. In total, ten Bahá'í women and fifteen men were incarcerated in Abu Ghraib Prison. The male prisoners included a youth named Redwan Saifi who had been a student in a Bahá'í class that Redwan taught.

Alone in his basement apartment, Redwan sobbed when he heard about the arrests. He was desperate for more information about his mother but couldn't talk openly to his siblings for fear their phones were tapped. He was sickened by the thought of his mother locked in a dungeon, blindfolded and subject to torture.

Four months later, on April 24, 1973, all were sentenced to life in prison. Shortly thereafter Redwan discovered that he too had been wrongfully convicted of espionage and sentenced in absentia to life in prison by the Iraqi Revolutionary Court. Now added to his distress was the very real fear that he might be suddenly snatched up by Iraqi agents in England. Sarmad warned him that agents might approach him saying that his mother was ill or dying and that he should return to Iraq immediately. His brother advised Redwan to ignore any such approaches.

---

1      Bahá'u'lláh, in *A Compilation on Bahá'í Education*, comp. the Research Department of the Universal House of Justice, 1976, p. 59.

**39**

After a year in England, Redwan had fully integrated into the Bahá'í community. But thoughts of Iraq were never far from his mind nor was the guilt that, of his family, he alone had escaped.

∽

In quiet moments, he often reflected on his earliest days in Khaneqin, a small town situated on the remote northeastern foothills of the Iraq/Iran border where he was born. Though seemingly an unremarkable town, Khaneqin holds special significance for Bahá'ís. In 1853, in the dead of winter, Bahá'u'lláh , the prophet founder of the Bahá'í Faith, His family, and a small band of His followers, all ill equipped, camped there briefly on the grueling three month, 4,079-kilometre trek into exile through the mountains from Tehran to Baghdad.

The Al-Wand River carves its way through Khaneqin and the dusty foothills that surround it. In his mind's eye, Redwan could see the river and the house his family lived in until he was five. It seemed large to him then. Its ancient wooden front door was positioned above a few steps. Inside was a small beige coloured stone courtyard. There was a simple kitchen with only a cold water tap, and an old-fashioned stove and two bedrooms. A balcony wound around the second floor.

In the winter they heated their bedrooms with a "sopa," a cylindrical paraffin heater with a kettle of water perched on top. From May to October the whole family slept on their roof. Each day at sunset they would fold up their cotton-stuffed mattresses and bedding and drag them upstairs to the roof where they would drape mosquito netting over them. By bedtime the sheets would be nicely cooled off. Redwan loved lying in bed watching falling stars before drifting off to sleep. His transistor radio, always tuned to BBC World Service, played discreetly under his pillow.

After they married in January 1944, Redwan's parents had moved to Khaneqin to help establish a Bahá'í community. For Bahá'ís, living in a Muslim country was, and still remains, challenging. Muslims interpret Muhammad's claim that He was the "Seal of the Prophets" to mean that He was the final Manifestation of God. Most Muslim clergy, therefore, condone, and even encourage their followers to persecute Bahá'ís, whom they consider to be blasphemers.

Compounding the religious persecution the Moqbel family faced was the fact that Kaykhosrow's name gave him away as a Persian. Iraqis did not take kindly to Persians, especially Persian Bahá'ís. As such, it was difficult for Kaykhosrow to get and keep a job. He was always the first to be laid off. Ultimately, he switched his first and last name around and became Moqbel Kaykhosrow. This was preferable because "Kaykhosrow" was a common name among Kurds who were slightly less detested than Iranians. The name Moqbel is Arabic for "one who is approaching the truth." Redwan thinks his family adopted it during Reza Shah's dictatorship when everyone was compelled to assume a surname.

It was under these precarious conditions that Redwan was born on August 14, 1947, in the Bahá'í month of *Perfection*.[2] His name is Arabic for "paradise" and is pronounced Ridhwan in Arabic and Rizwan (though it is spelled Ridvan) in Persian. His older sister's name is Sharaf, which is Arabic for "honour." Born prematurely on November 23, 1944, and not in the Bahá'í month of Sharaf, Hajer and Kaykhosrow named her Sharaf anyway. Their brother Sarmad's name is Arabic for "eternal" or "eternity." He was born March 9, 1952, in the month of 'Alá' ("loftiness").

Some time in the mid 1940s, news circulated of a job for a fluent English speaker at a new British Petroleum refinery. All seven of the Iranian Bahá'í men that lived in Khaneqin showed up for an interview. Surprised, but happy to see each other, they bantered about their chances of getting the job. Kaykhosrow's interview was last.

Immediately after greeting the British interviewer, Kaykhosrow said, "Sir, I want you to know that any one of the men who preceded me would make a much better choice than me. I just came to check out the waters and

---

2      The Bahá'í calendar is a solar calendar with nineteen months of nineteen days plus four or five (depending upon Leap Year) intercalary days.

once here decided to stay to meet you. Please ignore my application and offer the job to any of the others."

Dumbfounded, the man thumped his hand on the table and demanded, "What's going on here? Did you men rehearse this? Every one of you has come in here, sat down and said the very same thing."

In the end, British Petroleum created two jobs. Evidently the applicants' sacrificial attitude touched the interviewer. One went to Kaykhosrow.

∽

One time when the family was completely broke, Redwan's maternal grandmother, Melka (Arabic for "queen") Shoja'a Wakil, visited from Baghdad. She was gentle, loving, and the most encouraging person Redwan had ever met. She seemed regal and beautiful to him as he played with her long silver braids.

The family loved visits ordinarily but this time it was stressful because Redwan's parents refused to dilute their hospitality and hid their desperate financial situation. Each night after Melka retired to bed, one saleable item after another quietly disappeared out the door to be sold. When Melka left for Baghdad she seemed unaware of their desperate straits.

Then something strange happened. One afternoon about a week later, while the kids played in the courtyard, and their parents stretched out on a mat on the veranda floor, they heard the postman's distinctive knock. Hajer and Kaykhosrow jumped up. Kaykhosrow answered the door.

"Good afternoon Moqbel; there's a money order for you at the post office. You need to come and sign for it."

"That's impossible," Kaykhosrow replied. "I'm not expecting any money."

"Well, I don't know who sent it, but someone did, and it's waiting at the post office for you to claim it."

"There must be a mistake. Please go back to the post office and make sure the right person gets that money. It certainly isn't me."

"I assure you it is, but I will double-check," the postman replied before leaving.

Kaykhosrow spun around and shot a challenging glance at Hajer. Instantly, Redwan read his thought, that Hajer had divulged their financial situation to her mother and now their Uncle Munir was rescuing them. A wounded expression passed over Hajer's face.

"I didn't say a word to my mother," she said quietly.

"Well, if you didn't, who did? Who else would send money?"

"I don't know, but you need to go to the post office and find out. You can't assume that it isn't for you when the postman is sure it is."

Reluctantly, Kaykhosrow made his way to the post office and returned looking stunned. In his hand he clasped a money order for a substantial sum.

"This is a mistake," he said. "Someone sent this money to me in error."

"But, Kaykhosrow, we could surely use that money for food. What would the harm be in cashing it? After all it is in your name."

"Hajer, you know I can't do that. What if the real recipient came to collect his money and we had spent it. A fine state we would be in then."

As Kaykhosrow never budged in matters of principle, Hajer didn't pursue the discussion. Kaykhosrow filed away the money order. Two days later the postman made his distinctive knock at their door again.

"Moqbel, Moqbel, here's a letter for you from Tehran."

Kaykhosrow took the letter, thanked the postman, closed the door, leaned against it, opened the letter and read silently. As he did, he began to shake his head in disbelief. Tears ran down his cheeks. After he finished reading it, he dropped his head and held the letter out for Hajer. She took it from his hand and read aloud to her spellbound progeny:

> Dear Moqbel,
> For the past three nights I've been unable to sleep. Each night, just as I begin to drift off, Bahá'u'lláh appears to me in my dreams and instructs me repeatedly saying, "Pay Moqbel the money you owe him. He needs it."

The first time this happened I honestly couldn't remember that you had lent me money. The second time it happened I ignored it, but the third night I realized it was true. I borrowed money from you when you had your business in Tehran and I have an obligation to repay you.

Please accept my apologies for taking so many years to repay you. Again, I thank you for helping me out when I was in great need.

The family laughed and cried together for it was true; Kaykhosrow had lent the man money many years before. Its repayment meant not going hungry.

∾

Kaykhosrow frequently worked out of town, which made his time at home all the more special. He doted on his children, who missed him terribly when he was away. As soon as he walked through the door after a trip he would present each of them with their favourite treats, chocolate for Sharaf and Sarmad and bananas or apples for Redwan.

Though it didn't occur to them to ask while he was alive, Redwan and his siblings now realize to their regret that their dad didn't talk much about his life in Iran. Perhaps life before marriage and children, particularly in a foreign land, no longer seemed relevant. They don't know, for example, how far Kaykhosrow went in school but they knew he was extremely bright and had a photographic memory. He memorized entire books and taught himself to speak seven languages, including Japanese, and, in his earlier years, was known among his friends as a palm reader. He read dictionaries for fun and whenever his children approached him for the meaning of a word he would recite a whole roster of definitions.

Kaykhosrow had the sensitivity and temperament of an artist. He drew and painted well and composed remarkable poetry in Persian, and later in Arabic, which he sent to friends in Iran and abroad. Unfortunately, he didn't keep copies. His wisdom, generosity and gentle loving-kindness drew large numbers of people to him. Nothing and no one was too much trouble for Kaykhosrow. As such, their home was a magnet, especially for travellers. As a young adult living in Tehran their dad opened a shop called *The International*, where he sold men's wear.[3] His mother, Zarbanoo, claimed he chose that name because he wanted to attract people from all nations, which he did.

But after moving to Iraq, Kaykhosrow's work was always precarious, which rendered Hajer's salary, as a primary school teacher, the main income. She was one of the early graduates from a newly established Teachers' Training College in Baghdad. Her family took the Bahá'í teachings about the equality of men and women seriously, particularly the importance of education for girls. While never well paid, Hajer had a steady income, a rare thing for women in Iraq in those days, especially in a rural setting like Khaneqin. Hajer was loving but firm with her children, whom she expected to behave properly.

By the time Redwan went to primary school Hajer had been promoted to vice-principal of the primary school he attended. This cramped his style considerably. He recalls her swift slap to his face one day after he yanked the chair out from behind a blonde-haired girl who constantly pestered him. Revenge tasted sweet until terror dawned in Redwan's mind that if she were hurt he would be in big trouble. But, after her initial tears, the girl seemed fine. Most importantly, her ardour for Redwan cooled immediately, a turn of events he figured well worth the price of his mother's slap.

From grade three on, Redwan and his classmates had to memorize poetry in their Arabic classes. He found this a dull task and simply didn't bother to do it until the last minute while the four children who preceded him performed their recitations. In an adrenaline rush, Redwan always managed to memorize the poems just before his name was called. But, Hajer was nobody's fool. One night she asked him why he never had homework.

---

3    There is a discrepancy in the family's memory about what products *The International* sold. Redwan's cousin, Farahmand, believes it was stationery.

"I don't know, Mom, I just don't."

"Then why is it that I have seen some of your classmates looking like they're memorizing when they're walking home from school?"

"That's weird," he commented as nonchalantly as possible, given the serious level of her questioning.

Hajer glared at him and shook her head. The next morning in class, just before their regular poetry recital, she strode into his classroom, marched over to the teacher, Miss Su'ad, and whispered in her ear. As she listened, the teacher looked over at Redwan before returning her gaze to his mother. Miss Su'ad nodded at Hajer in approval. Hajer took a seat at the rear of the classroom.

"Redwan Moqbel, kindly come to the front of the room and recite your memorization work for us!"

It was a command, not a question. He sat frozen in his seat, completely unaware of even the title of the poem, let alone a single line of it.

"Redwan," thundered Miss Su'ad, "please come up here, now!"

Ever so reluctantly, he dragged himself out of his desk and took the necessary steps to the site of what he felt might be his execution. He faced the class but had nothing to say; his red face said it all.

"Please begin, Redwan," his teacher said firmly.

He was trying not to look at his mother but couldn't help noticing her rise out of her chair. His stomach knotted even tighter.

"Redwan," his mother commanded, "come with me!"

With that, she ushered him unceremoniously into the hallway and shut the classroom door firmly behind them. She grabbed him by the elbow and marched him along the corridor to her office where she pushed him through the doorway and closed the door behind them. She turned to Redwan and said with heated conviction, "You've disgraced me, yourself and the family in that classroom today, Redwan. Even worse, you lied to me when I asked you if you had any homework. Just because you think you're smart enough to fool your teacher you've become a lazy boy. From now on, you will do your homework every night! Do you understand?"

Tears trickled down his cheeks as he nodded solemnly.

"Now," she said, "I want you sit down here at this desk and write 100 lines that say, 'I will work hard and I will always tell the truth'."

With that, Hajer plunked him down at her desk and presented him with a pen and paper.

"And," she added, "tonight you will have two poems to memorize, the one from today and the one for tomorrow."

She left Redwan to labour over his lines and figure out how he would ever face his teacher and classmates again.

Another day at recess, Redwan and a friend were discussing the merits of something, perhaps watermelon, their favourite fruit. They continued chatting after the bell rang as they lined up and returned to their class to take their seats. Suddenly, the sound of their teacher's feet thumping rapidly towards him penetrated Redwan's consciousness. He looked up just in time to see her hand swinging through the air about to connect with his cheek. Smack!

As soon as her hand hit his face he overreacted, as was his wont, and reeled back in his desk, moaning loudly. Pleased his drama seemed to have achieved the desired impact on his teacher, he carried on a bit longer, finally settling on a look and a groan that proved effective, holding his jaw askew to the left as if he'd been paralyzed by her blow. She gasped.

"I'm so sorry," his horrified teacher said as the possible implications of her action dawned on her. She backed away from his desk, fled the room and was gone long enough that Redwan's jaw became sore from holding it in that position. Absentmindedly, he switched his paralysis to the other cheek just as his mother and teacher appeared at the door and swooped in on him.

As it turned out, his teacher was much more astute than he gave her credit for. She took one look at him and said, "He's changed sides. His jaw was facing the other direction when I left the room."

"I'll fix that!" his mother said as she swung her arm back and whacked him on the other cheek, then turned and marched out of the classroom, leaving him to deal with the inevitable fallout from his cheeky behaviour.

But while Hajer was strict, she adored her children. Sharaf maintains she favoured Redwan. Apparently, mother and son were similar in many ways and even looked alike until later years when Redwan came to look more like his father.

Life was difficult for Hajer and probably not much fun either. Not only was she a working mother, uncommon in that time and place, but often a single parent when Kaykhosrow worked out of town. As it was long before the age of instant food, or electrical appliances, cooking and housework took a great deal of time and energy.

Because their mother was so busy, the children had jobs around the house. Sharaf cooked from the age of seven and, at the same age, Redwan did the shopping. He learned to choose the freshest produce, haggle for the best price, and ensure he wasn't overcharged for anything. All this made him feel grown up.

While Hajer had to spend her evenings on household management and class preparation, when he was in town Kaykhosrow played games with the children. Their favourite was called "Geography." They had to identify the names of rivers and capitals around the world using their dad's two-volume world atlas and a large wall map. That was fun but the evening study sessions on the Bahá'í Writings with their dad were not. The only redeeming factor in Redwan's eyes was that his father was an excellent storyteller. Kaykhosrow enthralled them with such stories as this:

"As I sat in my shop in the market in Tehran late one afternoon, a good friend dropped by. Business was slow so he presented his palms to me and asked me to read them. I had been thinking of closing my shop early and going home to cook my favourite lamb dish, but as he was such a good friend and so entertaining, I obliged him. I motioned for him to take a seat. I was studying his palms when suddenly a handsome, large, hairy young man, obviously a Kurd by his style of dress, burst into my shop. He immediately perceived what was going on, thrust his palms towards me and said, 'Read my fortune too!'

"Something about this man disturbed me; I glanced furtively at his palms but everything in me railed against obliging him.

"'Oh, no,' I said, 'it's only a hobby. I'm not a professional palm reader. I was just looking at my friend's hands for fun and to pass the time.'

"'Well, why not pass the time with me too?'

"'Honestly, I don't know much about palm reading.'

"'Somehow, I think you do. I need to know what my future holds, so please oblige me.'

"I could tell he wouldn't brook any argument so I took his hands. They were large, and though red and rough, they were beautifully shaped. I flipped them over to examine his palms and immediately saw that imminent danger and that a violent death awaited him. My stomach turned and I pushed his hands away from me.

"'I'm really not a competent palm reader,' was all I managed to say.

"But the man persisted, 'You saw something. I know you did. Tell me!'

"Somehow this Kurd seemed to have guessed what I saw and almost seemed amused by it. Clearly, he wasn't going to let up on me until I responded. I sighed deeply and replied, 'All I can tell you is that you must take great care and exercise extreme caution for you may be in some danger.'

"The man was silent for a brief moment as that information registered, then he bowed his head slightly and backed out of the shop.

"The next morning, as I crossed the public square en route to my shop, out of the corner of my eye I saw something hanging. Almost involuntarily I lifted my gaze. To my horror I saw the Kurdish rebel from the night before hanging there. Everything went black. I fainted on the spot. When I came to, I vowed before God never to read anyone's palms again. Not because I'd caused his death for I had not: I'd just witnessed it in advance and I didn't want to experience anything like that ever again."

And he never did. In fact, Redwan recalls his father averting his eyes whenever his children handed him anything.

During their evening study sessions over the years, Kaykhosrow allowed Sarmad to fall asleep. This irritated Redwan to no end. He kept thinking, "Sarmad will never learn anything or remember any of these stories or Dad's wise insights." But his baby brother proved him wrong. One day, soon after Kaykhosrow died, Redwan overheard Sarmad, then fifteen, recount a long and complicated story that their dad had told them while Sarmad slept.

Redwan remains grateful to his father for persevering with them in studying the Bahá'í Writings. For him, those nightly studies provided a framework for life and grounding in the Bahá'í teachings. For Sarmad and Sharaf it went deeper. Their knowledge of the Bahá'í Writings, particularly those they memorized with their dad, sustained their children and grandchildren during the more than thirty years in Iraq when they were denied access to Bahá'í literature.

Kaykhosrow had an infectiously playful side as well. He would spare no energy when playing tricks on his family and friends, which explains why one morning when Redwan and his siblings looked out the window and saw that the ground was white, they assumed that their trickster dad had spent the entire night sprinkling salt on it. They had never seen snow before.

∾

From an early age, under his dad's tutelage, Redwan became a huge movie fan. Each summer the family frequented open-air evening screenings inside the brick walls of either the Roxi or the Al Hamra theatres. There they assembled on rows of chairs or wooden soda pop boxes set out on sunbaked earthen floors sprinkled with water to keep the dust down.

Vendors strolled up and down the aisles carrying soda, candy, an array of roasted pumpkin, watermelon, sunflower seeds and cigarettes. Redwan alternated between watching his dad's animated expressions, which vividly mirrored his response to the screen action, and watching the movie itself. Often he didn't know which was more engaging. If the film included kissing, Kaykhosrow would look embarrassed and turn to the children and say, "They must be related." The kids knew better but snickered at his sweetness in trying to protect them.

Redwan adored swashbuckler action movies with a hefty splash of romance, films like *The Crimson Pirate*, but Westerns were his favourite. Burt Lancaster was his hero but he was entirely taken by the swimmer Esther Williams. After a particularly lively film he would leap about in the courtyard with a fake sword, acting out various roles with enthusiasm.

In July 1953, after his family moved to Baghdad from Khaneqin, Redwan played a Kurd in a multicultural play. The next year they moved to Sulaymaniyyah. There, and years later back in Baghdad, he wrote and acted in historical plays for the Bahá'í community and at school. Redwan loved the stage and planned to pursue acting as a profession but Hajer and Kaykhosrow discouraged him. It was a hobby to them, not a solid career choice.

When it became clear that his parents wouldn't condone a future for Redwan in acting, he switched his allegiance to medicine. Soon he began to envisage himself as a first-class surgeon, well respected, well paid, and pleased to be of service to others. His cousin, Ikbal, who had recently returned to Baghdad after six years of pioneering[4] with her family in the Seychelles Islands, shared that dream. While she attained her goal, with fate only intervening later when she was incarcerated, fate intervened in Redwan's plans immediately.

It was 1963. Along with hundreds of other students, Redwan sat in a long row in the school auditorium writing his baccalaureate university entrance exams. Suddenly a wad of paper flew in through a window and landed on the floor beside him. He immediately raised his hand to attract an invigilator [a proctor].

"That bundle of paper just landed here, sir," Redwan said, pointing to it. "Please take it. It doesn't have anything to do with me."

The invigilator picked it up, opened and examined it and shook his head. He gave Redwan an inquiring look as if weighing his story, nodded and strode off. As soon as the invigilator was out of earshot, the young man in front of Redwan swung around in his desk, flicked open a switchblade and aimed it at Redwan's chest.

"You're in big trouble now," he snarled. "I'll get you outside after!"

---

4        A term used in the Bahá'í Faith for people that move to another location for the purpose of sharing the teachings of their faith.

Redwan had no doubt that the paper was intended for this young man. Nor did he doubt his threat. Fear overcame him. He'd never been in a fight and he never wanted to be. Desperate to clear out of the hall as quickly as possible, he hastily scribbled a few more answers before turning in his incomplete exam paper. He darted out of the building past the armed guards posted outside the school doors and made the half-hour run home at record speed.

Redwan knew that his exam results would be wretched but prayed for a miracle because his heart was set on becoming a doctor. While Ikbal excelled in her exams and went on to become the top medical student in the country, his results were below average, certainly insufficient to earn him a place in the School of Medicine in Baghdad, then rated the best in the Middle East.

Redwan tried to get into the Faculty of Science to study chemistry but it was oversubscribed. Reluctantly he accepted the only alternative, the Faculty of Education to study biology.

Ironically, the day Redwan lined up to register for his university program, he happened to stand behind his knife-wielding nemesis. Despite the fear welling up in him, Redwan took a deep breath, braced himself and tapped the foiled cheater on the shoulder.

"Hi," Redwan said, "remember me?" He saw the look of recognition in the young man's eyes.

"Yes," said the student, "I do, and I'm ashamed. I'm really sorry about what I did in that exam room. I was desperate to pass those exams. Please forgive me."

Redwan nodded, "Of course," he said as he exhaled the butterflies.

Surprisingly, Redwan became friends with that fellow, whom he described as kind and rather quiet. He credits him for unwittingly changing the course of his destiny. Had Redwan been accepted into medicine and remained in Iraq he would have been imprisoned along with his mother and cousin.

∽

In the mid 1960s, as part of his ongoing effort to support his family, Kaykhosrow left Iraq for Kuwait to work for an optometrist. The two years previous he'd worked in an underground warehouse where he was consistently exposed to toxic chemicals. In 1968, he returned to Baghdad because of a lump that had grown on the left side of his lower back.

Initially, Redwan, who worked at the university as a demonstrator of third year parasitology (among other subjects), hoped it was a hydatid cyst caused by a parasitic tapeworm that could be treated surgically. Kaykhosrow was confident it was benign. Redwan asked Ikbal, then in her final year of medical school, to look at it. She suggested he see the country's best thoracic surgeon, Dr. Yusuf-Al-Noa'man. The surgeon drained almost a litre of fluid from Kaykhosrow's pleural cavity and sent it to a pathology lab for diagnostic testing.

A few days later Redwan picked up the biopsy results. Even though he suspected cancer he was shocked by that diagnosis. At most his father only had a few months to live. That thought confounded him. Redwan staggered out of the lab, climbed into his beat-up yellow and white German Ford Taunus (not Taurus), and sat there in a tearful stupor for some time before driving to Ikbal's.

Ikbal and Redwan decided not to tell anyone about Kaykhosrow's diagnosis or prognosis. In those days, and in that country, people didn't utter the word cancer, especially to the patient. Sharaf, who adored her father, was teaching in Baquba and returned home on weekends. Redwan and Ikbal reasoned this news would devastate her. They considered Sarmad, at 16, too young to bear it. Hajer, they concluded, already shouldered enough with Kaykhosrow's care without having to deal with that diagnosis.

After Redwan left Ikbal, he sat in his car outside her house and sobbed uncontrollably. He didn't know how to hide his grief from his family. Fortunately, by the time he returned home it was late. Everyone was asleep on the roof. He tiptoed up to his father and stared down at the man who had always been the centre of his universe. Then he crawled into his own bed and wept. That day was August 14, 1968, Redwan's twenty-first birthday and one of the saddest days of his life.

Redwan kept his news to himself for the next two days but his mother detected something was wrong. He was relieved when she finally extracted the truth from him. Now she became a part of the informed group that also included his Uncle Munir. The doctor treated Kaykhosrow with radiotherapy but it was too late. Adenocarcinoma had metastasized to his lungs.

During those days, Redwan spent as much time as he could with his dad. Kaykhosrow accepted his declining health with fortitude in spite of the pain that was at times excruciating. He never complained. He lay in bed reading Bahá'í books, chatting with family and numerous friends who visited, some from Iran and some from as far away as the USA.

As wonderful a father as Kaykhosrow was, he and Redwan clashed on occasion. Redwan attributes this to youthful exuberance bumping up against his dad's concern that Redwan always say and do the right thing. Kaykhosrow would tell him, "Think of a man in a brand new, clean white suit. Now imagine a drop of ink on the front of that suit jacket. It would be spoiled wouldn't it? It's the same thing with your conduct. You must always protect yourself from making the kind of mistakes that will soil your reputation." Though Redwan knew that was true, he sometimes found Kaykhosrow's standards too high. But with his father's imminent death, he determined to resolve any old grudges he had against him.

From his deathbed, Redwan's father left him many parting gifts. Redwan remembers a particular Monday night when he must have looked glum. At the time, he was working as a lab assistant/demonstrator in a first year zoology class at the Faculty of Education at the University of Baghdad.

Kaykhosrow asked, "What's the matter with you, Redwan? You look troubled."

"Yeah, that's because I hate Tuesdays and Thursdays."

"Why is that?"

"Because Professor Fawzi Ismail verbally abuses us assistants in front of the students."

"What does he say?"

"Every day he finds a new way to humiliate and degrade us. He's disgusting."

"Really?"

"Yes!"

Kaykhosrow asked a few more questions and then said, "Redwan, clearly this man has never been loved and appreciated. His behaviour reflects his lonely and unhappy soul."

"Loved? How could anyone love a crazy man like him?"

"But Redwan, surely there's something good about him that you could love."

"Look Dad, you don't know Professor Fawzi. He's despicable."

"No! He sounds more to me like a man that desperately wants to be loved and appreciated. There's nobody in the world that doesn't have at least one quality worthy of admiration."

"You could be wrong on this one," Redwan replied.

"Redwan, you must find something about him that you admire."

"Trust me, there's nothing admirable about him; he's just plain vile."

"Don't gossip and call names. Just try to find one positive thing, even if it's small, and then focus your attention only on that, nothing else. You'll see things will change for you."

"That's impossible. He's a snake and you can't love a snake."

"Pray about it and see what you can come up with. I've got every confidence you can turn this situation around and then you'll feel better."

Even though Redwan knew his father would never give him bad advice, his suggestions sounded like platitudes. He felt annoyed by his dad's apparent lack of appreciation for just how nasty Professor Fawzi actually was. With reluctance, Redwan began to pray that night, eventually in earnest, to find a single positive thing about Professor Fawzi. When he was just about to give up, he realized that perhaps there was one thing worthy of admiration after all. Fawzi was extremely responsive to his students and would do anything for them. Redwan had frequently observed his rotund figure running from one side of the lab to the other in response to a student's raised hand.

With that thought in mind he knocked on Professor Fawzi's door the next morning to get his assignment. Something in Redwan's face must have softened because Professor Fawzi immediately acted differently towards him. Over time Redwan let Professor Fawzi know how much he appreciated his teaching skills. Thus began a profound transformation in their relationship that ultimately resulted in Professor Fawzi treating his teaching assistants with more respect. And when, sometime later, Redwan told Professor Fawzi about his plans to move away to continue his studies, his former foe wept. "You've been like a son to me," he said. "You showed me the value of caring for others."

∽

Meanwhile Redwan's father's condition deteriorated steadily. Despite his ill health, he continued to sit in a chair by his bed and recite Bahá'í prayers and passages. On the day he predicted privately to Hajer that he would die, Hajer invited Ni'mat 'Abdu'l-Waheed, a close family friend, to join them for prayers. If Kaykhosrow's expectation proved correct Hajer felt they would need his support. At approximately 2:30 a.m. Kaykhosrow asked Redwan to lift him onto his bed. Hajer woke up Sarmad to join the family. Once he was settled in bed, Kaykhosrow thanked each of them for their loving support and told them how proud he was of them. Then he closed his eyes, sneezed twice gently and passed away.

∽

Five years later, in England, Redwan struggled to pull himself out of his reverie. He was still sad about his father's death but he was sickened about what might be happening to his mother inside prison walls. He habitually peered nervously over his shoulder waiting for the long tyrannical hand of Iraq to snatch him up, drag him back and slam him into prison as well.

# Up Unto the Hills

Before heading to Newfoundland I looked forward to returning to Winnipeg. I was excited to share my experiences with Lionel Knight, a Métis man and the last in a succession of my grandmother Jessie's husbands. He was the only grandfather I'd ever known and always made time to listen to me.

Unfortunately, Lionel died of a heart attack just before my return. I was shocked and terribly disappointed. He had kept fit by walking five miles a day, even in the worst weather Winnipeg could dish out. But, in the midst of my grief, a powerful sense of reassurance washed over me; I was certain I would see Lionel again. In life he affirmed me and validated my worth. In death he imparted another gift; absolute certainty that life after death was a reality. I have no explanation as to how I knew that. I just did.

A few weeks later, in October 1971, I boarded a train headed from Winnipeg to Corner Brook, Newfoundland. Though accidental, my timing was impeccable. The performance of the fall colours outside the train windows mesmerized me, particularly the reds and golds of the maple trees that distinguish Eastern Canada in autumn.

I had been hired to work as a nurse in pediatrics at Memorial Hospital in Corner Brook. In terms of my main agenda, my search for love and unity, I soon observed that people were neither happier nor more united in Newfoundland. Corner Brook's economic recession and Newfoundland's isolation no doubt contributed to that.

My roommate, Barbara (not her real name), attempted suicide. I arrived home from work one day to find her cat, Link, hurling itself against the bathroom door. I struggled to open the door, eventually succeeding in dislodging Barbara's legs, which were wedged against the door.

She was out cold; a drained beer bottle lay beside her head along with

57

an empty container of sleeping pills, Mandrex, mine for when I worked nights. I called an ambulance. The paramedics gathered up a still-unconscious Barbara and loaded her into the ambulance. I rode along with her. I knew her family lived in St. John's but I didn't think to try to contact them.

My nurse friend, Joyce, who happened to be on duty on another floor that night, joined me in emergency. As soon as the attending nurse left the room, Joyce took charge and performed her own examination on Barbara. She quickly discovered and removed a tampon soaked with green discharge. Barbara, we later learned, had a fling with a biker, contracted gonorrhea, and couldn't face her boyfriend with the news that she had probably infected him.

Oddly, about a week before, as we sat around with a couple of friends smoking dope in our apartment, I'd looked into Barbara's eyes and seen with absolute clarity that she was going to kill herself. But that night, when she got up to leave, I was too out of it to stop her. Later, when she returned home I was surprised and grateful. After that experience, I never smoked marijuana again. I felt I had seen the future in that altered state and I was neither ready nor equipped to deal with it.

Barbara survived but I was becoming increasingly depressed. Not only had I failed to find love and unity in Newfoundland but the prevailing issues of the day, such as over-population, pollution, poverty and political corruption disheartened me. I longed to find something that would make sense of it all, some kind of master plan.

I had looked to Christianity, but I had long since given up finding answers there. Yet, every day as I exited the hospital doors after work, and looked out over the craggy hills that framed Corner Brook's harbour, unbidden Biblical words played over and over in my head: "I will lift mine eyes unto the hills from whence cometh my help. My help cometh from the Lord."[1]

One sunny winter day, as I walked along a snow-packed path in a downtown park en route to explore work alternatives at a drug crisis centre, a feeling of hope surged within me. At the centre I met Sean Gabriel, a Mi'kmaq

---

1    Psalm 121:1-2, KJV.

man my age. That afternoon he told me about the Bahá'í Faith. He said that it arose out of Islam in Iran in the middle of the nineteenth century in the same way that Christianity arose out of Judaism.

He said Bahá'u'lláh (pronounced Baha-oo-llah) was its Prophet founder. Born a nobleman, Bahá'u'lláh's teachings garnered Him 40 years of imprisonment and exile from country to country. During that time, Bahá'u'lláh wrote over 100 volumes of books and letters to the kings and rulers of the time, calling them to social justice.

Behind Sean stood a portrait he had painted of 'Abdu'l-Bahá, Bahá'u'lláh's eldest son, whom He appointed as the Centre of His Covenant. 'Abdu'l-Bahá's image captivated me. So did the stories Sean recounted. Over 20,000 of this Faith's earliest followers were martyred in the most barbarous fashion because Muslim clerics interpreted Muhammad's teaching that He was the "Seal of the Prophets" literally. Bahá'u'lláh taught that Muhammad was indeed the Seal of the Prophets that concluded the Adamic Cycle but that Bahá'u'lláh's forerunner, the Bab inaugurated a new cycle; the Bahá'í Cycle.

Sean took me to a few weekly Bahá'í meetings or informal chats called "firesides" at Patti and Doug Sheldrick's home. Despite my interest, I was reticent to invest much time or energy into learning about the Bahá'í Faith. I had been disappointed before by things that initially made sense only to later discover their fatal flaws.

One night, my nurse friend, Joyce, invited me to accompany her to a church where they spoke in tongues. She thought it would be "a laugh." It was a novel idea so I agreed to go along. I remember hearing people speak, what my mother would refer to as gobbledygook, but remember nothing else except our conversation afterwards as Joyce and I made our way down the hill in the dark. I mentioned that I was interested in the Bahá'í Faith. She dismissed it saying that she'd checked it out and found that it was similar to the Mormon Faith.

Though I was sure Joyce was wrong, I didn't know enough about the Bahá'í Faith to tell her otherwise. I felt badly about that. Despite myself, I was drawing closer to identifying with this Faith. At a certain point, I began to wonder if I was already a Bahá'í but I wasn't sure I'd be able to stick it out long enough in Newfoundland to find out.

Each day the notion of leaving held increasing appeal. For one thing, my new job was creeping me out. I had left the hospital to work at the drug crisis centre where Sean worked under the direction of Joe our paranoid boss. When my fellow workers and I compared notes, we discovered that Joe had claimed to be an Episcopalian priest and to have "run the numbers" for Tony Luciano, a renowned Mafia member from New York. He had an ample supply of rifles, and just like the cowboys in the Westerns we used to watch on Saturday afternoons at the Uptown Theatre in Winnipeg, he never sat with his back to a door.

Once, en route to meet up with a friend whose parents lived in Chapel Hill, I accompanied Joe to Nova Scotia and rode beside him as he test-drove a Porsche. He wanted a get away car. Some months after I returned to Winnipeg I understood why. Joe was charged and convicted with smuggling narcotics into the Atlantic Provinces.

At a nightclub one night, Sean introduced me to a Bahá'í named Gord Noseworthy. He was a rebellious character who, despite being totally blind, had hitchhiked alone across the States, including all through the Bayou. After a brief conversation with me he said he had figured out "my number." I liked to run away from things, he concluded, but if I'd make a commitment to stay until I'd figured out if I was a Bahá'í or not, he would be there for me day or night. I could call him any time I needed him. I had been unaware of my propensity to take flight but realized Gord was right; that was my pattern. For some reason I implicitly trusted his judgment and took him up on his offer.

I kept attending those weekly Bahá'í meetings because I was finding answers there. Years later, a friend told me, that when she came upon the Bahá'í teachings, it was like looking through a single keyhole and finally seeing the whole vista instead of fragmented components. Relieved and exhilarated, I began to comprehend a coherent new world order based on justice and unity in diversity.

Concepts like progressive revelation made perfect sense to me. Bahá'ís believe that approximately every thousand years, God chooses a certain perfect soul through whom to reveal teachings for that age. Humanity's job is to recognize these Manifestations (Messengers) and put their teachings into practice. The spiritual teachings of the great religions remain constant, such as the Ten Commandments, but the social teachings require renewal from age to age. So, while Christ was fully capable of revealing laws relevant to nationhood or even world citizenship, His followers weren't ready to receive them. Later, it fell to Muhammad to advance teachings about nationhood.

Other Bahá'í teachings, such as those on life after death, the equality of men and women, the elimination of all forms of prejudice, the harmony of science and religion, an international auxiliary language, and world government, seemed entirely relevant.

Bahá'u'lláh abrogated clergy. Instead, He made each of us responsible for our own spiritual development based upon our study of the Word of God. That was exactly what I'd been longing for, an updated, God-given standard. Bahá'í burial laws, however, presented an obstacle for me.

One day during my childhood, my grandmother, Jessie, took me to a graveyard (the only other place she ever took me was the race track) where she fussed about not having brought flowers for her brother-in-law, Tommy's, grave. Cremation was for me, I instantly decided. Cemeteries seemed such a waste of space. Later, when I heard that 'Abdu'l-Bahá said God would have created us self-igniting upon death if He favoured cremation, I had a good laugh.

A lesser stumbling block for me was the law against the consumption of alcohol unless medically prescribed. But since I believed Bahá'u'lláh's claim, that He was a Manifestation of God, I resolved to defer to His teachings, that is after one last drunk, compliments of cheap and infamous "Screech," Newfoundland rum. In the aftermath of that night I was happy not to touch alcohol again.

One evening Gord and I were walking along a snowy road, near the drug crisis centre discussing religion in general and the Bahá'í Faith in particular. Suddenly he turned to me and said, "You're sitting on the fence, Shar. This faith is like a bottomless ocean. If you believe in your heart that Bahá'u'lláh is

Who He says He is, jump in. You'll spend the rest of your life learning about His teachings so you might as well get started."

Again, Gord was right; I knew it in my gut even though my research was limited to one book: *Warriors of the Rainbow*.[2] It was about indigenous prophecies about One that would come to unite all people. From what little I knew, it seemed that all of the prophecies in that book pointed to Bahá'u'lláh. The real clincher, however, came when I read 'Abdu'l-Bahá's statement about the importance of the "indigenous population of America." He compared them to the warring tribes of the Arabian Peninsula who, after the influence of Muhammad's revelation "…became so radiant as to illumine the world. Likewise, these Indians, should they become educated and guided, there can be no doubt that they will become so illumined as to enlighten the whole world."[3] Based upon my previous interactions with indigenous people, I absolutely believed that. My immediate thought was that if it was good enough for them, it was certainly good enough for me.

I couldn't wait to attend the Sheldrick's next fireside. On the appointed night, March 27, 1972, Ann Schuster, a visiting Bahá'í from Ontario, was the guest speaker. She sat in an armchair to the left side of the living room picture window, which overlooked Corner Brook Harbour. I sat kitty-corner to her in an easy chair and listened intently. I'll never forget the passage she quoted from Bahá'u'lláh as it seemed to speak directly to me:

> Immerse yourselves in the ocean of My words, that ye
> may unravel its secrets and discover all the pearls of wisdom that
> lie hid in its depths. Take heed that ye do not vacillate in your
> determination to embrace the truth of this Cause…[4]

---

2        Brown, Vinson, and William Willoya, *Warriors of the Rainbow*, Healdsgraph, Naturegraph Publishers, 1965.

3        Abdu'l-Bahá', *Tablets of the Divine Plan*, United States Bahá'í Publishing Trust, 1993, pocket edition, p. 32.

4        Bahá'u'lláh, *Proclamation of Bahá'u'lláh*, United States Bahá'í Publishing Trust, 1978 reprint, p. 122.

When Ann finished her talk, I slipped into the kitchen, ostensibly to see if I could help Patti set out the refreshments. While I was busy arranging cookies I quietly told her that I wanted to become a Bahá'í. She froze momentarily. Her sweet face flushed with surprise. "That's wonderful!" she said, and gave me a hug. Patti asked me to wait while she got a declaration card for me to sign. Declaration cards (no longer used in Canada) are for the purpose of official registration. Anyone that believes in Bahá'u'lláh is essentially a Bahá'í. I knew about the registration process because a co-worker from the drug crisis centre had become a Bahá'í the week before. In fact, a few days later, he informed me that I should stop swearing now that I was a Bahá'í.

Patti returned to the kitchen with a small blue card in her hand. She laid it down on the table beside the cookies, gave me a pen and asked me to fill it out and sign on the bottom line. That done, she hooked arms with me and led me triumphantly out of the kitchen and back into the living room to make the "big announcement."

I couldn't figure out why everyone was so excited. I later learned that with my declaration I had become the ninth adult member of the Bahá'í community and therefore, automatically a member of the Local Spiritual Assembly of the Bahá'ís of Corner Brook.[5] The Assembly would not have formed at the upcoming annual election without a ninth adult Bahá'í.

Afterwards, with a prayer book that my admirer, ten-year-old Bevon Sheldrick, lent me, I headed out their front door. The Sheldricks always stood at their living room window to wave goodbye to departing guests. It was a touching sight, the five of them, shoulder to shoulder waving from that golden-lit room. I returned their wave and set out along the sidewalk into the dark night.

I was a bit jarred by the sudden turn of events, especially since I wasn't all that sure I believed in God. I felt the need for some kind of celestial confirmation. I crossed the road and lay down on the snowy hill overlooking the

---

5       The body that governs each local Bahá'í community.

port where I made a silent but adamant demand to God, if there was One, I wasn't sure there was, and fully expected to see some dramatic action in the night sky, at the very least a comet.

Eventually, as the chill set into my bones, I gave up waiting and tromped down one hill and up another to my apartment. Once home, I opened the prayer book and stared at the unfamiliar and very formal words. They felt awkward in my mouth but I kept reciting them over the next days because I promised the Sheldricks I would. They were so sincere that I couldn't bear the thought of disappointing them.

Patti had pointed out the section of the prayer book that contained three obligatory prayers. As I thumbed through the prayer book I noted there was a short, a medium, and a long one, but somehow I missed a notation that indicated choosing to recite one of these prayers a day. For some months I kept myself busy reciting all three.

In the short obligatory prayer or noonday prayer I discovered a hidden gift, what, as a teenager I had ached to understand; the purpose of my life.

> I bear witness, O my God, that Thou hast created me to know Thee and to worship Thee. I testify at this moment to my powerlessness and to Thy might, to my poverty and to Thy wealth. There is none other God but Thee, the Help in Peril, the Self-subsisting.[6]

What a relief! Finally, I knew why I was alive and what I was supposed to do, which was to learn about God and His will for us today through the writings of His most recent Manifestation, Bahá'u'lláh. According to His teachings, though the immediate future of the world looked bleak, the long-term picture, founded upon justice, would be brilliant.

My pact with Gord fulfilled, now that I was a Bahá'í, I could leave Newfoundland. I packed my trunk, shipped it off and soon followed suit. En

---

6      Bahá'u'lláh, "Short Obligatory Prayer," Bahá'í Prayers, United States Bahá' Publishing Trust, 1987 pocket edition, p. 339.

route, I read about Christian prophecies fulfilled by Bahá'u'lláh in the appendix of *Release the Sun*[7], a book about the early history of the Bahá'í Faith. As I read it, I realized I wasn't as disenfranchised from Christianity as I'd previously thought. In fact, Christ's prophecies about His return were deeply rooted in my consciousness. In my own way, I'd been on the lookout for Him during the decade that followed my initial intimation about His return. He had appeared and I had recognized Him, despite His new name.

It wasn't until I arrived in Winnipeg that I realized I'd left the Spiritual Assembly of the Bahá'ís of Corner Brook in the lurch in terms of its ninth member. I finally mustered the courage to call Patti to ask how they would manage. I had determined that if they needed me I would return even though I wasn't inclined to. I still remember my relief when she told me that a young woman named Corrie had pioneered from Ontario so they had their ninth member.

I had arrived in Newfoundland dispirited, despite the full blaze of East coast autumn splendor. As I departed, surrounded by snow and ice, my soul blazed with joy. Not even the theft of my cherished custom-beaded moccasins could dampen my spirit. My 23-year-old mind bubbled with excitement. Of course I had no idea that a century earlier, in what was then Persia, a woman named Zarbanoo had set foot on a parallel spiritual quest that resulted in her becoming a Bahá'í too. Without her pursuit of truth I can't imagine how I ever could have met her grandson, Redwan Moqbel.

---

7    William Sears, *Release the Sun*, Bahá'í Publishing, 2003.

# In the Meantime

To cope with the horrors of what was going on in Iraq, Redwan dove deep into his studies. By 1976 he held a PhD in Immunoparasitology that he followed up with a second masters degree in immunology from Brunel University in Uxbridge, Middlesex.

Within the Bahá'í community in London he had close friends, but he steered clear of other Middle Easterners because of the danger such association might bring to himself and other Bahá'ís in the Middle East. This included Iran, where the persecution of the Bahá'ís was on the rise again.

Religious persecution of a very personal sort was the primary reason Redwan decided to pursue his studies outside of Iraq. At the age of nineteen, the Biology Department of University of Baghdad offered him a job teaching lab courses, including Comparative Anatomy of Vertebrates, to fourth year students, just a year behind him. A beautiful young Muslim woman, Layla, (not her real name) joined the lab during the last year of her Master's degree. Redwan and Layla fell desperately in love. For both of them it was first love, pure and sweet. As dating wasn't an option in their culture, they saw each other only at university. But, Redwan's faith proved to be an insurmountable obstacle.

Soon after his father's death, he and Layla decided to marry. As a Bahá'í, Redwan sought and obtained the necessary consent from his mother. Hajer immediately liked Layla and approved of Redwan's choice. Although Kaykhosrow and Layla never met, she attended his funeral reception.

The evening that Layla intended to approach her family, Redwan was beside himself with excitement and could hardly sleep. He longed for his own life with the woman he loved.

66

But the next day when Layla failed to show up at school he began to worry. It wasn't proper for him to call or visit her home so he waited, suspended in fear. After another mostly sleepless night, he spotted Layla at a distance at the university. He stopped breathing. Her swollen eyes, visible even behind her dark glasses, told the whole story. Layla's mother would have supported their union but her deceased husband's brother violently opposed the notion of Layla marrying a Bahá'í. He immediately arranged her engagement to a Muslim.

"I would rather die than have to marry anyone but you," Layla sobbed to Redwan, "but they've threatened to kill us both if we try to get married."

Redwan knew this was no idle threat. He forced himself to rise above the searing pain of the moment to gain some perspective. His lips quivered and his voice shook as he said, "I can't bear the thought of not marrying you or of you having to marry someone else, but it would be even worse if you were hurt."

Suddenly Redwan saw fear in Layla's eyes. She was looking beyond him.

"It's my uncle!" she exclaimed.

Redwan turned to see an older man heading towards Redwan's office. He knew immediately that it was all over. He had lost his precious love in the very corridor where they had held hands and dreamed of a future together. Now there was nothing he could do to bring that fantasy into reality.

"Whatever happens, Layla, I will always love you," he said quickly while keeping an eye on the advancing uncle.

"Go now!" Layla urged.

Redwan obeyed and strode off in the opposite direction overwhelmed by a sense of desolation. Without Layla, life wasn't worth living.

∾

Redwan's thoughts increasingly centred on leaving Iraq, perhaps for America. Early in January 1971, he began applying to universities abroad. His mother strongly supported his initiative. She knew things were going to get tougher for the Bahá'ís in Iraq because, although not yet fully enforced, Bill 105, passed the year before, outlawed all Bahá'í activities.

The University of California at Berkeley, the University of Colorado in Boulder, and the University of Wisconsin in Madison all accepted Redwan. But he settled on England because at 250 British pounds a year it was a quarter of the cost.

On Sept. 10, 1971, as Redwan sat in the airplane on the runway in Baghdad awaiting his first departure from Iraq, he watched his family on the observation deck. Suddenly, he saw Professor Fawzi break through the small crowd. He held a large, brightly wrapped gift and looked bereft.

Redwan crammed his face closer to the window, silently willing his mother to turn around and recognize Professor Fawzi even though she had never met him. Tears slipped from under his closed lids as he prayed silently. When he finally opened his eyes his mother was talking to Professor Fawzi. Later, in a letter, she explained that Professor Fawzi had wanted to say good-bye and to present Redwan with a box of nougat but had misjudged his time.

As he settled back in his seat on the plane, and breathed a sigh of relief, once again Redwan contemplated the horrors he had witnessed during Iraq's numerous upheavals and the number of times he'd been assaulted by the police for no reason. He was profoundly grateful to be getting out of Iraq.

∽

Once in England, Redwan appreciated its sense of calm and order. His command of the language helped him feel at home immediately bar one Cockney professor whose lectures were incomprehensible to him initially. Still, he adored the English language and soon took delight in learning to pun, something that Arabic does not lend itself to.

He subsisted primarily on baked beans and toast so as not to squander the 200 additional pounds his mother sent him each month from her meager pension.

Just as Redwan's heartbreak over Layla was diminishing, her husband phoned Redwan. He explained they were honeymooning in England, and since Redwan had been such a great teacher and friend of Layla's, he hoped to meet him. Completely blindsided, Redwan failed to manufacture an excuse not to see them. En route to their hotel he stopped to buy a wedding gift: six multicoloured mugs. After all, it was the 70s.

The visit was excruciating for Redwan and Layla. At one point, she positioned herself behind her husband so that only Redwan could see her tears. Redwan left the couple as quickly as he could, but not before the unsuspecting groom extracted a promise from him to take them to the London Zoo the following day.

At the zoo, the husband slopped some food on his tie. As soon as he excused himself to go and clean up, Layla extended her hand to Redwan. He looked at it, but shook his head.

"No, you're someone else's now. I can't," he said.

When he finally bid them farewell, Redwan hoped never to see Layla again but destiny would decree otherwise. While in Iraq for Sharaf's wedding, Layla's younger brother, who adored Redwan, heard he was in town and insisted he visit their family. In the year that had elapsed the couple had produced a baby.

During that visit, once again Layla found an opportunity to speak to Redwan privately. "I can't love my husband," she confessed, "because my heart still belongs to you. I wish the baby was yours, I mean ours!"

Redwan left their home feeling even more dejected. Layla's predicament saddened him. He also felt badly for her well-meaning husband.

∽

Through the Bahá'í community in England, Redwan met and became captivated by a vivacious Scottish lass, Ann Macleod, who hailed from Glasgow. A striking pair, both tall, Ann with green eyes, fair hair and complexion, and Redwan with dark eyes, dark hair and skin, they married in

1973. For the first four years of their marriage they lived in London before moving to Glasgow. There, thanks to the prestigious Wellcome Trust, Redwan did a postdoctoral fellowship under Dr. Derek Wakelin, a leading light in immunoparasitology. In him, Redwan found "the epitome of a gentleman and a wonderful mentor."

∽

Meanwhile, back in Iraq, the Bahá'í captives endured six years and four months of imprisonment. They had been excluded from two amnesties afforded other prisoners but in August 1979, after he assumed Presidency, Saddam Hussein released them as part of a general pardon. Through accounts of Hajer's former cellmates, Redwan learned that his mother had sustained their spirits throughout those years of incarceration. To drown out the screaming coming from torture sessions in adjacent cells, Hajer would gather the women together in a tight circle and lead them in a loud chant or song.

Although Hajer was free, Redwan couldn't return to Iraq because of the life in prison sentence imposed upon him. He didn't see his mother until July 1980 when she managed to obtain a passport and visa to visit him and his family. Their first-born child, Samim, was two years old. Ann was in the final weeks of her pregnancy with Marianne.

At my request, Ann Moqbel kindly wrote the following description of her impressions of Hajer all those years ago:

> When Hajer arrived in London, it was the weekend of the men's final tennis tournament at Wimbledon and a total culture shock for her. But she hid any misgivings and enjoyed her time there meeting Bahá'ís who were in awe of her and her trials and experiences on behalf of the Faith in the Iraqi jail. I never heard her speak ill of her captors and her whole focus was on the plight of the friends back home. Her visit to the resting place of Shoghi Effendi[1] in London was particularly poignant and it was

---

1      Shoghi Effendi was appointed the Guardian of the Bahá'í Faith in the Will and Testament of his grandfather, 'Abdu'l-Bahá. Bahá'u'lláh was Shoghi Effendi's great grandfather.

a great privilege to be able to share that unique experience with her. When we took her home to Scotland she loved it and again met with many of the friends who came from far and near to meet her. She left a tremendously profound impression on all whom she met. During her stay with us, Redwan had to leave for the States (I think) and I was a little unsure of how we would manage but it was fine. She was a sweetly indulgent grandma to Samim and he tested her patience as only a two-year-old can. But she was wonderful with him.

She taught me to cook rice the Iraqi way and was a loving, kind and gentle friend. Her presence was greatly missed when she left. She was anxious to return to Iraq before the start of an Iranian conference in Spain so that she could not be accused of attending it. Such was her concern for the safety of those she had left behind. She was a remarkable and gracious lady.

Redwan recalls his mother saying that if she didn't return others would suffer. Four days after his departure to the US (for an interview at Tufts University), Hajer boarded a plane for Baghdad. Redwan never saw her again.

∾

Those years in Scotland were Redwan's happiest in the UK. He adored the Glaswegians whom he found to be open, accepting and fun unlike in London where he encountered prejudice because of his skin colour. Even his PhD supervisor called him a wog or worse.

Redwan continued to excel in his profession. In 1980, at a scientific conference in Edinburgh, he shared his observations about the role of the eosinophil, a white blood cell, in killing worm larvae. As a consequence, he was invited to join the conference speakers for supper. Over supper he was offered a job at the University of London's Cardiothoracic Institute, later named the National Heart and Lung Institute. So the family moved back to London where Redwan's successful scientific research catapulted him to international recognition as an authority on the eosinophil and its role in the inflammatory process in asthma and cancer.

He was also well known and respected within the Bahá'í community. All those nights of enforced study at his father's insistence paid off in terms of Redwan's knowledge of the Bahá'í Writings. His interest in people, and his outstanding skills as a speaker, kept him in demand. In 1979 he was elected[2] to the National Spiritual Assembly of the Bahá'ís of the United Kingdom where he served until 1992 when he was appointed an Auxiliary Board member for South East England.[3]

∞

Redwan and Ann's marriage, however, did not fare so well. They separated in 1988. Ann moved to the Isle of Lewis in the Outer Hebrides with Sam and Marianne. Redwan remained in London. He was heartsick about the loss of day-to-day contact with his children. Seven years later, when Redwan and children were accustomed to traveling to see each other, Redwan accepted a position as a professor at the Faculty of Medicine at the University of Alberta in Edmonton. He felt he needed a new beginning to rebuild his life.

---

2    Bahá'í elections are by secret ballot and without campaigning.
3    An appointed institution. All such service is performed as a volunteer.

# In Between Time

Freshly returned to Winnipeg from Newfoundland, I was keen to share my new-found discovery that Christ had returned but I must have been a little too enthusiastic because my dad made a point of informing me of the two subjects that make Canadians squirm: politics and religion. After his admonition I tried to share my discovery only with those that expressed interest, which turns out to be the Bahá'í approach.

In May 1972, I set off with a group of Bahá'ís headed to the Bahá'í National Convention held in Edmonton. There, old, young, hippy, executive, wealthy, impoverished, white, black, indigenous, Asian, you name it, we were crammed into a hotel lobby, engaged in animated conversation. I had read about the principle of unity in diversity in the Bahá'í Writings. Seeing it in action further confirmed me in the Bahá'í Faith.

Jalal, a new age rock band, performed that weekend. The combination of their lyrics counter-pointed against a backdrop of arresting images, had the audience on its feet.

One afternoon during the Convention, while sitting on the riverbank chatting with some new friends, Jack Lenz, Jalal's piano player, happened along. He introduced himself to me. Dressed in white, with shoulder length wavy brown hair. I was struck by his resemblance to the picture of Christ I'd studied on the wall at choir practice when I was a teenager at Westworth United Church.

∞

After the Convention I spent nine glorious days at the Bahá'í Centre in Fort Qu'Appelle, Saskatchewan along with eighteen other Bahá'ís, mostly my age, from across Canada. During the days, when we weren't immersing ourselves in a collective study of the Bahá'í writings, we meandered around the sage strewn hills in the early summer sun.

73

After that I set out for Camp Robertson, a United Church camp just north of Gimli on Lake Winnipeg. My friend, John MacLeod, hired me to work as the camp nurse. A close friend of John's family, Jean Hedley, formerly the camp nurse, became the elder caregiver. By the end of that summer John, Jean and ten more new friends became Bahá'ís. Every morning and evening we'd gather on the shores of Lake Winnipeg to pray. My soul soared.

Come September, I set out with a new friend, Julie Yates, to join a travelling Bahá'í teaching project in Quebec. The band Jalal performed at community halls we rented and invited the public to attend. Jack Lenz doubled as our bus driver. I positioned myself so that I could watch his face in the bus's rear view mirror. Ours eyes met with increasing frequency. One day I asked one of our project coordinators if she would pray for me, because I confided, I wanted to get married. Without hesitation she replied, "Oh, I have seen you and Jack together and I will pray for you!" For whatever reasons I tried to resist the pull I felt towards him but after a while I felt as if I was trying to swim against the current. I made a conscious decision to give in and go with the flow. Almost immediately, Jack approached me, asked if he could speak to me, and proceeded to tell me that he was attracted to me and wanted to know if I was interested in getting to know him with a view to marriage. His directness almost knocked me over but having made that decision to go with the flow, I went with it.

I returned to Winnipeg in the late fall of 1972. The following April, I moved to Ontario to be closer to Jack who lived with his band on the outskirts of Toronto. Jack had spoken to some Bahá'ís in Bridgenorth who said they needed one more Bahá'í to form the first Spiritual Assembly of the Bahá'ís of Smith Township. So, for a short time, I lived in that lovely lake country. I bought my first car there, a beat up old Ford that barely made the twenty minutes' drive to my job at a hospital in Peterborough.

When I think back to those days I recall how captivated I was by Jack's quiet charisma and the sound of his voice, deep and rich. We decided to marry in Saskatoon because his mother was battling cancer. The night before our wedding, however, I had misgivings and told him so. Jack placed his hands on my shoulders and said, "You're just nervous. It'll be all right." I opted to believe him.

We had a small backyard ceremony to which I wore a long white cotton dress I'd purchased in Peterborough for $35. I completed my wedding ensemble with school bus yellow patent leather clogs, with stumpy heels, and a yellow and white polka-dot barrette. Jack wore a dark green velvet embroidered Indian shirt and grey flannel pants.

He chose the readings and prayers for the ceremony. After the wedding, my father, who was somewhat annoyed at Jack for not allowing our family dog, Archie, to attend the wedding, asked if Jack planned to fly the plane back to Toronto as well, since he had handled everything else.

Later, my parents hosted a wedding supper in a hotel restaurant. For dessert we ate the log roll that dad ordered from Safeway in Winnipeg, especially for our wedding. It was most thoughtful and entirely out of character for him to do such a thing. Unfortunately, the writing on the cake smudged on the long, hot drive from Winnipeg. That wasn't surprising given how crammed our car was with my parents, my brother Don, Archie, Jack (who was allergic to Archie) me, and our luggage.

∽

Once back in Toronto, Jack's band manager, Ted Barris got me a job at CITY TV as an assistant to Ron Haggart, host of *The City Show*. As a typing student drop out, I was a dreadful assistant. Every morning upon his arrival, Ron would make a good-natured show of inspecting my garbage pail that by 10:00 a.m. was already half full with my aborted letter-writing attempts.

From there, thanks to Alex Frame, a Bahá'í friend and an executive producer with the CBC, Margaret Lyons hired me as a production assistant for the radio program, *As it Happens*. Those were heady days for me. After my work as a nurse, the world of creative production was like emerging from a mineshaft into the sunlight. I felt energized. But all too soon that chapter in my life closed because we moved to San Fernando, California. Jack had been hired as the musical director for Seals and Crofts, the number one duo in the

USA at the time. This was a major break for Jack. As exciting as it was for both of us, and as much as I loved the new friends we made in Seals and Crofts and their families, it marked the painful death of my short-lived career in the media for many years to come.

After failed attempts to find meaningful media work in LA, I volunteered as a road assistant to Seals and Crofts. Later, I elected to stay home when I became pregnant with our son Gabriel.

A year and a half later, Jack's musical acumen and charm led to an offer for him to join the duo that bumped Seals and Crofts out of first place that year, Loggins and Messina. So, instead of enjoying the long camping holiday en route back to Toronto that we had planned, we took a six-month detour to Ojai, California. There we rented a sweet little house on Cañada Street with a red wooden bridge in the backyard over what might once have been a creek. The long narrow back yard sloped uphill to the tallest cactus of its kind in the state, according to the owner.

We flew back to Toronto in December of 1975. Alex Frame had hired Jack to be the musical producer for a late night talk show, *Ninety Minutes Live*, hosted by CBC radio personality, Peter Gzowski.

My first order of business was to pay a visit to my former boss, Mark Starowicz, then executive producer of *As it Happens*. Blonde-haired, blue-eyed 11-month-old Gabriel rode along on my hip. Despite the excitement of the previous two years in California, I missed the creative camaraderie of my work on that show. "When are you coming back to work?" Mark asked me.

I could have wept. I longed to return to the job I sacrificed to follow Jack to LA but as I looked at my precious baby I couldn't imagine leaving him in the care of anyone else, even if I could find someone I trusted.

"Well, Shar," my friend Elizabeth Rowan later advised me, "you can look at it one of two ways. Either you can sacrifice and stay at home or Gabriel can sacrifice and you can go to work." My choice was clear.

Jack and I produced two more wonderful children, Colby and Asher. Having the prayers and teachings of the Bahá'í Faith, and the diversity of the Bahá'í community, were a huge support to our child rearing. How can it be anything but helpful to raise children to believe that there is one race, the human race?

Our various homes bustled with all manner of people. In fact, I credit Buffy Ste. Marie for helping us to sell our house in Toronto. This famed singer and songwriter happened to be playing the baby grand piano in our living room the evening prospective buyers came through. She made her song, "God is Alive, Magic is Afoot,"[1] come true for us that night.

Jack and I knew that our children would benefit greatly from widespread exposure to other cultures. We took them to India for the dedication of the Bahá'í House of Worship in New Delhi. We endured hardship together in the Australian outback where we went to meet Aborigine Bahá'ís. Wherever we travelled, including Cuba, Jack entertained Bahá'ís and their friends with songs and prayers he set to music. Our children were always enthusiastic participants.

Jack's work also involved substantial travel and when possible he took our children with him in turn. Asher accompanied him to Lima, Peru. Upon their return I exclaimed, "Asher, you're so lucky. You're only five and you've already been to Peru. I'm 32 and I've never been there!"

Obviously shaken by the poverty he'd witnessed, Asher replied solemnly, "I don't think you'd want to go there, Mom."

One year, when Gabriel was about five, Jack took him to a weekend gathering just outside of Port Hope, Ontario. They stayed with Bahá'ís in Port Hope who were also hosting a guest from London, England, Redwan Moqbel. While the momentum of those years has blurred many details in my mind, I have a hazy impression of a restaurant scene where I may have met Redwan at the end of that Port Hope weekend, though Redwan has no memory of meeting me. If we met then, perhaps that was when I heard a story about his father and the robber.

∽

---

1    The lyrics to "God is Alive, Magic is Afoot" were excerpted from Leonard Cohen's poem of the same name in his 1966 book *Beautiful Losers* (published in Canada by McClelland & Stewart and in the United States by Viking) and set to music by Cree singer Buffy Ste.-Marie for her 1969 Vanguard album *Illuminations*. —ED.

When Asher started kindergarten I enrolled in a Native Studies history class at Trent University in Peterborough, Ontario. Initially I was terrified of failing, but I loved the whole process, including the solitary hour and a half drive each way along country roads. The next year I signed up for more classes. One night a week, I stayed in a cabin motel along the Otonabee River. After many intense years of childcare, including seven consecutive years of diapers, the intellectual stimulation and the time alone was heavenly. Ultimately, it took me 18 years to finish my bachelor's degree because my life took a sharp and unexpected turn.

One day in 1989, while driving my children home from French immersion school in Uxbridge, Ontario I shared news of a marriage breakup of some friends. I concluded by saying, "Don't worry kids, that'll never happen to you." Soon thereafter I discovered to my horror that my marriage was in serious trouble. Though the blame appeared to rest squarely on Jack's shoulders, I've had enough therapy and years of processing our breakup to believe that, among other things, had I been better able to accept the love Jack had to give me, in the way he wanted to give it, perhaps our marriage of sixteen years wouldn't have been so vulnerable.

If I'd heeded my intuition the night before our wedding, I wouldn't have married Jack. That night, an insistent inner voice kept repeating, *I don't think this is a good idea.* Those words didn't surprise me because, despite our love for each other, we were mismatched in terms of lifestyle. After my love affair with the north, I'd vowed never to live in a big city again, but Jack's musical passions tied him to large cities. When I think of Gabriel, Colby and Asher I cannot imagine that our marriage was a mistake. I think that we just weren't up to handling the challenges our union brought forth.

In the aftermath of my marriage breakdown, horrible nightmares plagued me. I was terrified to fall asleep. Dr. Hossein Danesh, the psychiatrist I was fortunate to see over the next three years, assured me that the insights I gleaned from my dreams, however wretched, were gifts of understanding to which I needed to pay attention and for which I should be grateful.

My agony for my children, and my role in our personal catastrophe continued to torment me, but Dr. Danesh helped to ease it by asking, "Shar, would you say that you did the best job you could in your marriage with what you knew at the time?" After some consideration, I replied that I had. That realization helped to quiet that nagging inner voice.

A friend of mine, Brenda Kotras, practiced Neurolinguistic Programming (NLP). Like a mind engineer, she guided me through a process that resulted in banishing the soul-shattering images that haunted my psyche. The books *Codependent No More* and *Beyond Codependency* by Melodie Beattie[2] helped me to understand the unhealthy dynamics of my relationship with Jack. Still it took years for my wounded soul to recover.

One day, when Dr. Danesh and I were discussing the potential of a new love relationship for me in the future, he said, "Shar, before you can put on a new coat you have to take off the old one." That image remained with me as I worked towards removing my *old coat.*

---

2        Published by Harper/Hazeleden in 1987 and 1989, respectively. Some years later, my son, Gabriel, married Erica Carlisle whose father, Roy Carlisle, edited those very books.

# *There's a Plan After All*

In the messy wake of my marriage breakup, bumping into my ex-husband and his new wife, who lived in the same neighbourhood, didn't exactly help my healing process. So, in the end I took my mother's advice. "Shar," she said, "it's always a good idea to move away from the scene of the crime if at all possible." As a huge consumer of murder mysteries, she ought to know.

It was possible for me to move. Gabriel had finished high school and was travelling that year. Colby was in her second year at Maxwell Bahá'í School on Vancouver Island. She'd begged to go there after she watched a hip-hop dance troupe from that school perform in Toronto. I was offered a contract position on a daily CBC television talk show, *What On Earth*, produced in Regina. Asher, who was fifteen, agreed to attend Maxwell with Colby, more out of a desire to help me than a wish to go there. He knew such a job offer for me was a rare and major break as I'd mostly been out of the workforce since before my kids were born. It still saddens me that he made that sacrifice for me. It should have been the other way around.

Nevertheless on September 13, 1993, I landed at Regina Airport. As I descended the steps onto the tarmac I wondered if I'd landed in hell. Massive mosquitoes navigated their way through the largest snowflakes I'd ever seen. They reminded me more of floating communion wafers than ice crystals. I settled into an apartment sparsely furnished with two borrowed thin foam mattresses, some plastic cutlery and utensils and dove into my work with great intensity. I was elated but terrified by this opportunity. I felt I needed to prove, not only to my bosses, Clark Donnelly and Michael Snook, but also to myself, that I could do the job. I also desperately needed to fill the enormous gap formerly occupied by my precious family of five, our large house and assorted pets.

Over my years as a Bahá'í, wherever I lived or travelled I had an instant community to explore and serve. Regina was no exception. In a by-election in June 1994, I was elected to the Local Spiritual Assembly of the Bahá'ís of Regina. At the Unit Convention a year and a half later I was stunned to be elected one of two delegates to represent Regina at the annual Canadian Bahá'í National Convention on April 26, 1996. I can still see myself at the opening of that conference at the Toronto Bahá'í Centre on the corner of Bloor and Huron Streets. Karen McKye was seated to my left. We had become close friends in 1990 when we travelled through Russia and Ukraine as part of a video project I co-produced and directed. I traced down a list of the 153 names in my delegates' package with my index finger. My finger stopped when I came upon the name Redwan Moqbel. I pointed it out to Karen.

"Look," I said, "Redwan Moqbel's here."

"Who's he?" she asked.

"I don't know. All I know is an amazing story about his dad and a burglar and also that he was married and lived in England."

" Is he still married?" she asked. I immediately read her mind. Karen was keen to see me remarried. She had stood by me through the anguish of my marriage breakup and subsequent years of legal fallout.

"I don't know."

"Well, find out!"

"No," I said. "If you're so interested, you find out!"

I wanted to put a face to that name I'd long associated with that story about the robber so I asked a Persian delegate if he could identify Redwan for me. "Oh," he said, pointing across the room, "he's behind that booth over there."

I consulted my watch and decided that with ten minutes remaining before the afternoon session there was time to speak to him. As I approached the booth where Redwan stood I couldn't help thinking about the bread booths in Marrakech where, on cold mornings, I had lined up to buy the most delicious hot bread served with melting, unsalted butter. But instead of a Moroccan bread lady, there stood an entirely unfamiliar looking man. He was tall, rather sturdy, with a full head of black hair.

"Hi," I said, "My name's Shar. I don't remember meeting you but I know a story about your father."

While I recounted the tale, Redwan listened, seemingly disinterested. (*Oh no*, he later confessed to thinking, *not another woman after me!*) When I finished the story Redwan acknowledged it was indeed about his father.

During the convention the next morning I felt Redwan's eyes on me. I was seated directly in front of the podium, though several tables back. Redwan sat to my left on the other side of the room where he faced the podium at a right angle.

On one of the breaks he rushed over to me and said, "I've been watching you," he paused, "and wondering when we might have met."

As he talked I noticed he had unusual pale, mottled marks within the borders of his lips, rather like the sucking pads of nursing babies. Unlike the day before, there was an intriguing twinkle in his warm brown eyes. Like Superman, Karen shot across the packed room of some 250 people just as someone diverted my attention from Redwan. This gave Karen a thirty-second exchange with him; just long enough to discover he was no longer married. As Karen and I made our way to our seats she announced in a voice I feared was too loud: "That's him! That's your next husband!"

Years later, when I asked her why she said that, Karen replied, "I hadn't even processed that thought. I just knew it."

On the last night of the Convention, while I was chatting with an elderly woman who was attached to an oxygen tank, I saw Redwan making his way towards me. Truth be told, my eye was secretly on him most of the weekend. By this point, however, I was irritated with him for not talking to me since our short encounter two days earlier. As he drew near, he said with some urgency, "I need to talk to you." I noted his emphasis on the word "need," obediently bid my friend goodbye, and turned to him.

"Let's sit over here," he said, pointing to a group of empty chairs out of earshot. There, Redwan preceded to display his virtual feathers, something like a peacock and the Leo he turned out to be. (An Iraqi later told me that bragging is a cultural norm, whereas Canadians, like me, endeavour to find more subtle ways to show off.)

I learned that he had moved from England the previous year and had just received the highest ranking in a Canadian national grant competition on asthma research. I countered that I had recently won a grant to do a documentary about the Bribri in Costa Rica. But mostly I didn't help him out one bit. I just sat back and let him talk. He later confessed he was trying desperately to find some point of connection with me. Sometime during our conversation my nose began to run.

"Would you pass me my purse, please, my nose is running," I said.

As Redwan bent forward to retrieve it, he said, "Don't run after it."

*How pathetic*, I thought. Eventually, Redwan asked if I'd like to exchange emails. I agreed but without enthusiasm, saying I would send him my address. I wasn't about to admit I didn't have an email account. He bid me farewell and left.

As Karen drove me to the Shepherd Subway Station the next day, she asked what had transpired between Redwan and me.

"Not much," I said. "He's way too formal for me."

"Oh, Shar," she said, "Persians are formal at these types of events. See him outside of that kind of a gathering before you dismiss him."

Another friend said, "He's great! I worked with him in England. At least go out with him three times before you write him off."

Though I was annoyed with Redwan, I had not lost interest. Back home in Regina I opened an email account post haste.

I enrolled in a Spanish immersion intercession class at the University of Regina in preparation for my project in Costa Rica. One day, a group of Bahá'ís were gathered in the cafeteria when Dr. Pierre-Yves Mocquais, a

Bahá'í and a professor there at the time, appeared. I knew him and his wife, Laura, a little. Pierre-Yves asked if he could speak to me privately. I thought that was a bit strange but agreed. He opened the door for me and we began to stroll in the university courtyard in the mid-June sun.

"I don't know how to say this," Pierre-Yves said, "and I must say I find it extremely uncomfortable, but there's someone from out of town who is quite smitten with you. He's asked me if I'd approach you to see if you'd have lunch with him if he came to town."

I laughed out loud. How quaint for Redwan to send a runner to check things out with me first. I wondered if that was some kind of Middle Eastern thing.

"I know exactly who you're talking about," I said, "and I think we may have a serious conflict ."

"Oh, really," he said, "what's that?"

"I think that we're both looking for a wife!" Pierre-Yves chuckled. What I meant was that after years of looking after others, the notion of someone looking after me was most appealing. Nonetheless, Redwan and I began to email back and forth. He called a few times too. We had long and surprisingly direct conversations about what we were and weren't looking for in a partner. I told him that if he had any leftover baggage from his first marriage or his life in general he better deal with it. After all the counselling I'd had trying to sort myself out, I wanted to make it absolutely clear that I wasn't interested in taking on someone else's problems. To his credit, Redwan had already begun to tackle his issues with a counsellor. Though terrified to remarry only to discover that I made a bad choice, I began to think there might be possibilities for us, even though at most we had spent half an hour together.

In the meantime, CBC cancelled *What on Earth* so my job vanished. I didn't mind. After three years of such intense work, I was ready for a change.

On May 23, 1996, on an airplane headed to Michigan to visit Asher, who was now studying at Interlochen School for the Performing Arts, I ruminated about a conversation I had earlier that day with my mother during a brief visit to Winnipeg. We were in my parents' basement bedroom. It was a good-sized room with off-white shag carpet. Numerous family pictures of my brothers, all our children, and me featured on the pallid pink walls. On the wall above their king-sized bed hung a large square print of oversized magenta flowers. My mom wore her comfortable faded sage green jogging suit with flowers embroidered on the top. She lay on a heating pad to get some relief from her arthritic hips and back. I stretched out beside her on Dad's side of their bed. I was anxious to cut to the chase because I only had an hour before my taxi ride to the airport.

"I've met someone named Redwan Moqbel. He's a professor of Medicine at the University of Alberta. He seems to be interested in me but I'm not so sure. He's pretty serious," I added.

"Well," she promptly replied, "what did you expect? Medicine is a serious business."

"I know it is. It's just that if I'm going to get married again I sure would like it to be to someone who is fun-loving." I pictured an adoring, light-hearted, accomplished and handsome man dressed, in off-hours, in faded jeans and a red plaid lumber jacket, someone who longed to spend time with me.

My mother levied one of those looks of hers that translated into something like, Give your head a shake! "What are you after?" she asked, "Some kind of loser with a sense of humour?"

My mother is nothing if not pragmatic, I thought, as I settled back into my airplane seat, looked out the window then down at my watch, closed my eyes and heaved a long sigh. Suddenly, a Persian man's face from a dream several years before surfaced in my consciousness. At the time I had a terrible crush on someone. In my sleep I demanded three times that God tell me if that relationship was going to work out. That's when I was permitted to see that Persian man's face in a framed picture and at a great distance. I scoffed at that notion but now I laughed out loud. Just maybe there had been a plan all along. I just had to wait for it.

Something else nudged my subconscious. In my hasty departure from Regina and then Winnipeg, I hadn't paid any attention to my flight schedule. I reached into my burgundy leather bag under the seat in front of me, pulled out my airplane ticket and studied it; a four-hour stopover in Chicago, more than enough time to make it to Wilmette.

I made my way through O'Hare International Airport, caught a cab and headed towards the House of Worship in Wilmette, Illinois, on the shores of Lake Michigan. An hour later I was seated in that magnificent structure, gazing up through the lofty, cement-laced dome to the blue sky above. Three hours and a second $70 cab ride later I arrived back at the airport with time to spare. I found a pay phone in the centre of a vast and empty concourse and decided to place my first telephone call ever to Redwan in Edmonton. As it happened to be a Bahá'í Holy Day, it occurred to me he might be at home. I picked up the phone and dialed. He answered.

"Hello, Redwan? It's Shar."

"Shar! How wonderful to hear from you." He sounded pleasantly surprised.

"I'm calling from the airport in Chicago. I've just been to the House of Worship."

"Oh, how special for you! And on a Holy Day too."

"Yes, actually I said prayers for my children, and yours too."

"Thank you, that's wonderful" As we talked, I imagined him on the other end of the line dressed in a bathrobe and leather slippers with the backs folded down and squashed under his heels like I'd seen other Middle Eastern men do. I wondered if I could bear to live with a man who walked on the backs of his shoes.

Before we hung up Redwan reiterated his promise to call me in Regina as soon as he returned from Rio de Janeiro where he was organizing an international bio-medical conference on the role of the eosinophil. I reminded him I would be leaving for Mexico immediately after that for a two-week video production course on indigenous cultures under the tutelage of a veteran 60 Minutes TV producer.

I smiled to myself as I headed towards my gate and thought about what I hadn't mentioned-that I also prayed to discover if it was the Will of God for us to marry.

I looked forward to talking to Redwan. On the appointed evening, my boss Clark and his wife Debbie invited me out for coffee. I declined so as not to miss Redwan's call but he didn't call; for weeks. I was extremely annoyed as was my daughter, Colby, who was staying with me during her university summer break. When I talked to her from Mexico, Colby said, "Redwan called." I'd primed her that he might. "He seemed surprised that you were away. I thought he knew you were in Mexico."

"Oh, who cares," I said with bravado. "I've already written him off."

While visiting Pierre-Yves and Laura in Regina a few weeks after my return, Pierre-Yves asked how things were developing between Redwan and me. He was shocked to learn I had heard nothing from him and immediately offered to check it out. I didn't care either way and said so.

A friend from Saskatoon mentioned she'd heard that Redwan was interested in a woman who lived in Regina. She was positive it was me. I didn't think so and, again, was nonplussed by the news.

Redwan called one evening in mid-July. I took my friend Laura Burkhart's advice and informed him I was not to be trifled with and that if he ever promised but failed to call me again he could forget about any kind of relationship with me, that I was unaccustomed to being treated disrespectfully, which was more a statement of intent than truth. In short, I would not tolerate it. He listened up and told me he had meant no disrespect but that he had to bring closure to another relationship first. By the end of our long conversation I believed he was sincerely sorry and definitely interested in me.

∾

A few days later, on July 19, 1996 Redwan arrived in Regina. Unfortunately, in my desire to ward off a threatening attack of irritable bowel syndrome, I risked a gall bladder cleanse that my reflexologist indicated might help. (He later clarified he had not meant I should do it that night.) What clear-thinking person could expect to drink ten ounces of olive oil and three ounces of lemon juice and then sleep peacefully? I was up the entire night trying not to throw up, which I hate more than anything. Anne Lamott's book *Hard Laughter* got me through that night in my old-fashioned apartment bathroom. The next morning, and several fluorescent green stones later, I was completely exhausted and could barely manage to stand up at the airport where I waited for Redwan. As it happened, a massive papier-mâché dinosaur loomed over the luggage rack, a testament to a recent find in Eastend, Saskatchewan. Redwan later confessed that when he caught sight of me as he descended the escalator he didn't know who looked worse, the dinosaur or me. But despite my wan appearance, he also later confessed that his immediate thought was that he was going to marry me.

Laura and Pierre-Yves were out of town that weekend and offered their home to Redwan. On Saturday morning I took over a fruit and yogurt salad. Redwan and I sat out on the Mocquais' back deck where we conducted, by Western standards at least, a most peculiar exercise; something between a job interview and a visit with Santa. On the phone in advance of Redwan's visit, we agreed that we would both prepare an itemized list with the following four categories: what we were looking for in a partner, what wasn't essential but would be a bonus, what qualities or attributes we didn't want in a partner but could live with, and what we absolutely couldn't tolerate.

Among Redwan's more interesting specifications was that he was looking for a homely woman who was a bed-breaker. By homely, I ultimately discovered he meant a woman who took pride in her home. A bed-breaker felt rather ambitious, but oh well.

During those few days I put him to the test to ascertain if he was open-minded, flexible, spontaneous and most importantly, fun. To that end, I dragged him around on a series of visits to a fortuneteller, my astrologer friend, my reflexologist, some restaurants and a movie. We had a fabulous time.

By Sunday afternoon, as I stood outside the Regina Airport and watched the tail of the plane carrying Redwan vanish into the cloudless blue prairie sky, I felt as if my heart was being pulled along behind it.

Two months later, on September 9, I had a stopover in Edmonton en route home from my Uncle Dick's funeral in Vancouver. Redwan greeted me at the airport with flowers. Back at his apartment, he invited me to sit on the green and white striped couch in his living room. On the coffee table he had arranged a collection of family photographs, his in Iraq and mine in Winnipeg, a prayer book, an eagle feather that an indigenous friend had given him, a dried orange from the House of the Báb in Shiraz, Iran, parts of a Parker pen that Shoghi Effendi, the Guardian of the Bahá'í Faith, used, and an illuminated book of Writings of Bahá'u'lláh.

With Kitaro's recording of "Caravansary" playing in the background, this dear man got down on his knees and, in tears, proposed to me. His reverent and sincere pledge of love and faithfulness won my heart. I knew that for the past several years Redwan had been heartbroken and lonely. Certainly I had been too. We could scarcely believe our good fortune.

Meanwhile, my boys were checking out Redwan, Gabriel through common associates and Asher in person on a visit to Regina. From her room at Wellesley College, outside of Boston, Colby asked, "What about me?" I assured her I would never marry anyone who wouldn't afford my children priority. A few weeks later she met Redwan at the Edmonton Airport. Within minutes she had her arm draped over his shoulder. Though Gabriel thought it was a bit of a speedy decision, he was on board too, as were Redwan's children, Marianne and Sam.

My parents fully approved of our match. My dad reminded me of a time, in the midst of my heartache over the demise of my first marriage, that I had assured him that one day my knight in white armour would appear. He marveled at how I'd had such confidence. As for my mother, she was totally in favour of this match and said, "Well, if you don't marry him, I will!"

Confirmations abounded. They gave me the courage to take this monumental and life-changing step including this one from Redwan's mother, which Sharaf kindly translated from Arabic for us. It read:

My dear son Ridhwan, dear Shar,
As you know, one's marriage is decided by His Lord's
fate. It seems that your fate is destined in Canada with Shar, for

whom your love is obvious, so I send my consent of marriage and bless this love.

Also I inquired from you if your marriage will have any effect on your children. You said that they were happy for you and would attend the wedding. I wish you the best. Hajer

In some mysterious way, and for reasons unknown to me, I have a feeling that from the next world Kaykhosrow chose me to marry his son. That's why I believe I heard and then carried that story about his encounter with the robber in my heart all those years.

# Orchestrating Glory

*Tropical Pas de Deux*

*Jamaica late afternoon*
*bird warbles waft through sweet scented air*

*I sit legs dangling in cool pool water*
*and ponder passionate you versus fearful me*

*A sudden gust of wind pelts my back*
*thrusts two petals into the water*

*From stage right, a dusty rose azalea*
*and from stage left, a fiery orange frangipani*

*Side by side pink and orange blossoms glide diagonally across the stage*
*tiny yellow leaves follow*

*The performance finished*
*the lesson clear.*

∾

I will never forget that magical moment when nature demonstrated for me that, despite our differences, Redwan and I could make a very good match.

∾

Though he had only lived in Canada a year and a half, word of Redwan's strengths as a speaker had already reached British Columbia. A couple of weeks before our wedding, a Bahá'í from the Vancouver area called to ask Redwan if he would do a marriage workshop for their Bahá'í community. I happened to be in the room at the time. "Well," Redwan responded, "I'm about to marry Shar Mitchell. I'd want to include her."

"Of course," the man replied.

"What would you like us to talk about, our failed marriages or our honeymoon?" The man laughed and so did I.

On Saturday, November 9, 1996, Redwan and I married. A few weeks before, I packed my Toyota Corolla with all my belongings, including an eight-foot plant I named Gabriel after my eldest son, and set out on the ten-hour drive from Regina, Saskatchewan, to Edmonton, Alberta, the city of my birth. I'd never expected to live there again.

Before our marriage, Redwan and I saw a marriage counsellor several times to work through some issues. I was skittish about remarriage, to say the least, and needed to know that if we had difficulties Redwan would be willing to work through them with me. During those counselling sessions he impressed me with his openness and honesty. Outside the sessions Redwan impressed me even more with his determination to apply his learning.

Sharing a common faith, though not a prerequisite for Bahá'ís has provided a helpful foundation for our marriage. Because Redwan had lived in the West for almost 25 years by the time we met, there wasn't much in the way of obvious cross-cultural adjustment for us. Before marrying him I talked to a Canadian friend who was married to a Persian. I wanted to know if issues had come up because of their divergent backgrounds. She said that one of the things she cherished most about her husband's approach to life was his incredible sense of hospitality. I already knew that to be true about Redwan.

Since we were well beyond childbearing years, I suggested to Redwan that we adopt a fictitious child as a symbol of our newborn marriage. He agreed. We both thought it should be a girl and wanted to name her after an attribute of God. I silently sang the names of the Bahá'í months, nineteen in total, thanks to a melody my first husband composed to amuse our young children one day on a road trip. When I got to "Glory" I knew that was it. Redwan concurred. Based on our previous marriages we understood that Glory would wither and die if denied proper attention, nurturing and love.

Thus committed, we carved two weeks out of our busy lives for a proper honeymoon. Money was tight but for $69, Redwan's travel reward points, and a generous wedding gift of money from my parents, we could realize my dream of visiting Greece. It seemed a perfect place for Glory's first critical weeks of life. Managing the rest of the trip on a tight budget didn't concern us. We were both accustomed to travelling frugally. We booked the flight and began planning our wedding.

Our five far-flung adult children, my brother Don and many of our dearest friends joined us for the elegant candlelit ceremony we held in the spacious country home of some friends. It was marred only by a blizzard that began that morning and was still blowing three days later when we left for our honeymoon.

We organized every aspect of our wedding ourselves, from booking flights to renting chairs, decorating the space, preparing some elements of the supper and planning the program. Our exhaustion after the wedding was nothing compared to how we felt when we finally staggered off the plane in Athens at dawn, after an eight-hour flight to London and a ten-hour layover.

Since our boat to Crete, which we were told was the warmest island that time of year, wasn't scheduled to leave until evening, we chose not to invest in a room for the day in the semi-seedy port of Piraeus. Instead we took a day trip to the nearby island of Hydra. It was a sunny but cool morning as we climbed aboard the passenger boat. Dressed in woolen sweaters and down-filled jackets, we sat alone on the deck in orange plastic bucket chairs and held hands and watched as we passed intermittent greenery on rocky islands. The cold wind finally drove us inside to join the local inhabitants.

Seconds before the boat docked at Hydra we decided to use the facilities. Seated inside the bathroom stall, I was startled to hear the boat engine rev. *That's strange*, I thought, *aren't people disembarking?* Then my inner alarm bells began to ring. I rushed out to find a desperate looking Redwan pacing back and forth on the deck terrified he'd never find me if I had disembarked.

Now we had a dilemma; we had to be back in Piraeus by evening to catch our over night boat to Crete. We scoured the vessel in search of an English speaker to help us sort out our problem, but it wasn't until we met the captain at the helm that we succeeded. Two islands (with the briefest of touch downs) later, we disembarked on a small island called Poros with the assurance we could make it back to Piraeus in time for our connection that night, but our mistake would cost us.

As the late fall sun rose in the sky, its warmth gained a degree of ascendancy over the wind, but we were still grateful to be wearing our Canadian winter gear. With no place to lie down, and only time on our hands, we set out to explore our surroundings.

Rows and rows of white-washed buildings with faded red roofs wedged their way up the sloping hillside that led back from the port. A collection of small shops and restaurants comprised the first row. We strolled along the winding seaside road, stopping every now and again to examine the assorted collection of floating items bumping against the cement-faced shoreline, rusty anchors, containers and puffy transparent globs, presumably jellyfish, to name a few of the floaters.

By noon we were hungry and circled back to the port in anticipation of real Greek hummus and pita. But our search yielded nothing as we wandered from one posted menu to another, scanning their English translations. Still we refused to believe they didn't serve hummus and pita so we questioned the restaurant staff. After a series of cold, blank stares we finally realized that they really didn't know what we were talking about. And if they had, they would have been offended as hummus and pita are actually staples of their despised neighbours, the Turks.

Mid-afternoon found us hovering close to the port for fear, that of the many boats passing in and out of that harbour in rapid succession, we would miss the only one that could deliver us back to our destination on time.

In a misty drizzle that evening at the port in Athens, we reclaimed our heavy baggage and dragged it for what seemed to be miles in search of our ship. Redwan, being the stronger and more chivalrous of us, carried the bulk of our stuff and worked up a sweat in the process especially after scaling a vertical mountain of stairs to reach the upper deck of the ship. Eventually, we wound our way into our miniscule room buried deep within the ship's bowels. In the fog created by his exhaustion, Redwan's depth perception must have been out of whack. I lost track of the number of times he banged his head on the upper bunk. By morning, when the boat docked in Crete, the lack of sleep and stress caused by the ardours of our wedding, plus the endless journey to our honeymoon destination (and who knows about the effect of the blows to his head), culminated in Redwan coming down with a severe sinus infection and fever.

But we were on the north side of Crete and wanted to be on the south side because we presumed it would be warmer. Certainly, the bustling port city of Iraklion was not our idea of a romantic setting for our days of Glory. Our plan, if you could call it that, was to rent a car and hunt for an appealing location. Since it was dawn, nothing was open. A taxi driver offered to take us to a local coffee shop where we could wait until a car rental place opened. As no other clear option presented itself, we went along for the ride and provided, it seemed, the conversational fodder for the local Greek men who assembled to drink their early morning coffee.

Some time later we pulled up in front of the rent-a-car office (no doubt owned by the taxi driver's relatives). I was keen to do the driving so Redwan could rest but soon realized I had neglected to bring my driver's license. Our journey along endless winding mountain roads, banked by olive trees, fell to a fevered Redwan.

It wasn't until late afternoon that we pulled up at a seaside resort called Matalla. A fine white sandy beach stretched out before our eyes. Sandstone hillsides pitted with cave doors flanked the sheltered beach. Heaven at last!

We soon discovered, however, that the majority of tourist houses were closed for the season. Those that were open weren't heated. A friend warned us before we left Canada not to settle for unheated accommodation. Despite the odds, we eventually scored, or so we thought. In the middle of the night, however, when we realized the heat was off, we understood why the blanket weighed half a ton. Indeed, with its pressing weight it felt more like a dead horse than a blanket. It didn't keep us warm and we could hardly lift it let alone roll over underneath it. By early morning's frigid light we concluded we needed to press on. The negative reception we had received from local Cretans (their name for themselves, not ours) at a restaurant the night before further cemented our decision.

While Redwan rested in the car with the heater on full blast, I decided I must explore at least one sand cave before leaving. Once inside, however, the stench of stale urine hastened my departure.

Before vacating this resort town, I ventured into a store to pick up some food for our journey. Though I was the only person in the shop, and hence the only immediate potential source of income, the shop attendant buried her head in her book and pretended I wasn't there until I barged through her silence.

Eventually, it dawned on us that we'd missed the tail end of the tourist season by a week or two. If we felt we were unwelcome it was because we were, especially if we were American as the Matalla restaurant owner incorrectly surmised.

Hours, and miles of sheep (not sleep) later we arrived in Ierapetra just before nightfall and checked into the only affordable hotel open off season. Honeymoon suite it was not. Tiny, but clean, with its double doors opened directly over the ocean save by a narrow balcony just large enough for two small chairs. Two single beds, framed like sandboxes were pushed together in the middle of the room with barely enough room to walk around the edges. Redwan immediately set to work with a blanket trying to pad the wooden ledge that separated our beds. It didn't work; the frame was too high. The owner assured us he would keep the heat on throughout the night. He seemed like an honest man and, as it turned out, he was. Now we could settle. Once Redwan was feeling better our honeymoon would begin.

The next morning, when I glanced at my face in the bathroom mirror, I got a terrible shock. During the night, I had acquired something in the range of seventy to eighty bug bites on my face. Indeed, one eyelid was swollen half shut. Poor Redwan, not only was he ill most of our honeymoon, he also had to look at my face. Some bridal transformation, I thought, whenever I inadvertently caught sight of myself in that mirror.

Despite his wretched physical condition, Redwan delighted me with a steady stream of timely jokes. Towards the end of our honeymoon he even managed to entertain me with his creative running commentary on a Greek ruin when he adopted the role of my tour guide to avoid paying the tour guide fee of USA $50.

Sometimes over lunch we studied a book I'd brought along on how to make a good marriage. We already decided that if Glory could endure Redwan's incessant sneezing and snuffling and my gory mug, she was made of pretty hardy stuff.

We were soon to make it up to Glory, though not by our design. Seven weeks after our ill-fated honeymoon, my daughter Colby and I set off for the Costa Rican rainforest. In the mid 1980's Jack and our kids and I had attended a music conference in San Jose, Costa Rica. There I became captivated by some Bribri Bahá'ís from Mojoncito, located deep within the rainforest, who performed a traditional corn dance before speaking about how they fashioned their community life around the Bahá'i teachings. About ten years later, while working at the CBC in Regina, I came upon a notice about a competition for a FOCAL Media Fellowship in Central and South America and seized the opportunity to apply. I was thrilled to win a fellowship that paid my way there and back, my travel expenses as well as a broadcast quality video camera. Colby, God bless her, accompanied me for the first month. Ultimately, I produced a video the Bribri named *Skowak*, which aired on VISION TV in Canada. It focused on a sustainable educational project at a centre the Bribri built called the "Boowoo," their word for light.

My travel plans were arranged before Redwan and I fell in love. I suggested waiting until my return from Costa Rica to marry, but Redwan couldn't wait. So, beyond the reach of telephone or electrical wires, we were separated for two long months.

In the rain forest, I scored the prime sleeping spot, the second floor of a new wooden structure with a roof and waist high walls, minus glass or screens. All other available structures in the Boowoo were old and thoroughly bug infested. At bedtime, about 7:00 p.m. each evening, in the pitch black, I slithered under that mosquito netting, endeavouring not to dislodge my improvised tent pegs: cans of paint, books, shoes, stones and whatever other heavy objects I could find to hold down the netting, as I raced to beat the lurking bugs inside.

Once inside I lay there on my thin mat completely surrounded by jungle night sounds, cooing, calling and bats feeding on bananas in the cook room below me, as a variety of unidentified creatures made their clumsy way en route across the open kitchen shelf, knocking our meagre food supplies onto the floor.

While the jungle nights were alive with sound, I took particular delight when, on occasion, my cameraman, Rick Gustavsen, lent me his tape recorder. I'd slip into my makeshift boudoir, clamp on the headset and listen to the two tapes Redwan had recorded and sent along with Rick as a surprise Valentine's Day present. Nothing could have raised my spirits more. One of the tapes was a compilation of songs he knew I loved. The other, by an Irish-Norwegian group, was called *Secret Garden*. The richness of those haunting scores amidst the mysterious jungle backdrop transported me to another realm, somewhere where rapture fused with the pain of my longing for my husband.

After what felt like an eternity, Redwan met up with me in Costa Rica at the end of my scheduled stay in the rainforest. My plan was to travel into the capital, San Jose, to meet him and then bring him back to Mojoncito, but days of torrential rain foiled our plans. Roads were flooded and bridges washed out. I barely made it to San Jose.

My friend and host in San Jose, Ruby Seals, took me to the airport to meet Redwan. I was beside myself with anticipation. We hadn't known each other long before we married and had only been together for a few weeks after. I was half afraid I wouldn't recognize him.

On that warm night, as Ruby and I waited behind a fence that separated swarms of other would-be greeters from passengers, I held my breath each time a man approached the exit doors. Finally, my man walked through those doors. I had no trouble recognizing him. In fact, I can still see the look of expectation on his face. He had endured his own hardships during our separation. It was as if each of us had run a long and arduous marathon. We finally made it across the finish line we feared we would never reach. Bashful at first, we held hands tentatively in the backseat of Ruby's car.

It was a strange thing but earlier that afternoon in my mind's eye, I saw Redwan present me with a replica of his wedding band. He knew I regretted my choice of a wedding ring. On the way to the airport that night I shared my premonition with Ruby. Later, the moment Redwan and I were alone he said, "I want you to close your eyes and hold out your left hand." My vision, and in fact, my unspoken whim became a reality. I was touched deeply by his thoughtfulness. Inside the band he had engraved REDWAN and SHAR ETERNALLY + 2. During our courtship when I dragged Redwan to that palm reader in Regina she had said, "Oh you'll be together for eternity, plus a day or two." We had joked about that.

Since we couldn't go back to the rainforest as planned, we decided to head for the west coast. Rick wanted to come too. The next morning the three of us piled onto a crowded bus pointed towards the sunshine. Redwan unfolded a scrap of white paper on which he had listed all the news he wanted to share with me over those two long months. During the entire journey we conversed with the intensity of magnets, entirely oblivious of the bumps, jolts and excessive heat on that overcrowded bus.

Once at the coast we found an inexpensive but charming beachfront hotel. Mercifully, Rick chose other accommodations. We spared him only one supper with us and hogged the rest of the time to ourselves. Despite my severe sciatica from the rigors of the rainforest, we reveled in the sunrises, the sunsets and each other. At dawn each morning, we carved our way into luscious, vibrant orange papaya and the most spectacular watermelon, savouring each bite before heading to the beach to greet the morning sun. Under those starlit nights and sunbaked days, days of playing in the ocean and staring into each other's eyes, Glory began to flourish.

These days we don't think as much about Glory. It seems she has reached a certain level of independence and is not so much in need of our watchful eye. In fact, now she seems to give more than she takes. As we reflect back on her beginnings, we're grateful she was our priority.

# Casting My In-Laws in Words

*"O My Brother, journey upon these planes in the spirit of search, not in blind imitation. A true wayfarer will not be kept back by the bludgeon of words nor debarred by the warning of allusions."* [1]

Like a kid whose eyes are glued to the candy store window after the shop is closed, in the early days of my marriage to Redwan I yearned to meet my new Iraqi family. Travelling to Iraq was out of the question. As a Westerner I would've attracted too much attention and put the family in danger. Redwan's life imprisonment sentence meant he couldn't go either. As Bahá'ís, his family weren't allowed travel documents.

It was after a surprising prompt that I began to prod Redwan in earnest to tell me his family stories. In September 1998, Redwan and I, along with his daughter Marianne, were concluding a three-day visit to the Bahá'í World Centre in Haifa, Israel. We were praying in the Shrine of Bahá'u'lláh. As I lay my forehead upon the scarlet rose petals arranged on the carpeted threshold of that inner sanctum, a commanding male voice inside my head said, *"You should pray to become worthy of your association with Redwan's family."*

*Of course I should,* I thought. *Why haven't I thought of that before?*

Despite agreeing with that sentiment I couldn't figure out what praying to become worthy actually meant. Since work carried out in the spirit of service is deemed worship in the Faith, I determined to strive to discover and record the stories that link Redwan's family to the earliest days of the Faith. It was the only way I could think of to get to know his family. Gathering that history for Redwan's children and grandchildren, and mine, further propelled

---

1      Bahá'u'lláh, *The Seven Valleys and The Four Valleys* (Wilmette, Illinois: United State Bahá'í Publishing Trust, 1991 pocket edition), 65.

my drive. Also, I believe that in the realms beyond we will associate with those we have loved in this world. As I contemplated the mysteries of my future beyond the grave, I decided I didn't want to miss out on the opportunity to meet Redwan's deceased family on account of my laziness in not making an effort to get to know them.

My initial research source was Redwan, of course. Like his father before him, he is a great storyteller. Later on I came across published material about family members and met others, like Latifa Toeg and Ahmad Motlagh, who knew his family in Iraq. I began to keep a diary of my findings. I even rented a humble room, with chinks in the wall that let the cold air in, in a church in Edmonton where I took refuge to work on what had become my passion, capturing Redwan's family in words. My approach to this task, however, was so far from systematic that over a prolonged number of years I felt as if I were trying to collect and preserve melting snowflakes. What follows is a sketch of my discoveries about Redwan's family, some of which he didn't even know! I take full credit for any inadvertent errors or omissions that I have no doubt made.

∾

Redwan's maternal great grandfather, Mirza Muhammad Wakil, moved from Isfahan, Persia to Baghdad, Iraq, some time before 1853. That same year, the Emperor of Iran, Nasir'u'l-Din Shah, banished Bahá'u'lláh to Iraq. Thus began forty years of incarceration for Bahá'u'lláh. But this ten-year period in Baghdad was the only time when He was permitted to associate freely with the public. People thronged to meet Him, often in search of His advice. It is easy to imagine that Mirzá Muhammad Wakil, Redwan's great grandfather, was one such person.

Redwan's maternal great-uncle, Mirzá Haydar-Alí, kept a diary that was later published under the title *Stories from the Delight of Hearts: The Memoirs of Hájí Mirzá Haydar-Alí*.[2] In it he describes his first, and most surprising,

---

2    Hájí Mirzá Haydar Alí, *Stories from the Delight of Hearts*, trans. and edited by Abu'l-Qásim Faizí (Los Angeles: Kalimát Press, 1980), 12-13.

meeting with his uncle, Mirza Muhammad Wakil (Redwan's great-grandfather) in Baghdad.

> ... most of the friends did business in a market place called the Suqu'l-Haraj. When I reached Baghdad, I immediately made for this market and with the help of friends sought Jinab-i-Zayn.
>
> An uncle of mine, whom I had never seen, had decided to transfer his residence from Iran to the holy cities of Karbila and Najaf. His name was Mirza Muhammad-i-Vakil. I did not know that he had become a believer.[3] Through Jinab-i-Zayn we met each other. He took me to his house and showed me such kind hospitality. I later learned that among the more than eighty believers who had been imprisoned and exiled from Baghdad to Mosul were my uncle and Jinab-i-Zayn.[4] After some years my uncle returned to Baghdad...[5]

'Abdu'l-Bahá describes Redwan's great grandfather's life this way:

> One of the captives who were sent from Baghdad to Mosul was Mirza Muhammad-i-Vakil. This righteous soul was among those who became believers in Baghdad. It was there he drank from the cup of resignation to the will of God and sought his rest in the shade of the celestial Tree. He was also an extremely capable and energetic administrator of important affairs, famous in Iraq for his wise counsel. After he became a believer, he was distinguished by the title of Vakil-deputy.[6]

In the spring of 1863, Naser al-Din Shah Qajar[7] ordered Bahá'u'lláh's further exile to Constantinople. Grief struck at the thought of losing such

---

3        By "believer" he meant a Bábí (i.e., a follower of the Báb).
4        'Abdu'l-Bahá, *Memorials of the Faithful* (Wilmette, IL: National Spiritual Assembly of the Bahá'ís of the United States of America, 1971) 150-153. Jináb-i-Zayn was also known as Zayn-Muqharribin and Zaynu'l Abidiyyin. He was a remarkable calligrapher.
5        Hájí Mirzá Haydar Alí, *Stories from the Delight of Hearts*, 12-13.
6        'Abdu'l-Bahá, *Memorials of the Faithful*, 108.
7        Ruled Persia from 1848 to 1896.

a revered figure, the governor of Baghdad, Najib Pasha, offered Bahá'u'lláh the use of a garden, on the banks of the Tigris River, to bid farewell to His followers. It was in the Garden of Ridván[8] that on April 21, 1863, Bahá'u'lláh publicly declared His mission and thereby inaugurated a new era in religious history, the Bahá'í Era. Though Redwan's family has no specific information about this momentous occasion, it's hard not to fathom his great grandfather being in attendance unless he was still in prison in Mosul.

After His exile to Constantinople, the government in Baghdad seized Bahá'u'lláh's properties. Redwan's great grandfather filed a complaint with the court claiming to represent Bahá'u'lláh. Evidently, he felt dreadful about his false claim but couldn't think of another way to protect Bahá'u'lláh 's property. Of this 'Abdu'l-Bahá wrote:

> Mirza Muhammad went to the Government authorities and said to them: 'I am the deputy (vakil) of Baha'u 'llah. These properties do not belong to Mirza Musa. How is it that you have taken them over?
>
> But he had no documents to support him, for the title deeds were in Akka, and on this account the government rejected his claim. However, in the process, he became known to all as Mirza Muhammad the Deputy.[9]

Bahá'u'lláh effectively gave Mirza Muhammad his surname. A hand-delivered letter to him from Bahá'u'lláh address him with, "O my

---

8    The Garden of Ridván ("paradise") was a formal garden with an attached palace to the north of the city walls of Baghdád. Built by order of Muhammad Najib Pasha (governor of Baghdád 1842-1847), it was purchased by the government in 1870 and underwent further modification. The site was cleared in the early 20th century to make room for the Royal Hospital. [Ed.]

9    'Abdu'l-Bahá, *Memorials of the Faithful*, 115.

deputy ... " or "wakil." In that letter Bahá'u'lláh praises Mirza Muhammad Wakil for his efforts. How relieved he must have felt.

In later years, on a return trip from Akka, Hájí Mirzá Haydar-Alí wrote this touching account of how Redwan's relatives lived in captivity:

> I also met my uncle, Jinab-i-Vakil. As one of the captives, it was necessary for him to earn a living in order to provide for his family. At his advanced age he found no other way but to learn shoe making. Though in a state of near poverty, he took me to his home. The love and hospitality that family showed put me to shame, especially when I could only express my gratitude in words and promises of prayers on their behalf and on behalf of the deceased members of their family. These people lived in such unity, love, and peace that they mirrored forth the same light as one beheld in the Bahá'i community of Akka.
>
> They vied with each other in serving the Cause and had no ultimate aim in life except to have a glance of His countenance. Though poor, they had established a fund to which the adults and children would contribute any extra amount from their daily income. In time of need the friends were allowed to borrow, but with the stipulation that they would pay back the loan with interest.[10]

'Abdu'l-Bahá encapsulates Redwan's great grandfather's life in this memoriam:

> Mirza Muhammad was taken prisoner and sent away from Baghdad to Mosul, where he fell prey to fearful ills. He had been rich; in God's path he was now poor. He had enjoyed his ease and comfort; now, for the love of God, he suffered pain and toil. He lived on for a time in Mosul, suppliant, resigned and lowly. And then, severed from all save God, irresistibly drawn by the gentle gales of the Lord, he rose out of this dark world to

---

10     Haji Mirza Haydar Ali, *Stories from the Delight of Hearts*, 74.

the land of light. Unto Him be salutations and praise. May God shed down upon him the waters of forgiveness, and open before his grave the gates of Heaven.[11]

Redwan and his family know only that Mirza Muhammad Wakil is buried in Mosul but not where.

In another diary entry, Haji Mirza Haydar-Ali states that in 1899 or 1900, Redwan's grandfather, Husayn Wakil, assisted in moving and concealing the sacred remains of the Bab.[12]

When the time came, the beloved Master[13] issued orders that the body should be transferred from Persia to the Holy Land.

Those responsible were advised to travel first to Iraq. They arrived in Baghdad with their sacred cargo, entrusted it to the hands of friends there and, after visiting the Shi'ih shrines, returned home. My cousin, Husayn-i-Vakil, acted as the custodian of the casket in Baghdad.[14]

Soon after it was published in 1980, I read *Stories from the Delight of Hearts*. It touched me deeply. I heard Shoghi Effendi's widow, Rúhíyyih Khánum, comment in a talk that parents should read this book to their children because Hájí Mirzá Haydar-Alí was such a remarkable role model. Despite brutal persecution, and years of imprisonment for being a Bahá'í, he retained a delightful sense of humour, even after being hung upside down from a camel for days while crossing the desert en route to prison in the Sudan. Of that experience he wrote:

A more torturous way to travel cannot be imagined!... Although we were in great pain and torture, as we watched each other hanging from the camels, the sight was so ridiculous that we could not help laughing.[15]

11      'Abdu'l-Bahá, *Memorials of the Faithful*, 116.
12      Forerunner to Bahá'u'lláh.
13      Bahá'u'lláh referred to Abdu'l-Bahá as "the Master."
14      Hájí Mirzá Haydar Alí, *Stories from the Delight of Hearts*, 108.
15      *Stories from the Delight of Hearts*, 47.

Hájí Mirzá Haydar-Alí describes their prison cell in the Sudan as

> ...small, dark and putrid... There were so many people
> crowded together that we could not even breathe, let alone move.
> The slightest gesture would arouse the anger of the jailers. We
> were surrounded by darkness, mosquitoes, fleas, lice, all manner
> of filth, and prisoners who were worse than scorpions...[16]

As a very old man Hájí Mirzá Haydar-Alí still continued to make everyone laugh. Western Bahá'ís who met him referred to him as The Angel of Carmel. Requests for him to visit poured into the Holy Land from all over the world but 'Abdu'l-Bahá would wrap Hájí Mirzá Haydar-Alí up in His cloak and lovingly repeat, "Hájí is ours! Hájí is ours!"[17]

Hájí Mirzá Haydar-Alí is buried in Haifa. We've been fortunate to visit his grave on a few occasions. By marriage I guess I am related to this remarkable man; now that is truly humbling.

Husayn Isfahan Wakil (Redwan's grandfather) married Melka Shoji's. They had two sons, Munir and Shoghi, and four daughters, Munira, Shoghia, Munawar and Hajer (Redwan's mother).

For a period of time Redwan's maternal grandparents, Husayn and Melka and their youngest children, Munirih and Munir, served in Bahá'u'lláh's daughter, Bahiyyih Khanum's home in the Holy Land. There, Munir played with Shoghi Effendi, Bahiyyih Khanum's nephew, who later became the Guardian of the Bahá'i Faith. Shoghi Effendi was a year older than Munir. Evidently, they wore each other's clothes. Later, when Hajer, Redwan's mother, was born, Shoghi Effendi suggested they call her Hajer after a nanny he adored.

When I mentioned to Sharaf that her great-grandfather was a shoemaker she said, "Yes. He and his son, Husayn, made shoes for the Master ('Abdu'l-Bahá) and for Shoghi Effendi. Each year our grandfather went to the Holy Land for pilgrimage with a new pair of shoes for Shoghi Effendi and

16     *Stories from the Delight of Hearts*, 48.
17     *Stories from the Delight of Hearts*, 162.

returned with the used pair for Munir. Uncle Munir had the blessing of having the same size of feet as Shoghi Effendi. He wore Shoghi Effendi's old shoes until such time as his grandfather Husayn passed away."

∾

Apart from a trip to Tehran with his mother and sister when he was three years old, Redwan had no opportunity to get to know his father's side of the family.[18] As an adult, Redwan met his cousin, Farahmand Moghbelin, twice briefly. But in 1996, while attending a medical conference in Barcelona, Spain, Redwan had an opportunity to spend some time with Farahmand and his wife, Ashraf. On that occasion, Farahmand stunned Redwan with news that their paternal great grandfather, Khosrow Mehraban, though not a Bahá'í, had received a letter from Bahá'u'lláh that is published in Persian.[19]

It seems that Bahá'u'lláh wrote in response to greetings from Khosrow Mehraban, conveyed to Him by Manokji Sahib, a Parsi[20] who had become a Bahá'í. In His letter, Bahá'u'lláh indicates that He planted a seed in Mehraban's family that will last forever. In part it reads:

> In the name of Merciful God, O Mehraban, A friend among friends mentioned you so we remembered you ... This memory is like a fresh plant, which was planted with the hand of Generosity. Soon it will burgeon in abundance with fresh leaves and fruits.

Apparently, Redwan's paternal grandmother, Zarbanoo, had no idea her father had communicated with Bahá'u'lláh before she undertook her search for truth at the age of 10 or 11, when she was a just a fresh plant.

In May 2005, we visited Farahmand and Ashraf in Spain. I was captivated by Farahmand's stories about Zarbanoo and wrote the following

---

18      By virtue of moving to Iraq, Kaykhosrow Moqbel relinquished his Iranian nationality and could never return to Iran.

19      Bahá'u'lláh, "Adiyeh Mahtub", 303.

20      A term used to describe Zoroastrians from Persia who moved to India.

piece,which incorporates every detail Farahmand shared about her.

∾

*Zarbanoo Trails an Angel*


*By 10, your spiritual antenna was on alert, your intuition strong. While others saw a man, you saw an angel pass you on the street in Amiriyeh on the outskirts of Tehran. Transfixed, you watched in amazement as he entered your friend's home. You longed to follow him. You sensed he had information you needed.*

*Did your eyes meet?*

*Did the look in his eyes allow you to read his soul?*

*Or did he read yours?*

*That night you dressed carefully in your chador. You were invited to listen to that man whose name was Mirza 'Abu-Fadl. Your cheeks flushed with excitement but your feet took root and refused to approach the door. Desperate to hear him, you scaled a tree, perched on a branch, and listened keenly. That night the seed of a new faith took root in your spirit.*

*Thereafter, whenever Mirza' Abu-Fadl returned, you would settle on your neighbour's roof and bask in his words in the moonlight.*

*Though you thirsted for knowledge, you only attended school for two months. You never learned to write but you read everything including scraps of paper you salvaged from the street.*

*One day, you happened upon a man selling a complete book of Hafiz's poetry for pennies. In tears, you raced home and begged your father to buy it. Then you drank in Hafiz's words with a comprehension that astonished all.*

*Poetry fueled your veins. You committed entire books to memory. Your nimbleness at rhyming even garnered you first prize in Sherjangi[21] in Tehran.*

*Years passed. You married Khoda Morad, a building contractor, gave birth to 11 babies, loved them faithfully, and lost many fatefully. You cried for all of them, and for the yearning planted deep in your soul on those starry nights so long before.*

*When you could no longer bear your grief, your father's trusted friend, a Bahá'í,*

---

21      Sherjangi or "Battle of the Poems" is a competition in which a competitor reads a poem. Their opponent must respond within sixty seconds with a verse that begins with the letter that ended the first poem.

*Feridun Khoosh-nu-Dian, visited. His words became your lifeline. You insisted he visit often despite your husband's disapproval.*

*You didn't know your father had sent a message to Bahá'u'lláh with Manokji Sahib[22] or that Bahá'u'lláh had called you forth with these words: "Soon this seedling will burgeon with fresh leaves and fruits in abundance." And, just like a seed, you burst into blossom. Bahá'u'lláh, you declared, was the return of the Shah Bahram and the establisher of a new world faith. More and more fresh leaves and fruits appeared amongst your offspring: Sarvar, Golbanu, Faraydoon and Kaykhosrow. The newfound joy in your home melted your husband's frigid heart.*

*"I can no longer deny Bahá'u'lláh," he said, "for He has transformed all of you. Surely Bahá'u'lláh is the Shah Bahram for whose return I've prayed all these years."*

*Though you didn't tell him, he found out about the teachings forbidding alcohol.*

*"If my Lord forbids it, no wine shall pass these lips again," he exclaimed. With that, despite your pleas, he rolled his wine filled barrels off the roof of your house where they smashed onto the road below. Then you loyally nursed him to an early death caused by his abrupt withdrawal from alcohol.*

*Sick only two months of your life, you outlived all but one of your children. You filled your life with service and learning. And when at 105 you could no longer read the daily newspapers, you played with dolls.*

*"Look," you said gleefully to your grandson Farahmand, "I've returned to my childhood!" And you smiled the sweetest smile*

*Did your eyes meet?*

*Did the look in his eyes allow you to read his soul?*

*Or did he read yours?*

∽

My son Gabriel was born in 1975, the same year Zarbanoo died in Iran. Technically, I could have met her because by that point I'd been a Bahá'í for three years. Sadly, Redwan doesn't remember meeting his grandmother when he was three. Since Zarbanoo and Kaykhosrow became Bahá'ís at the same time, Redwan is a second generation Bahá'í on his dad's side and fourth on his mother's.

---

22      Zarbanoo's father's friend. Manokji Sahib travelled to see Bahá'u'lláh while He was imprisoned in Akka.

# Hajer's Gift

A black and white photograph of Redwan's mother, Hajer Wakil, hangs on the family gallery wall in our bedroom. Redwan took it at his sister's wedding. Hajer would have been in her mid-fifties. Her long graying hair is parted on one side, her dark eyes warm and penetrating. Despite the hint of a smile, Hajer's face portrays long suffering. Soon after this picture was taken her suffering would intensify with her arrest and an imprisonment in the now notorious Abu Ghraib Prison for six years and four months.

Not surprisingly, it seems Hajer's life before marriage was less burdensome. Evidently she'd been longing to marry but wouldn't settle for anyone whose faith wasn't as paramount in his life as it was in hers. About 1943, Kaykhosrow, approximately 37 years old, left Tehran by train for Baghdad where he met Hajer through the Bahá'í community. Twelve to fifteen years her senior, Kaykhosrow's good looks, gentle and loving nature, and deep faith, swept Hajer off her feet. In him she found a strong and devoted Bahá'í who shared the same level of commitment to their Faith.

Hajer was alive but unable to travel outside of Iraq when I met and married Redwan. I was fortunate to be able to talk to her briefly on the telephone on a few occasions. Though she studied and taught English, it had been some time since she had spoken it. I heard and almost felt her searching for words. During a conversation one day, Hajer worked particularly hard to convey a message, but the only words she could summon to her command were, "Rethwan good boy." I agreed and my heart broke for her. My middle-aged fiancée was still her little boy. Out of love, she sacrificed being with him for his entire adult life, apart from a few weeks in Scotland in the summer of 1980.

Just after our wedding, an Iraqi colleague of Redwan's, Qutayba Hamid, returned from Baghdad with gifts for us from Hajer: deep, smoky-blue fabric for me and a child's small keyboard. Those tokens of her love touched us deeply.

Sharaf said her mother clung to life for years in the hope she would be able to see Redwan once more. But it was not to be. In the fall of 2000, Redwan and his mom had a long heart-to-heart chat. I recall that afternoon clearly. Redwan sat on our bed on the side closest to the window that overlooked the north west side of Edmonton's river valley. Though I can't understand Arabic, it was obvious from Redwan's tears and tone of voice that he and his mother were emptying their hearts to each other. Afterwards, Redwan confirmed my assessment but added that despite her grief his mother remained strong.

A number of weeks passed before Redwan could get another call through to Baghdad. When he did he was anxious to explain to his mom why he hadn't been in touch.

"What's the matter?" Hajer asked. "We said everything we needed to say. Nothing has been left unsaid." As she had detached from Redwan so many years before when she sent him off to England, she had made peace with letting go of him one final time.

During that conversation, Redwan mentioned he was going to the Bahá'í World Centre in Haifa, Israel, on January 5, 2001. Because of the likelihood that her phone was tapped what he actually said was, "I'm going to see Uncle Ali."

Hajer immediately replied, "Take me with you." Perhaps it was at that moment she prayed to die in the hope that she would be permitted in death what she was denied in life, a visit to the Holy Land and a reunion with her beloved son. In the Middle East aging parents customarily live with their eldest son. As such, Hajer lived with Sarmad, Shatha, and their four children. Some time in December 2000, she went to stay with Sharaf's family for a few days but on the morning of December 31st (my 52nd birthday), she announced her intent to return to Sarmad's home. She spent that evening, New Year's Eve, visiting with Sarmad's family. When Sarmad left for work the next morning he didn't say goodbye to her because her door was closed. At 10:00 a.m., Hajer still wasn't up so Shatha knocked on her door. When there was no answer she entered and found Hajer lying peacefully in her bed having passed away some time in the night. Though no records were kept the family believes Hajer was 83 years old when she died. Redwan was grateful that his mother died in the bosom of her family. To him it was significant that it was on the first day of the new millennium.

A few years previous, during a phone call with his mom, Redwan said he would pray for her health. "No, don't," Hajer immediately interjected. "The longer I live the more tests I have." She wasn't referring to medical examinations. When the U.S.-led invasion of Iraq began two years later, Redwan and I were grateful she was spared that particular test.

For three days after Hajer's death, Sharaf and Sarmad tried to contact us but Iraq was completely sealed off from the rest of the world; they couldn't make calls out or even send a fax. On the fourth day, Redwan happened to call his family and got through. By that time Hajer's funeral had already taken place as the deceased in the Middle East are generally buried the day they die.

Truth be told, I visited a fortuneteller the summer before Hajer's death when I returned to Regina to visit my friend, Laura Burkhart. As a surprise, Laura took me directly from the airport to see a friend of hers who read Tarot cards.[1] This man described to me a group of people bearing a body aloft on a stretcher en route for burial. I felt certain he was predicting Hajer's death. In fact, my prompting sparked the farewell conversation Redwan had with his mother.

For some months after that reading I worried about how Redwan would react to Hajer's death, particularly as it was so long since he'd seen her. I stood by our bed when he made that call to Baghdad. When he heard the sad news from Sharaf he cried out, sobbed briefly, and then chatted quietly with his sister for a few minutes. After he hung up he cried some more before he pronounced stoically: "She's coming to Haifa with me."

---

1    Seeking out one's fate through fortunetellers is discouraged in the Bahá'í Teachings.

Redwan immediately sent word of Hajer's passing to the Universal House of Justice, the international governing body, at the Bahá'í World Centre in Haifa, Israel. They kindly sent the following message:

> We were deeply grieved at the news of the passing of your dear mother, Hajir al-Wakil (Moqbel). We recall with deep appreciation her devoted services to the Cause in pioneering ... in Khanegin and Sulaymaniyyah, in her active support of community activities, and through her exemplary steadfastness in the face of persecution. Be assured of fervent prayers in the Holy Shrines for the progress of her noble soul in the Abha Kingdom, and kindly convey to the dear members of the family our heartfelt condolences.

The next day, Redwan set off for Haifa. Soon after his arrival he was waiting to visit the Shrine of the Bab on Mount Carmel to pray when he happened to see Mr. Ali Nakhjavani[2] (Uncle Ali). As Redwan embraced the man whom he had always looked up to as a role model, Mr. Nakhjavani whispered in his ear, "She's here with you, you know." Redwan took that as a confirmation of his mother's presence from the spiritual realms.

The timing of Redwan's trip to the Bahá'í World Centre couldn't have been better. No other place on earth could have cushioned the blow of Hajer's death like a visit to the spiritual centre of his beloved faith.

When he returned from the Holy Land we planned a memorial service for Hajer at the Edmonton Bahá'í Centre. Redwan's son, Sam, then 24 years old, was visiting from England at the time. We were happy he could share in honouring the grandmother, who, when she met him as a toddler, nicknamed him "Creamy," because of his light-coloured skin.

Redwan put his heart and soul into producing a wonderful memorial program for his mother. It included befitting prayers, writings and soul-stirring music. Redwan's heart-rending eulogy introduced and endeared the Edmonton Bahá'i Community to his mother.

---

2    He served as a member of the Universal House of Justice from 1963, when National Spiritual Assemblies worldwide first elected it, until his retirement in 2003.

Redwan Moqbel and his mother Hajer Wakil. Redwan used a pen to doctor this picture of himself as a swashbuckler.

Redwan (Ridvan) Moqbel on a field trip to Egypt during his studies at the University of Baghdad, approximately 1967.

From left to right: Hajer Wakil, Aqeel Khasibi, Sharaf Moqbel, Redwan Moqbel and Ikbal Wakil. Photograph taken at Sharaf and Aqeel's wedding on Nov. 6, 1972.

Shar Mitchell, taken in approximately 1966.

Gerry Mitchell (left side, back row) and Shar Mitchell (left side, middle row, far right), in front of Reverend Simpson, at their confirmation service at Westworth United Church in Winnipeg, Manitoba, in 1964.

Shar Mitchell's mother, Donna Catherine Mitchell (née Morrison), approximately 1945.

Shar Mitchell's father, Lieutenant John (Jack) Mitchell, approximately 1947. For his bravery he was awarded the Military Cross and later the Legion of Honour from the Government of France.

Redwan Moqbel and his father Khaykhosrow Moqbel, circa 1967.

LEFT: Redwan Moqbel's mother Hajer Wakil, Redwan, and his son Sam, July 1980 in Scotland one month before Marianne was born.

RIGHT: Redwan Moqbel's cousin Ikbal Wakil and Redwan's mother Hajer Wakil, 1975. Taken inside Abu Ghraib Prison grounds in Baghdad where they were incarcerated because of their faith for six years and four months.

Bernice and John Lenz, Shar Mitchell, Jack Lenz, Donna and Jack Mitchell, June 16, 1973, at Shar and Jack's wedding in a backyard in Saskatoon, Saskatchewan.

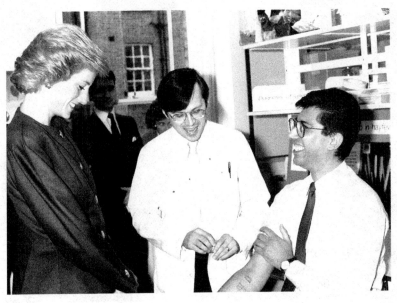

Princess Diana and Redwan Moqbel, 1990, at the National Heart and Lung Institute, London, England. Her Royal Highness was a Patron of the British Lung Foundation. Redwan was demonstrating an allergic response. (Tony Frew stands in the middle.)

Shar Mitchell and Redwan Moqbel, November 9, 1996 at their wedding just outside of Edmonton, Alberta.

ABOVE: Shar Mitchell and Redwan Moqbel reunite in March, 1997, Costa Rica after Shar spent 2 months in the rainforest making a documentary.

BELOW: Sam Moqbel, Aqeek Khasibi, Sharaf Moqbel and Amy Constable, August 28, 2006 in a meeting room at Heathrow Airport in London, England. Sharaf and Aqeel were en route from Baghdad to Edmonton to see Redwan before his surgery for sinus cancer.

ABOVE: Redwan Moqbel and his brother, Sarmad Moqbel, Istanbul, Turkey, November 2007.

BELOW: Marianne, Redwan and Sam Moqbel, November 2007, Haifa, Israel, just outside the Bahá'í graveyard where their relative, Haji Mirza Haydar-Ali is buried.

Shar Mitchell's daughter Colby Lenz, Shar's daughters-in-law Emily Dragoman and Erica Carlise, Shar's son Asher Lenz (holding the picture), Redwan Moqbel (seated in a chair), Shar and her son Gabriel Lenz (seated on the floor), December 2008, Winnipeg, Manitoba. Photo taken by Keramat Momtazi of Arc Studios.

Shar Mitchell and Redwan Moqbel, Riverview Health Care Centre, Winnipeg, Manitoba, August 2013.

# Shock and Awe Diary

Early in January 2003, our anxiety for our Iraqi family mounted daily as talk of a U.S.-led invasion of Iraq heated up. I began to scribble down everything I could from our phone conversations with Sharaf and Sarmad. That same month, Sarmad's eldest daughter Ouj gave birth to a baby boy, Anwar. I recalled how protective I was of Gabriel, my firstborn, and how I needed to believe that the world into which we brought him was safe. My heart ached for Ouj. I couldn't imagine how she could bear the anxiety of the mounting threat of war.

Mail service to Iraq had been spotty at best since I'd come on the scene, but as a token of our solidarity, we bought a gift for Anwar and sent it anyway. Miracle of miracles, on the eve of the war our parcel arrived!

On March 16 we managed to reach Sharaf. In preparation for the invasion, her family had converted a car battery into a generator so that they could cook when they lost power, which they inevitably would. They also dug a well and stored food and water. In the midst of discussing their situation Sharaf said, "You know Shar, the people here are really very brave. We are believers in God and we thank Him all the time." Her words weren't bravado. Six and a half years of sporadic telephone conversations with Sharaf had convinced me that she has complete trust in God.

Sharaf and Sarmad are fluent English speakers. In fact, Sharaf has a degree in English literature from the College of Arts at the University of Baghdad and had taught English at a high school level. I took Arabic as an elective to complete the bachelor's degree I dragged out for 18 years. Although at the time it seemed like a good, and even noble, idea my results were less than stellar. If I had to rely on my Arabic to communicate with my Iraqi family I wouldn't even be able to talk to them on the phone.

**115**

My conversation with Sharaf continued, "People are staying at home because they don't know when the war will start. I can't visit Carmel [her daughter] because she lives across the city, about twenty minutes away. This is really very difficult, not knowing how, when or what to expect. We're on alert all of the time. We hope for the best and prepare for the worst." Then she added with a determined optimism, "We pray for the best." She took heart from witnessing mass protests against the war in Iraq on television, "even in Chile!"

Sharaf longs for us to visit Iraq and plans to cook us a fish recipe from Basra, Aqeel's hometown. She hopes it will be in date season, her favourite time of year, so she can prepare some special treats from their backyard harvest.

As we were wrapping up our conversation Sharaf said, "Baghdad means the City of God. One day it will be the greatest city in the whole world." Her certitude about the future of a city that might soon be blasted to dust wowed me. Redwan later clarified that Bahá'u'lláh, who lived in exile in Baghdad from 1863 to 1873, had renamed it Madinat'u'lláh, which means "City of God." As we bid her a reluctant goodbye, Redwan and I had no idea if we would ever be able to talk to her again.

On March 23rd, just three days after the Iraq war commenced, we reached Sarmad on the phone.

"You must be very worried about us as you watch television and see things falling from the sky on us," he said, "but really, we're better off than you can imagine. We know how to live with this situation because God has given us courage and strength."

Sarmad's family has decided to remain in Baghdad for the duration. Five families have moved in with them. "One family's roof was rocketed," he said. "I took Manar[1] to see that house. When he saw it Manar said, 'Oh, it's only a little bit destroyed.'" Sarmad laughed heartily.

He was amazed that on the first day after the bombing all of the shops and bakeries were open. "You wouldn't believe it!" he said in awe of his

---

1    Manar, aged 10, is Sarmad and Shatha's youngest son.

compatriots' courage, "people are really trying to live normally." Sarmad and his family have stored a thousand litres of water and aren't concerned about running out because several of their neighbours have granted them access to their wells. Sharaf and Aqeel have three families staying with them, including their cousin, Ikbal[2] and her husband, 'Abu'l-Razak, and their children. 'Abdu'l-Razak's brother, Adel and his family moved in after an explosion shattered their windows.

Sarmad laughed as he explained that his father-in-law came to visit them that day. En route, a rocket shot past him travelling in the same direction as his car, fortunately not quite on the same trajectory.

"Are you close to the centre of the bombing?" Redwan asked.

"There's no near and no far; it's everywhere," he said.

Sarmad said they phone their friends in various cities around the country every day to see how they're managing. So far they're all fine. "We still have telephones, electricity and water and we pray for two hours each day."

As far as he is concerned, since their physical and spiritual needs are met, they're content.

Two days later we reached Sharaf. She said, "For the three nights previous everything shook. The raids begin with very hard bombing, with rockets and military planes every twenty minutes. Then it eases for an hour or two before continuing right through until morning when the sounds of the day begin."

"How are your nerves holding up, Sharaf?" I asked.

"We are a little bit used to it from the Gulf War but we're a bit shocked. We wake up with the sound of bombing and we pray until the bombing stops, then we go back to bed and try to sleep for an hour or so until it starts up again." For the first time, Sharaf sounded distressed, not only because of the

---

2      Redwan's cousin, Ikbal, was amongst the younger women imprisoned with her maternal aunt, Hajer (Redwan's mother).

military attacks but also because of a blinding sandstorm that infiltrated her home.

"You can't imagine the mess!" she exclaimed. "Everything is covered in at least an inch of sand, inside and out. But we're obliged to keep our windows open or the force of the explosions will break the glass. Carmel and I are tired of cleaning."

Sharaf seemed more comfortable venting about sand than the war. Certainly it was the first time I ever heard her utter anything that sounded the least bit like a complaint.

Somehow Carmel and her children managed to visit during the day, which cheered Sharaf considerably. They have enough to eat because the Iraqi government gave everyone a three-month store of supplies. As well, her family had been "hoarding" food for a while. She offered no more details.

∽

We weren't able to speak to our family after that for a number of weeks. One night on the news there was a story about foreign correspondents lending their mobile phones to Iraqis so they could contact family outside of Iraq to let them know they had survived. I allowed myself to hope that Sarmad would get such access to a phone. A few days later, in the middle of the night, our phone rang beside me. I reached over and answered it. I recognized Sarmad's voice immediately. "Hello, Sheeyar, this is Sarmad." *Oh my God, he did it* I thought.

"Oh Sarmad, you're okay!" I said, and immediately handed the telephone to Redwan. Sarmad quickly explained that everyone was fine and that a journalist had lent him his phone to make a brief call. That was it. He said goodbye and hung up. Our relief and gratitude to that unknown journalist knew no bounds. Our fears for the family abated slightly.

On July 26 we had cause for celebration. That day we spent two and a half hours talking to every single member of Redwan's extended family, the majority of whom he hasn't met. Despite the chaos and confusion in Baghdad, which they didn't mention, they somehow managed to gather together for that historic phone call.

After that journal entry, I have no record of any calls until February 2004 when Sarmad and Redwan enjoyed a long chat. Sharaf's phone had been out of service for ten months by then. Finances were scarce, especially for Sarmad, whose engineering firm couldn't get work. In May we sent some money, which the family divided into ten lots and distributed to the children.

Manar is eleven now. Sarmad describes him as their own CNN. "He knows every single American military vehicle and provides a running commentary as they drive past our house," he said.

On May 5, 2004, while passing by the newspaper box outside our condo building, I happened to catch sight of a colour photograph of Abu Ghraib Prison on the front page of the *Edmonton Journal*. The faded yellow trim above white prison walls captured my attention before my eyes moved to an American soldier who posed for the camera with a smirk on his face. He (I later discovered he was a she) was yanking a dog collar attached to a naked Iraqi prisoner's neck.

My eyes returned to the prison walls. Inside that very prison some three decades previous my mother-in-law, Hajer Wakil, along with 24 other Bahá'ís, endured imprisonment for six years and four months. I know little about their ordeal. If those walls could speak what would they tell me about her character, her resilience, the nature of her suffering, her will to survive and why the other prisoners claimed she sustained them throughout their imprisonment. It is interesting to note that every one of them could have been released if they had recanted their faith, but none did.

I have a vague memory of a photograph of Hajer and her fellow prisoners, half older, half younger, dressed in striped prison attire and standing in the prison courtyard. Perhaps I dreamt it. All of the older women have passed away, but if I'm ever able to visit Iraq, I'd love to interview any living cellmates of Hajer's. Their stories would be like different facets of a prism, each providing a fuller store of impressions of Hajer, the extraordinary mother-in-law I never met.

∽

After fifteen months with no phone service, we talked to Sharaf on June 23, 2004, when her line was finally repaired. I asked how they were doing. She replied, "With God's will and God's grace we are all doing well."

Later that month I called again. We were discussing family birthdays when Sharaf said, "My mother was only seven months pregnant when she fell and I got born. You see, when women have backaches they give them hot baths. So that's what they did for my mother, which made it easier for her to go into labour. There were no, what do you call them ... "

"Incubators?" I offered.

"Yes, there were no incubators," she said. "We were living in Khaneqin in the north near the Iranian border. It was a poor place so they put hot water boxes…"

"Bottles?" I interjected.

"Yes, bottles, on me and covered me with olive oil and cotton."

"Then you grew up into Redwan's hero," I said. He had told me that just a couple of days before the call.

"You know Shar, I adore Redwan," she continued. "We were friends. He was very close to my heart. He even told me his secrets and his feelings. He was always very serene. That's Redwan."

Redwan told me that he talked to Aqeel about meeting the family in Turkey. I mentioned that to Sharaf. "Turkey is what we're discussing," she said. "After July 1 we hope to have new government passports. We have no travel documents now. Please pray for us for the next few days. Things here are terrible and horrible. Two days ago our cousin Ikbal's car was stolen from the pavement in front of their door. Someone opened the car door, pulled the switch and drove off in the daylight at 1 p.m."

"I saw something about this on television," I said. "People from other countries travel to Iraq in order to fight the Americans."

"Yes, they do" she said. " Ikbal's car is a bit old. It is the type of car that is stolen and used by suicide bombers."

In early October as Sharaf and Aqeel prepared for their son Moqbel's wedding, Sharaf told me that things were very bad in Iraq. "People are feeling helpless, they've lost hope. They say, 'What have we done to deserve this?' They ask us how we cope. 'You always have a smile on your face,' they say. 'You give us courage.'

"But really," she added, "they [the Iraqis] are getting tired."

A few days later, while listening to Redwan speak at a memorial service for the mother of some friends, I noticed an increasing amount of gray amidst his black hair. A disturbing thought followed: might he die of old age before he is able to reunite with his family? Given the mess in Iraq, that is entirely possible. Yesterday, for example, we heard part of a CBC radio interview with a Baghdadi woman who recently visited her homeland. She reported that Iraqis still don't have regular access to electricity. Even worse, their water supply is mixed with sewage from the Tigris River. Neither Sharaf nor Sarmad mentioned this.

I heard another disturbing clip on CBC radio today. An Iraqi man admitted to honour killing his sister and his sister-in-law for shaming his family. Then he bragged about strangling one of their children. Evidently, such killings are becoming increasingly common.

∽

Later in October we travelled to Ottawa for Redwan to receive an Excellence in Research award in immunology from the Canadian Society of Allergy and Clinical Immunology. There we visited with the Toeg family, close friends of the Moqbels in Baghdad. The Toegs moved to Canada in the early 1970s. Latifa Toeg, and her late husband, Daoud Toeg, were first generation Iraqi Bahá'ís from a Jewish background. Latifa is 87 and in poor health. I sat with her in the dialysis unit at the Ottawa Hospital. There, within the labyrinth in a dimly lit "L" shaped room, patients sat in two rows of reclining chairs facing each other. Each was attached to tubes, bags and electronic machines that must have chilled them because they all had blankets pulled up to their necks. With her thick, black-framed eyeglasses and short brown hair, I quickly picked Latifa out of the line-up.

She was delighted to see me and eager to reminisce about her family history, such as how Daoud had heard about the Bahá'í Faith, how they got together, her conversion from Judaism, and their service to the Bahá'i Faith, followed by a rapid summation of Redwan's family when she learned I had to leave.

"The family of Redwan was the top of the Faith, very strong Bahá'ís. His uncle Munir rotated as chairman of the Bahá'í National Spiritual Assembly with Daoud."

Then she spoke about Kaykhosrow. "Day and night he gave his soul to the Faith. He couldn't find a job because he was from Iran. I would always see him with lots of people talking and laughing. He gave people his soul."

"And Hajer," Latifa said, shaking her upper body to demonstrate Hajer's impressive inner strength, "would say, 'I am Hajer Wakil'. They were the first real Bahá'is with love."

"Then the first time I saw Redwan, when he came to Canada, and I knew that he had been a member of the National Spiritual Assembly in the UK, I said, 'You see what happened to you? It was all from the suffering of your dad. It was a gift your father couldn't have.'"

In later years in Iraq, Latifa was appointed to serve as the chairperson of the Education Committee of Baghdad and asked to provide names of youths with whom she wanted to work. She had given Redwan's name, along with her sons. She said they enjoyed working together as a team to educate children and junior youth.

∽

We talked to Sharaf on Halloween for the first time since Moqbel's wedding on October 6.

The day before, she had returned by taxi from a weeklong trip to Mosul. I asked if the taxi was expensive, assuming it must have been.

"No," she said, "I shared it with two other passengers. The trip there took three hours. It was smooth and easy but on the way back there was a three-hour delay because of explosives that had to be detonated."

I asked her if that was scary. She admitted it was, though everyone is used to that process. "Yesterday," Sharaf added, "there was a huge explosion in Mansoor."

In the taxi en route home, Sharaf and another passenger discussed the Iraqis' need for spirituality. She commented, "These poor people have no hope and no aim and need to focus on character development through practicing good deeds."

Her fellow passenger turned to her and said, "What is your work? You say these things. You must be well educated." Sharaf replied, "No, these teachings are from God."

As Sharaf had just visited Mosul I asked if she knew where her great-grandfather, Mirza Muhammad Wakil's, grave is located.

"All I know," she said, "is that he was a prisoner with Bahá'u'lláh and was exiled to Turkey and that he died there." (Mosul was formerly a part of Turkey.[3])

---

3      Ottoman rule over Mosul ended in 1918, when the area was occupied by British forces following World War I. In 1926 a border settlement transferred Mosul from Turkey to Iraq. ("Mosul", *Encyclopedia Britannica Online*, https://www.britannica.com/place/Mosul.)

# Birthday in Baghdad

*You Give Me Heart\**

Hopeless eyes locked behind windows
Explosions jolt our bodies
Bounce us wall-to-wall
Ashen smoke leadens blue skies
Fear shocks our hearts
Terror grips our souls

You suffer too but still you smile
Your smile consoles me
Don't worry, you say, everything will work out
For this is the City of God
Pray for a spiritual solution

Your words reassure me
Your embrace comforts me
And you, dear friend, give me heart.

\* Inspired by Roo Borson's *Short Journey Upriver Toward Oishida*

I placed a call to Redwan's sister in Baghdad on her 60th birthday, November 23, 2004, while she was visiting her neighbor, Um Cahlil. What follows are my imaginings of how they might have interpreted my call.

∽

**Sharaf:**

Today I turned sixty. Soon it will be four years since my mother died. If someone told me what would happen in the years since her death, I wouldn't have believed them. Our lives were difficult then but I had no idea how much worse they would become. The situation here is really terrible with no security, limited electricity, and water only occasionally, and even then it is frequently contaminated. Still, in the midst of this chaos my whole life has been transformed. I was so bored after I retired from teaching. Maybe I shouldn't have retired early but, after thirty years of enduring religious prejudice, I needed a change. That was also when Aqeel began to manage the pizza shop. He and Moqbel worked there day and night. Someone needed to take up the slack at home and I preferred it be me.

Still, other than housework and visiting with Um Cahlil, there was little to do. The only highlights were visits from Carmel with her babies and the occasional visit with my mother. So today I turned sixty. I can hardly believe I'm entering old age. Well, that's what everyone thinks of sixty. But, I don't feel old, apart from a few physical complaints. In my mind I'm still 25.

Um Cahlil invited me for tea and cake tonight. What a wonderful woman she is. God has blessed me with such a neighbor. There isn't anything she hasn't or wouldn't do for us, nothing! So I accepted her invitation. Aqeel was at work. Moqbel and Sama went to see her parents after supper so I was free to go. In any case, it has kind of become a tradition for her to treat me to date cake on my birthday. Her timing had to be perfect or she might have had a half-baked cake, because for every two hours of electricity there are four hours without.

We were enjoying the last of our cake when Um Cahlil's phone rang. It was right after a huge explosion. I think most of Iraq must have heard it. I went outside to see what was going on while Um Cahlil answered the phone. But it turned out the phone call was for me. It was Shar. Redwan was away and she was calling to wish me a happy birthday. Somehow she called that number by mistake. Shar was worried about interrupting my visit with Um Cahlil but I told her that it was all right for us to talk.

She asked how things were and I told her frankly. Then she asked if it would be okay for her to pose some questions to me about our family. She wanted to know my dad's father's name as well as those of his siblings but I told her I didn't know. She heard that my father had a sister who was very ill and that he looked after her until she passed away. Then he pioneered to southern Iran. My father rarely talked about his life in Iran or his birth family but he did tell us one of his sisters was martyred by a neighbor because of her faith. Mother would have known more details about his family but it's too late to ask her now. What a shame.

It sounded as if Shar was writing a book so I asked her if that's what she was doing. She said she was trying to. I told her to keep writing because we need to gather together our family history.

Before we hung up I told Shar how much I hope she and Redwan will be able to come and visit us in this City of God, even though things are certainly horrible right now. In the future, I said, this gentle city will be quiet again and everything will be great. En shah' Allah.

∽

**Um Cahlil:**

As my good friend and neighbor, Sharaf, sat sipping tea and eating cake, I asked Sharaf how the newlyweds were doing. She beamed at me. I swear to Allah, she is the only person I ever see who smiles these days.

"Oh, Um, Cahill, they're very happy," she said. "Moqbel likes his job and Sama has begun her computer studies. They're so in love with each other. I'm delighted for them, and so is Aqeel. They remind us of when we were first married."

"You lived in Sulaymaniyyah then, didn't you?"

"No, that was when 1 was still in high school. My first teaching job was in Baku but I moved back to Baghdad after we got married."

Just then we heard a huge explosion. My hand shot up accidentally and sent some tea flying over my right shoulder.

"Oh dear," I said. And we laughed. That's still what I do with Sharaf, laugh, I mean. It's not the same with my family and other friends. They're entirely hopeless. All I see in their eyes is a reflection of the smoke-filled sky.

While Sharaf was talking to her sister-in-law I listened carefully. I'm so glad I learned English. From what I understood her sister-in-law's name is Shar. It is very close to Sharaf's name.

Before Sharaf hung up, I heard her tell Shar she hoped they could visit her in Baghdad very soon. I doubt that, given the constant explosions going on around here. But it was Sharaf's birthday after all; she deserves that wish.

Sharaf amazes me. She's still so full of hope despite our desperate situation. She's convinced that the only way for our country to resolve its problems will be through what she refers to as a 'spiritual solution.' I don't understand how we could ever arrive at a spiritual solution to our problems, not that I would object, I just can't imagine how it's possible. But Sharaf believes that will be the outcome. We'll see.

In any case, she adores her brother Redwan and it's been 32 years since she's seen him. She's never met Shar. My birthday wish for Sharaf is that before she turns 61 her wish will come true, even if they have to meet somewhere outside of Iraq. It would mean the world to her to see Redwan. She last saw him just after her honeymoon and now she's a grandmother!

Ꮿ

**My account:**

This morning I called Sharaf in Baghdad. Redwan is away and I wanted to wish her a happy 60th birthday. I've never remembered to call her on her birthday before so this time I was determined to do so. I have a whole ritual I perform before I call our family in Baghdad. First I have to find my purple notebook, the one in which I've jotted down every conversation we've had with family members since January 2003. That was right before the war, when we knew it was imminent and that we might never talk to the family again. Those were agonizing days.

I find a pen or two, position the telephone on our bed and then kneel down facing the bed, notebook open and ready to capture as much as I can manage to scribble down. Then I scroll down the telephone directory through the phone numbers that Redwan has programmed.

Today I went through that list backwards. Sharaf's name was there with Um Cahlil's written after it. I didn't stop to figure out what the Um Cahlil part meant, I just hit speed dial. After a few rings a woman answered with an Arabic word I didn't catch.

"Sharaf?" I said, "Is this Sharaf?" I knew it wasn't. The woman seemed slightly confused but quickly processed everything and replied, "No, but she's here. One moment please and I will get her for you."

"Thank you," I said. Then she came back on the phone to tell me Sharaf was coming. She seemed to want to hang onto me with her words.

When Sharaf answered she sounded troubled and heavy-hearted. This was unusual for my sister-in-law who, despite everything, normally sounds positive.

"Happy birthday, Sharaf! How are you?" I asked.

"I'm fine, thank you. Thank you very much except the situation is horrible."

Sharaf and I chatted a bit about an upcoming trip she planned with Aqeel. Then she told me I had actually called her at her neighbour's, Um Cahlil's house, but that it was just as well since her own phone line had been down for about ten days. "I offered to pay a repair man to have it fixed but he hasn't come. Everything here is running out of order. We pray to God that people will be able to fix it." I knew she meant the mess in Iraq.

"We have a lack in electricity with a four-hour cut and two hours on. There's no security. We hear explosions all day and all night; those are mostly on the street. People are getting tired."

I told her how sorry I was about their living conditions, particularly because it comes on the heels of over three decades of untold oppression caused by political sanctions against Iraq.

Sharaf replied, "But as for us, we know that the closer the circle becomes the quicker it will re-open and that the darkest hour is closest to the dawn. We're getting to the darkest hour. The only thing that we can do is pray. I tell people, the only solution is a spiritual solution. People tell me we're strong. They say, 'You're the only ones who believe there is hope.'"

Though her words were confident and sincere, I felt Sharaf's frayed nerves through the telephone line.

I wanted to ask her about her father's family because I was trying to reconstruct the family's early connection to the Bahá'í Faith. Sharaf said she thought he only had one brother, whereas Redwan says there were two, Gushtasp and Faraydoon. He said Faraydoon pioneered to Iraq with Kaykhosrow some time in the 1930's or early 1940s after their sister died. Faraydoon returned to Iran after two years.

"I know that his brother Faraydoon had two sons: one in Persia and one in Portugal that Redwan was in touch with," said Sharaf. I told her the latter cousin actually lives just north of Barcelona, Spain.

The only thing that Sharaf knew was that her grandmother's name was Zarbanoo. (Redwan thought his grandfather's first name might have been Morad.)

I told Sharaf that despite everything, I hoped her sixtieth year would be a much better one. Then she reminded me about how she got her name even though she wasn't born in the month of Sharaf. I told her that perhaps that's why my name is Shar because I was born on the first day of the month of Sharaf, or Honour. This made her laugh because she knows my parents aren't Bahá'is.

As we were wrapping up the call, Sharaf said, "I had great parents." Then she went on to express more strongly than ever how very much she hopes we would soon be able to visit them in the City of God.

"Even as horrible as it is right now, it is still a gentle city," she said. "In the future it will be a quiet city and everything will be great."

As we said goodbye, my heart wrenched for our dear brave Sharaf on her 60th birthday.

# Going Down Under

Redwan had been postponing his sabbatical for a number of years because of my frequent trips to Winnipeg to care for my parents, but by the spring of 2005 he was feeling some pressure to get on with it. So, for three weeks in July we toured parts of Australia to nail down his choice of locations. He settled on Perth and Brisbane. My brother, Gerry has lived his entire adult life in Australia. He and his family live on the Gold Coast south of Brisbane. Given Redwan's enforced separation from his siblings he understood my longing to spend time with my brother.

After months of dreading telling my parents we were leaving Canada, we finally told them in person in mom's room at the nursing home. She was well into dementia by that time and didn't understand what we were saying but my dad did. His face blanched. He didn't say anything for some time. When he did it was by way of encouragement to us. My parents have always made a point of not guilt-tripping their children and for that I shall always be grateful. We assured them that we would phone regularly and return for a visit mid-way through the sabbatical for Mom's 85th birthday.

∽

**November 14, 2005**
**Journal Entry, Perth, Australia**

I was unable to get through to Sharaf but reached Shatha, Sarmad's wife. She apologized for her English and passed the phone to Sarmad, who happened to be at home. Sarmad said, "When everybody loves someone, they don't see their shortcomings," referring to Shatha's English. Sweet.

I told Sarmad that our friend Terri is slated for bowel surgery because of cancer and asked if he and his family would pray for her. He thought out loud about when they could do that and then said, "We thank you for this honour."

**December 11, 2005**
**Journal Entry, Perth, Australia**
Redwan's present sinus infection aside, we're doing well. We've been here for six weeks now. Had a great time in Hong Kong en route. Sean Lee, whom we got to know in Edmonton when he was doing his PhD, arranged for us to stay with his friend who is a professor of translation at the University of China and a sweetheart of a guy. They cooked for us and took us to so many interesting places. We had a fabulous time.

We have only three weeks left here in Perth and I am just now getting rolling on my book again, *The Bridegroom from Baghdad*. I need to finish it so I can move onto other things, such as figuring out when I am going to give birth to this turkey that seems to have made its way into my abdomen. Honestly, you'd think that when your uterus was getting ready to call it quits it would shrink, not blow up. I look several months pregnant. Ugh.

Gabriel just finished his last of 10 job interviews yesterday. That one was at Duke. He's had three offers so far: NYU, U Penn and Minnesota. He's still hoping Yale or MIT will come through. My daughter-in-law, Erica, is rooting for New York University so they can remain in New York.

**January 15, 2006**
**Journal Entry, Gold Coast, Australia**
We're staying with my brother, Gerry, his wife Ann, their almost 21-year-old youngest son, Brad, and Alfie, their highly entertaining dog. We arrived before Christmas and then did a twelve day driving tour of the North and South Island of New Zealand with Gerry and Ann.

I can't believe it has been two months since we talked to Sarmad. Last night Redwan tried both Sharaf and Sarmad's numbers but there was no answer. I was doing my face in the bathroom at the time and heard that overpowering voice in my head tell me to get Redwan to dial Sarmad's mobile phone. He did and got through.

Sarmad's engineering firm hasn't had any contracts since the invasion, which adds financial pressure to an already untenable mix of tests and difficulties.

I'm ashamed that we haven't kept in better touch. Even though their phone lines often don't work, we've known at least since November 14, truthfully, before that, that Sarmad's cell phone works. We are so caught up in our own lives that we let the most important, keeping in touch with our long-suffering Iraqi family, slip by.

**January 17, 2006**
**Journal Entry, Gold Coast, Australia**

Redwan called Sarmad again on his mobile. Apparently, Sharaf's phone has been fixed again so we called. What a thrill to talk to her after so long.

Her son, Moqbel, already an engineer, is back in school studying computer science. Sharaf's daughter, Carmel, continues to amaze her and Aqeel, "She is a gift from God," Sharaf told Redwan. Carmel's son, Furat, is in Grade 5; Bahji is in Grade 2 and Shoojah will be two in February.

Sharaf sounded so joyful. "I've been missing the sound of your voice," she said. "Our phone line was out for 10 months. We finally had to do things the way they're done here. We had to bribe the repairmen to fix it. It was only a very small thing that was wrong with it," she said, laughing.

Sharaf asked about me, my children and my parents and then inquired as to what I was working on.

"I'm still trying to finish the book I'm calling *The Bridegroom from Baghdad.*"

"How's it going?"

I scrambled for a response because I had not worked on it since we left Perth a month ago.

"We went to Spain in May and I interviewed your cousin Farahmand Moqbeline," I said.

"Who?"

Redwan, who stood close by me, corrected my pronunciation of Farahmand's name. This time Sharaf understood.

"In Portugal?" she asked. She didn't seem to remember our previous conversation about Farahmand. *Little wonder, given her life,* I thought.

"No, Spain. They live in Barcelona."

I told her we had also talked with their cousin Irradj Farrok Tehrani in Germany. After his mother, Kaykhosrow's sister, died, Kaykhosrow looked after him.

"Did he tell you about his mother's death?" Sharaf asked.

"From malaria?"

"No, she was poisoned," she said. "I remember my dad telling me that. Poisoned by her neighbour because of her faith."

"Poisoned?" I asked.

"Yes."

"Was her name Golbanu?"

"I don't remember."

Sharaf asked again how far I was with the book. I told her that I had been trying to put together a chart of names and dates. She gave me Moqbel's email address so I could send him that chronology. Hopefully, Sharaf will be able to show it to Sarmad and Ikbal to see if they can fill in any of the gaps.

I asked Sharaf how she was doing. Instead of talking about herself she focused on the Iraqis and what she sees or doesn't see in their eyes when she passes them on the street.

"Nothing, almost as if they are beyond despair," she said. "These things happen in cycles. I pray that God will relieve them of their suffering."

As if she isn't suffering! Certainly she is, but her entire focus is on the well-being of others. Sharaf must dwell in part in the world of the spirit, somehow mitigating some of the more unbearable aspects of her life. I've never heard her sound so light and giggly. In part, she was happy because just the day before she had asked Sarmad to tell us to call her. She said, "When Aqeel answered the phone he called out to me, 'Redwan!' We could hardly believe you would call so soon."

It seemed an apt example of just how patiently they have to wait for anything they want or need including our phone calls.

### January 26, 2006
### Journal Entry, Gold Coast, Australia

Today was Australia Day. We went to a "Barbie," on an acreage not too far from here, with Gerry and Ann and a group of their friends. En route they tried but failed to find some Lamingtons, coconut covered chocolate cake that Ann explained is a traditional holiday dessert. When we got home we "vegged out" on movies. As for my writing, I'm having trouble making time for it.

Gerry sawed off the top of his thumb at his window manufacturing factory the other day, had surgery and is now recovering. I am enjoying spending more time with him and am trying to be useful.

Unlike Redwan's sabbatical time in Perth where he was working on a new finding: the presence of the eosinophil in infant and child thymus glands, the Brisbane component of his sabbatical was a disappointment in that it was neither interesting nor productive.

Soon we will book a trip to Canberra, which will be interesting for both of us as we've not been there. We also hope to make it to Alice Springs and Uluru (formerly Ayers Rock), maybe in April. In March we will be in the US and Canada. Redwan has a conference and I want to see my kids en route to visit my mom in Winnipeg for her 85th birthday. She's been through a tough time, probably another transient ischemic attack, which severely interferes with her brain function for a time.

### February 27, 2006
### Journal Entry on a plane from Brisbane to Los Angeles

Iraq is on the verge of civil war. Civil war there was everyone's fear. Certainly, there is no hope of visiting Iraq any time soon. I overheard Redwan tell someone recently that when Sarmad leaves his house he says a special goodbye to everyone just in case he doesn't make it home. God help them! I think it would destroy Redwan if any of his family were killed before he gets to see them. He has been tested so much already.

When we were packing last night at Gerry and Ann's, Redwan tried to reach Sarmad. It was late because we attended a memorial that an Australian, Huda Granfar, held in her late father's honour. She'd asked Redwan to speak at it. As it turned out, Huda's father, Golmohamdi, had been another of Kaykhosrow's students. His widow, a 79-year-old, gorgeous woman with the most loving face, told me she had heard stories that as a child her husband was constantly in trouble with his parents for arriving home late from class. He protested that it was because he wanted to talk to his teacher, Kaykhosrow. Ultimately, his parents discovered that the other children were late too. They all adored Kaykhosrow and wanted to prolong their time with him.

**March 13, 2006**
**Email to Jean**
**Subject: Both of you**

We're in Winnipeg and from here we'll go to Edmonton to see our doctor, dentist, accountant, etc. We are desperate to see Terri Flanagan and Pierre-Yves. Redwan visited with my parents for an hour on Thursday night when we arrived but has been in bed at the Holiday Inn since. He has a severe sinus infection, a fever, vomiting, etc. He has been right out of it. The fever abated yesterday and he ate a bit, so hopefully, he'll be able to fly tomorrow morning. I fly out later in the day. We're booked to leave for Australia via Japan on Friday, March 17. I hope Redwan will feel well enough.

Today is Mom's 85th birthday so I'd better get moving. My aunt Fran, Dad's brother's widow, is here from Vancouver for the occasion. We are very fond of her.

Thank you for your concern and especially for your prayers for Redwan's family. We haven't talked to them for a few weeks now but pray they are okay.

Much love to you both,

Shar

**March 16, 2006**
**Email to Jean**
**Subject: Prayers**

I forgot to reassure you that Terri is doing well. Now she has to come to terms emotionally with her bowel cancer; it all happened so quickly.

Redwan's immunity is good but his sinuses suck. They've plagued him for years. We may end up returning to Canada early, partly because of that and partly because of his work commitments.

We're off to Japan on Friday. I need to see if I can find out where their Naw Ruz (New Year) will be held in Tokyo. I really hope we can attend.

Much love to you both and hugs to that 79-year-old man with the cute smile,

Shar

**March 16, 2006**
**Journal Entry, Edmonton**

In the midst of packing to leave for Japan en route back to Australia, Redwan called Sarmad. I wish I could get Redwan to take notes when he talks to him but it's just not his style. Unlike me, he usually has good recall, but it's all a matter of me asking Redwan the right questions at the right time to get any information. I often hear the news when he's relaying it to others.

Sarmad told me that one of his neighbour's sons was killed. When he and Shatha went to visit that couple the bereaved father said, '"Muhammad also lost his son. My eye must look to Muhammad. "'

"I told myself," Sarmad continued, "that we must encourage ourselves and become even stronger than this man. It is natural to cry, to feel sad, but we must be strong. I'm not only talking about individuals but also the community. We must not think that this suffering is in vain. At the same time, when all of this is going on is when you feel God's mercy."

I told Sarmad we thought about him on his birthday, March 9. I asked if, in the midst of the chaos around them, there was a birthday celebration for him.

"Shatha is so sweet," he said. "She got me a gift and baked me a cake. I ate five parts of it," he said laughing.

During my conversation with Sarmad, Redwan passed me a note that said, "Ask about what happened to him yesterday." I did, but Sarmad suggested that Redwan tell me later because to him it is an everyday occurrence. Before we hung up, Sarmad asked me to pray for the people of Iraq. I assured him I would.

After I got off the phone, Redwan explained that Sarmad and a hundred or so Iraqis were caught in a crossfire. He crawled under his car for protection. As he watched the action from under there, an engineering concept came to mind. When heated, metal becomes almost like plastic. Iraqis, he said, have been through the fires of tests and difficulties and now are as malleable as plastic.

My God, this man is a philosopher, too!

**March 23, 2006**
**Email to Terri**
**Subject: Needs/wants**
It was so great to have seen you, Ted and your family. Of course it was too short but as you said, even a week wouldn't have been long enough. I wish that the supper idea with Pierre-Yves would have worked too. As it turned out, we really didn't get to visit with him until late afternoon and then we needed to go to bed by 10 p.m. because we all had to be up by 5 a.m. Argh! It was a good visit but, again, too short. He's in France now. Tough year for Pierre-Yves.

I've thought so much about what you said about needing to process what you've been through. You will know what to do, just listen to those "needs" and make sure you don't dismiss them as just "wants."

As to Japan! Yes, it was great but we stayed at Narita International Airport, which is too far away from Tokyo. It equated to 12 hours of commuting being hacked from that brief visit.

Naw Ruz was held in an American pioneer's home. A mix of fun people attended. We had a great time but had to leave at 8:30 to catch the last train but didn't arrive back at our hotel until after 11. Let it go, Shar.

The majestic sloping roofs we saw on our little foray to Japan captivated me.

Much love to all,
Shar

**May 4, 2006**
**Email to Terri**
**Subject: Thanks for the newsy note**

I was planning to phone you just now but after I called my mom I realized I don't have a voice today. I caught a bad cold after spending four and a half hours at an outdoor restaurant in Brisbane in the pouring rain. I was really chilled but Redwan was having such a delightful time with his old buddies from the UK, Naysan, and his wife Zoreh, and their friends that I just sat it out. Anyhow, today I have laryngitis.

My mom had no idea who I was when I called her. On the topic of Mom, we're trying to sort out a safety issue. She wears an alarm bracelet because last January she slipped out of Deer Lodge without a coat! It was -20C. She wandered down Portage Avenue quite a distance before a man found her and brought her back to the nursing home. "Oh, what a kind young man he was," she said with something approaching wonder in her voice.

Redwan is sick in bed. It is noon and he's still asleep. He's got the same cold thing I have but his is on top of his horrific sinus situation. Jean Hedley saw a documentary on sinus problems and mentioned that it rarely results in cancer. My stomach sank because it confirmed that, even though it is rare, there is such a thing as sinus cancer. That had been Redwan's fear.

Last night both of us had our laptops in bed. I began to go through web sites looking up sinus cancer. I got scared because Redwan has so many of the symptoms. It puts our trip to Asia in question, which we haven't organized yet, though we will set off for Singapore within a week or so, and then make our way overland through Malaysia and possibly Thailand, Cambodia and Vietnam to Macau, Hong Kong, Tianjin and Beijing, Korea and San Francisco. There we plan to stay a few days with Colby after which Redwan will return to Edmonton about July 15. I intend to stay in California for an extra month, in a monastery or some such place, to work on my book until Redwan returns to San Francisco to attend the Association for Bahá'í Studies Conference. Then we will return to Edmonton.

I wonder if Redwan should just go to Edmonton so cancer can be ruled out. In March when he was sick and saw a doctor in Winnipeg, that wonderful man suggested Redwan have his sinuses thoroughly checked out. I don't want to be selfish, but I really don't want to return to the chaos of my life in Edmonton without making great strides with my manuscript.

I know what you mean about longing to do something big. I often pine about that too and wonder how I could manage to do such a thing and why I haven't thus far. But Terri, you have done BIG THINGS! Really big things. You pioneered in Haiti and India for years. That wasn't easy. Then, despite the torture of the dying days of your marriage, you continued to serve others through every means possible and you raised the MOST AMAZING children. Maybe your current sacrifice is your sadness at being unable to set off for parts unknown because of your present circumstances. Do you think God doesn't know that you and Ted long to serve in that way?

I feel lousy and this note is cumbersome and likely incoherent. My apologies. I need to go outside for my 10 minutes (or more) of vitamin D therapy. I'll lay on the dock in the sun in full view of all of the neighbours that overlook this watery cul de sac.

Love to you all,

Shar

**May 8, 2006**
**Email to Jean**
**Subject: Sinus story**

God bless you. You're a saint. Thank you very much for going to all the trouble of finding that article on sinus cancer. I won't show it to Redwan just yet. I'll wait until he gets back to Canada (mid July). I will set the alarm for the middle of the night tonight, though, and get him to call our GP to arrange for an appointment with a specialist, or for a SCAN as soon as he returns home in mid July.

We had supper with an Indian doctor and her family on Friday night in Brisbane. I took her aside and mentioned my concern about Redwan after reading about sinus cancer on the internet. Honestly, he has most of the signs of it. She said we're probably all right to carry on with our travel to Asia. He is on painkillers at least two to three times per day because of his excruciating headaches and face pain.

It will be very difficult to say goodbye to Gerry and Ann. It has been just wonderful to have this time with them.

So much love, Jean,
Shar

**May 12, 2006**
**Email to Terri**
**Subject: Redwan**

We are on the highway en route to Brisbane for Redwan's MRI. (Don't worry he's driving as I type.) We've been running around like crazy all day trying to tie up loose ends. I just had time to do a quick email download so I could catch up with my email in the car. Redwan thanks you so much for the loving and thoughtful message and advice. He says he is as calm and content as a koala. We'll let you know the results as soon as we know them.

A few hours, and a little poorer, we have great news. Redwan's sinuses are a mess, and flying will be tough on him but there is no cancer or anything that warrants returning to Canada early. The doctor who read the MRI explained the images to us. He suggested Redwan also have a PET SCAN.

While Redwan was having his MRI the hospital parking lot closed with my niece Jacqui's little car in it! We paid $40 to a roving parking lot attendant, who had never been in the lot before, and had no idea how to get us out. Eventually we sped out through two sets of doors on the bumper of an obliging female hospital employee.

Another bit of good news is that Redwan's colleague in Montreal will arrange for Redwan to have the same high tech sinus wash in Montreal that we saw on TV here.

Anyhow, it's late. Tomorrow we have an all day sailing lesson with my brother Gerry and his family.

Much love and gratitude,

Shar

P.S. Redwan says to tell you he succeeded in lying totally still for 17 minutes under the MRI.

**May 20, 2006**
**Email to Marlene**
**Subject: Miss you in Malaysia**

A quick hi from an internet cafe in Kuala Lumpur. We are figuring out this trip one day at a time. Tomorrow we fly to Bangkok, Thailand. After hours of standing around in a ticket office we just booked those flights. We're going to meet up with a young friend who is doing a year of service there. Next Saturday we fly to Cambodia for a few days and then on to Vietnam, if we can work out how to get there, and then to Singapore for our flight to Beijing on June 6. We hope to stay until July 6, and then go to Korea for a few days, but we'll see.

Redwan's sinuses are a mess and he has a bad cough but he's not dead yet. I know that for a few reasons, one I'll mention. He suggested we try to see the *Da Vinci Code* tonight.

Love to Michael and Ben and you, and big hugs,

Shar

**May 22, 2006**
**Journal Entry, Nathambury, Thailand**

We just arrived in Nathambury on the outskirts of Bangkok to visit Naisa, a Bahá'í youth from Edmonton. She left a key with the security guard outside her building because she wouldn't be home from the Catholic school where she volunteers until after we arrived. The key let us into the room that resembles a garage. On the right side two tired beds were hemmed in by old filing cabinets, broken lamps, bikes and assorted clutter. To our delight, in the far right corner there was an old computer with a sign on the top that hints at potential internet service, coupled with warnings about exercising patience while it fires up and struggles to carry out commands. By the time it was up and running Naisa arrived. Fortunately for her, this was not her room but a spare one owned by some Bahá'ís who lived down the hall. A few minutes later, an Irish Bahá'i that Redwan knew in the UK knocked on the door. He had just returned from northern Thailand. Ultimately, we let him have that room and booked a hotel in Bangkok that we hoped would have functional air conditioning.

∽

*Reflection*

From Thailand we flew to Phnom Penh where my friend, Laura Burkhart's son Chris picked us up and showed us around. We attended a Bahá'í gathering there. After a few days we took the bus to Battambang where we spent five days in the remarkable company of Bahá'ís engaged in social and economic development projects.

We couldn't go to Cambodia without exploring the ancient ruins of Angkor Wat in Siem Reap, even though the heat and humidity were intolerable. There we were invited for supper, along with two Cambodians, to the home of a Malaysian Bahá'í we'd met in Phnom Penh. We returned to Singapore to hang out with friends before heading to China. In Beijing other friends hosted us royally.

During those travels Redwan became increasingly ill. He had to stop mid-climb of a section of the Great Wall of China. I was afraid he was having a heart attack but his pulse was normal. We didn't travel to Shanghai with our Beijing hosts as planned because of Redwan's poor health.

Redwan had previously committed to completing a Bahá'í project that required his total focus. If he returned to Edmonton before finishing it he knew he wouldn't meet his deadline. He told me he would rather die than not finish it so we cut our time short in SE Asia and only spent one night in South Korea. There, a Chinese family, whose relatives we'd met in Beijing, hosted us. Though not Bahá'ís, they arranged for us to visit the Bahá'í National Centre in Seoul as a surprise. When our young, hip hostess learned that we'd never tasted fresh Krispy Kreme donuts, she promptly took us to an outlet. After consuming at least half a dozen donuts each, Redwan and I gave the remaining dozen to our hostess' chauffeur who drove us to the airport.

Once in San Francisco, we stayed near the airport for a week before renting a house in Novato in the Napa Valley. Both locations afforded us opportunities to catch up with Colby.

**June 21, 2006**
**Journal Entry, Novato, California**
Now that we are settled into our Novato retreat, we need to go out in search of a long distance phone card to try to call the family. We anticipate news of more people being mowed down in this dreadful, interminable Iraq war.

**June 25, 2006**
**Journal Entry, Novato, California**
Last night Redwan failed to get through to Sarmad, but Sharaf and Aqeel were at home. In fact, Sharaf said Aqeel commented over their breakfast, not a half an hour before our call that it had been about a year since they'd heard from us. Then, voila! There we were on the end of the line. He has done that before. I told Sharaf, "I think Aqeel's intuition is very strong." She laughed.

Sad news from Iraq. Sharaf said 100 to 150 people are carted to the morgue each day in Baghdad.

"We're coping but we're tired," she said. "All the population is tired. Most Iraqis are fleeing from the country anywhere they can go where they have relatives."

I told Sharaf that an Iraqi friend had asked why they don't leave. She replied, "If something happens to me, then it is my time to go. It could happen to me just as easily in New York City as it could here. Many people who move away from here die in Amman or other places. We always remember that we are in a city that Bahá'u'lláh loved. He shed tears when He left. All the Bahá'is of the world envy us for living in a city that Bahá'u'lláh graced for ten years. When I see the bridge over the Tigris River I salute it. This is the river that Bahá'u'lláh loved. I am proud to be here."

Sharaf and Aqeel finally have passports. If they can obtain visas they can travel outside Iraq.

"We already have an invitation from our neighbours to visit Egypt and Syria," she said. "They have homes in both places." They hope to go for two or three weeks in July or August. Sharaf has only been outside Iraq once. That was in the summer of 1968 when she accompanied her mother to Kuwait to visit Kaykhosrow, who worked there the year before he died. She described the weather there as "hellish".

I was thrilled to hear they had passports. "This is wonderful news, Sharaf!" I said. "Now we have to find a way to get you to come to Canada."

"I'd be there tomorrow if I could," she said.

Sharaf thinks that it will be more difficult to get a visa to visit Canada than Egypt and Syria but said for us to go ahead and try. I have no idea how this works but I will ask our travel agent, Arasteh.

"You know, it is ironic," Sharaf added, "I want to travel and you're tired of it."

I had to agree with that. During the past year or so we have stayed in over thirty different places. I'm tired of being constantly on the move. Not that I want to go home yet because I don't; I want to finish this book first. It's just that when we go home it would be nice to stay put for a while. But with trips to Winnipeg to see my parents, a visit to Boston to see Gabriel and Erica, and one to Toronto to see Asher, oh and a potential return trip to China, and now possibly Turkey to meet up with our Iraqi family, it's not likely I will retire my suitcase any time soon.

Sharaf gave me a little more information about her maternal grandparents. Her grandfather, Husayn Wakil, is buried in Eskandaroon [Iskenderun, Turkey]. After her maternal grandmother, Melka Wakil, died, Shoghi Effendi gave instructions for her tomb to be built in Baghdad.

Sharaf pleaded with me to keep her informed about Redwan's sinus problem. I managed to dodge her question about "my projects" as I really wouldn't know how to respond appropriately. Today, I am having a difficult time believing that this manuscript will ever, ever see the light of day. Part of my purpose was to learn about the family in advance of meeting them. Now it seems it might be possible to at least meet Sharaf and Aqeel!

**June 25, 2006**
**Email to Pierre-Yves**
**Subject: How's it goin' mate?**

We wonder how you are and how your parents are faring on the slippery slope called old age. Yesterday, when I asked my dad how he and Mom were doing he said, "It sure is different being 85."

Redwan is feeling so lousy. I managed to get him to speak to two doctor friends in Canada who are going to look for the right kind of surgery for him, and the right surgeon. If something can be set up soon, we'll return to Canada early.

Much love,

Shar

**June 30, 2006**
**Email to Laura Burkhart**
**Subject: Your timely call and comments!**

Your call and encouraging words were so helpful. Also, I needed to tell you how much I LOVED Ann Patchet's book, *Truth and Beauty*. It chronicles the journey of two women writers to success. I'm thinking about sending it to you but feel I need to hang onto it for a bit first. There is much learning in it for me, given that it is non-fiction.

Back to the editing process here.

Love you so much,

Shar

**July 4, 2006**
**Journal Entry, Novato, California**

Redwan just got off the phone with Sarmad. He had trouble telling me what Sarmad said because he couldn't stop sobbing. Almost every day one or two people are killed in his neighbourhood. Gruesome would hardly describe what he sees on his own street. At the threat of their lives people are prevented from removing dead bodies from where they were killed. Dogs feast on them.

"There are dead bodies everywhere," Redwan said to me with a look of disbelief and terror in his eyes. Then he choked out, "I told Sarmad that I just want God to ease up on their trials a bit. It has been too long. My prayers are that the horrendous cloud of oppression and severe testing will be dispelled and that a period of ease and tranquility will be ushered in." Later, Redwan told me Manar is in a gifted program at school and that Sana passed his exams. It was 48°C in Baghdad today. Imagine.

Redwan asked his brother about the wisdom of us trying to meet Sharaf and Aqeel in Turkey or trying to arrange for them to come to Canada. Sarmad said he didn't know what to say about either option.

"How could they come to Canada and then return to Iraq?" I asked Redwan, knowing absolutely they would return out of loyalty to their country, but what havoc would that play on their psyches? Redwan agreed. He felt it would be almost cruel for them to experience peace and order and then have to return to the exact opposite.

**July 4, 2006**
**Email to Pierre-Yves**
**Subject: When are you going home?**
When are you going home? That's what we both want to know, though you've likely told us several times.

We have new developments in our lives as a result of Redwan's health, or lack thereof. His blood pressure reading at the Safeway here in Novato was 160/102. His buddy at McGill, Qutayba Hamid said, "Go home! You've got too many problems going on," he said. I agree.

The sinus doc in Edmonton isn't back in his office until next Tuesday, July 11, but he does do computer-assisted sinus surgery.

As soon as Redwan gets off the phone we'll call Air Canada and try to book our return. It is the right thing for me to return with Redwan as he has a lot to deal with, but when I think of unpacking our bedroom closet in Edmonton I begin to twitch. I am also grieving the loss of my dream to have time to write and to spend two weeks at that health retreat Laura went to in Southern California. But as Muhammad said, and I know this quote is correct because Redwan looked it up for me, " ...they plotted and God plotted; and God is the best of plotters."

We really miss you.
Much love,
Shar

# *Fire and Vengeance*

*"My calamity is My providence, outwardly it is fire and vengeance, but inwardly it is light and mercy..."*[1]

∽

### Reflection

On a lovely prairie evening, July 11, 2006, as the setting sun gave birth to puffy pink clouds in a darkening sky, we slipped quietly back into Edmonton. Our faithful friend Pirooz picked us up at the airport.

Once home, Redwan's health crisis trumped unpacking, dealing with nine months of mail, or catching up with friends. The first Friday evening we were home Canadian Revenue Agency called to say they were performing a "random" audit on us for every deposit over $100 for the two previous years. And with that another thousand pound burden landed on the shoulders of someone who had nightmares about grade 12 math until she reached the age of 35.

I could barely remember the infrastructure of our lives after being away so long; it urgently needed to be re-established. Matters that should have been sorted easily became major obstacles. Our so-called "personal bank manager" kept bungling things and wouldn't return my frantic calls or emails. Redwan's UK insurance policy was in danger of being cancelled because our bank kept forgetting to mail the funds to London. We couldn't get an answer from the banker as to whether or not we'd signed our rights of survivorship when we opened our accounts. Our investments were in the toilet and needed to be salvaged. Our wills needed work. I needed a Power of Attorney for Redwan. As my urgent list mounted I tried to cover up my panic but inside I was freaking out.

Perhaps worst of all was how the ENT surgeon—I'll call him Dr. X—

---

1    Bahá'u'lláh, *The Hidden Words*, trans. Shoghi Effendi (Wilmette, Illiois: United States Publishing Trust,1985), Arabic 51, 22.

dealt with Redwan. The day after our return to Edmonton this doctor ordered a CT navigational scan of Redwan's sinuses. The results were so alarming that the lab made a point of calling the surgeon but he made no effort to inform Redwan.

While Redwan languished in bed enduring terrible pain, I was overwhelmed with fear that if he didn't get immediate medical attention he would die. It fell to me to make sure that didn't happen but it was as if I was trapped in a burning house with an invalid. No matter whom I called I couldn't get appropriate help. Each day he lost more ground. I called the surgeon's office twice and told his secretary that in the evenings, when Redwan was always worse, I was afraid he was dying and considered taking him to Emergency. "Well," she huffed, "I don't know what good that would do."

Late one night, a week after that sinus scan, Redwan said quietly, "I'm not sure I'm going to make it." I became desperate. In tears I said, "I feel as if I'm failing you." With his eyes still closed he replied, "Don't worry, Bahá'u'lláh will guide you." That night I prayed as earnestly as I ever had.

I woke up at 4:00 a.m. with the thought that I needed to call Negar Asdaghi. She was a neurology resident and former graduate student of Redwan's. In the morning, however, I reconsidered and endeavored to contact more experienced colleagues of Redwan's but none was available. When I finally dialed Negar it was as if she was waiting for my call. She went online immediately, read the CT report and was alarmed. "Get him to emergency this afternoon, Shar! This is very serious. I would not wait out the weekend on this."

But Redwan resisted. He had organized a meeting with his graduate students at our place that afternoon. Eventually, and with great reluctance, he cancelled that meeting. Within a half an hour of Negar's call I dropped him off at the University of Alberta Hospital Emergency Department. By the time I parked the car and joined him there he was incensed. "Let's go," he said impatiently. "They say Negar is only a resident and isn't even working in Emergency." I prevailed upon him to remain. Soon Negar arrived and managed to get him out of the waiting room and onto a chair behind a curtain.

No stretchers were available. Then she set about getting him admitted.

ENT refused saying it was Friday and nothing would be done until Monday. But Negar succeeded in persuading the Emergency doctor to allow her to go over his head and approach the Pulmonary Department. In the end, one of Redwan's colleagues in that department agreed to admit him for "pain management." Eventually, Redwan was moved onto a stretcher and into the cast room where he spent the weekend. Despite the constant interruption of staff rushing in and out for supplies, I could have cried from relief.

Even though it was the weekend, Negar and that pulmonary doc got things moving. On Sunday evening, an ENT doctor on call for Dr. X, the surgeon who'd left Redwan in the lurch for 10 days, visited Redwan and offered to speak to Dr. X.

The next morning at a previously arranged appointment with Dr. X in his hospital-based clinic, he showed us Redwan's navigational scan but made no mention of the gravity of the report. Just then his phone rang. It was the other ENT doctor. In our presence Dr. X said, "I have neither the time nor the inclination to handle this case." Our jaws dropped. Redwan and I stared at each other in disbelief. Then, to our indescribable relief, we heard Dr. X agree to pass Redwan on to the other doctor.

After that visit, as we approached a bank of phones in order to call Redwan's children, Marianne and Sam in the UK, Redwan commented, "If this is how he treats a colleague, how would he treat 'Joe Public?'" Nonetheless, we were joyful. Finally, Redwan was going to get the medical attention he needed. For the next couple of months, he was in and out of hospital but at least he was "in the system." When Redwan was hospitalized I spent my waking hours with him and, when necessary, advocating on his behalf. Throughout, I was thankful for my ancient nursing training.

We were also profoundly thankful for the abundant support we received from others. When word got out that we were back in Edmonton, and that Redwan was ill, friends like Ezmina Samaroo devoted hours to helping me un-stuff cupboards I'd crammed full before we left for Australia in order to make storage space for our renter. My daughter Colby came to our rescue from San Francisco, not once but five times during the ensuing ordeal. All of our kids and siblings (except Redwan's brother, Sarmad, who couldn't leave Iraq) came too. As well, we are blessed to have supportive former spouses, Ann and Jack. Although we are all Bahá'ís, and divorce is highly discouraged in the teachings of our faith, 'Abdu'l-Bahá advised that if divorce occurs former couples should forge new sibling-like relationships. We are grateful to count Ann and Jack as such.

Apart from supporting Redwan, my main role was communicating with family and friends. Redwan had travelled to over sixty countries. Literally hundreds of his friends wrote with promises of healing prayers. Our late friend, Andrew Pemberton-Piggot, coined the term "joonami". It is a cross between "joon", which means "dear" in Persian, and tsunami. Those prayers were like a joonami for us. They lifted us above the tidal wave of tests and held us there and then safely re-deposited us.

Among the loving messages we received, those from some youth touched us most deeply. Like his father before him, Redwan has a strong heartfelt connection with the youth and has served as a mentor for numerous young people both at work and in the community at large. He is deeply steeped in the Bahá'í Writings and often conducts classes for youth.

What follows are a selection of my reflections and journal entries as well as my emails, and those of others, that tell the saga of Redwan's illness, the unexpected bounty that came with it, and the stupendous support and "confirmations" we received along the way.

### July 18, 2006
### Journal Entry, Edmonton

I'm extremely worried that Redwan's terrible headaches and stabbing pain in his head, which increase in severity almost daily, is cancer. This hit home after I saw the growths inside his nose on the television monitor while the surgeon was scoping him. He referred to the growths as polyps.

Redwan was reluctant for me to tell Sharaf because he didn't want to worry her. I refrained from saying that it wasn't fair not to tell her. (Back in the day, she wasn't told that her father was dying of cancer.)

When I asked Sharaf how things were, she replied, "The situation is not very good. There are dozens of killings every day. People are killed by identification; the Sunni kill the Shi'a and the Shi'a kill the Sunni. Sometimes people get killed haphazardly. Yesterday, fifty men entered a busy market and killed 100 people. There are explosions all day long. You don't know if your sons and daughters will arrive home safely or not."

**July 19, 2006**
**Journal Entry, Edmonton**

CNN reports that 14,000 civilians have been killed in Baghdad already this year. They described the conditions as approaching civil war. I'd say so! How long can our family escape death?

**July 22, 2006**
**To Karen, Marlene, David and Meim**
**Subject: Prayers for Redwan, please**

Dearly loved friends,

I'm sorry that I don't have time to call you but I need to ask for your prayers for Redwan. He was admitted to the hospital here in Edmonton yesterday. He is currently undergoing tests to see what is going on in his sinuses that has caused bone erosion. He has been in agony.

Now Redwan is getting the attention he needs. He may have an angiogram on Monday in advance of a biopsy of the lesion (under general anesthetic). Then they will know what they are dealing with and can treat it. He was scheduled for sinus surgery August 29. After the directional CT scan the surgeon put him on top of the emergency surgery list, but he is on holidays part of the summer and operating room time is tight. Now that Redwan has been admitted, and ENT (Ear, Nose and Throat) and Pulmonology are involved, maybe the surgeon will feel some pressure to move up the surgery date.

Redwan is content with the Will of God and not scared. I'm scared. I need to say some prayers and then call his siblings in Baghdad and try again to get his kids on the phone tomorrow, and with them all, sound positive and cheerful, like I did with my parents today. There, you've got the scoop. Thanks for being shoulders to lean on.

So much love,

Shar

**July 22, 2006**
**Journal Entry, Edmonton**
I returned home from the ER about 8:30 p.m. exhausted but had much to do around the apartment. After some prayers I called Sharaf around midnight hoping she wouldn't answer. I dreaded telling her that Redwan was in the hospital. He agreed I could if I made it sound positive. I tried, but she cried the moment she heard the news. Still, I kept focusing on the positive; he is finally getting the attention he needs.

Between sobs Sharaf said, "I haven't seen my brother for more than thirty years. I just want to see him before ... " Her voice trailed off. In her mind it was clear he was dying. I felt so sad for Sharaf. Truthfully I shared the same thoughts as her as I walked home from the hospital tonight. I want Sharaf to see her brother so badly. After I hung up with her I called Sarmad. He sounded light and happy and reassured me.

I also talked to Negar who brought up some concerns after she extracted a promise from me not to do any more internet research on Redwan's illness. I already freaked myself out by looking up Wegner's Disease, the organ-eating, etiology-unknown disease that destroys sinuses.

**July 27, 2006**
**Journal Entry**
Day six of Redwan's hospitalization at the University of Alberta Hospital. Today, after three or four unsuccessful attempts to get through to Sharaf, I managed to talk to Sarmad. This time he sounded somber and worried.

Though he seemed fearful of what I might say about Redwan's condition, he extracted the possibilities from me. I tried to assure him that Redwan is fine, happy and content with the Will of God.

"It's not a problem for him," Sarmad replied, "but it is a problem for you."

**July 28, 2006**
**Journal Entry**

Redwan went to surgery just before 4 p.m. My stomach is in knots. According to the orderly who came for him, there isn't anywhere for me to wait where I might interface with the surgeon after the biopsy. Negar said the surgeon would know from the look of the lesion what it is and how extensive it is. So, here I sit, in Redwan's hospital room wearing my jacket and his slippers. My feet and ankles are freezing.

Since they came for Redwan, a number of friends have called including my brother Gerry from Australia. That bank clerk finally returned my innumerable frantic calls. Apparently, we have signed the right of survivorship on our bankcards after all. He admitted the bank attached insufficient postage to the UK bank payment for Redwan's insurance policy, which is why the funds didn't arrive. What a piece of work he is.

I need my stomach to calm down. I started to write an email to Sarmad and Sharaf but I'm too on edge.

It is 8:50 p.m. Redwan is back from surgery. He is moaning and groaning. He passed a mega clot from his mouth that attracted a flurry of attention because of the potential to hemorrhage. Mercifully, the bleeding has slowed up. His moustache bandage has not needed to be changed for almost an hour. He's had sips of apple juice and says he is hungry.

I just remembered something that Sarmad said on the phone yesterday.

"'Abdu'l-Bahá said sometimes we have to turn." There he paused, struggling for a word to describe the opposite of good, "that which is bitter into something sweet." I told him that that's clearly what he and the family had been doing in Iraq all along.

## August 1, 2006
## Journal Entry

I've just spent the last hour in the kitchen cleaning up after company. My back is breaking and my heart is heavy. I am suspended over the edge of a cliff hanging onto Redwan's ankle. He is about to drop into a deep abyss, and me with him I fear, when we hear the biopsy results. "Bunches of biopsies" is how the surgeon described what he removed.

Right now Redwan is trying to reach his brother and sister in Iraq. "What am I supposed to tell them?" he asked me. "That I'm out of hospital and waiting for the biopsy results?" I nodded. "Sharaf will freak out," he said.

I nodded again. "She needs to know. She deserves to know."

Reluctantly, he picked up the phone while I returned to the kitchen.

Now he is speaking in Arabic trying to explain what is going on inside his head. He was in such terrible pain this morning my heart broke for him. He couldn't sleep because of it. Now, he must be talking to his sister and she must be crying. Oh, it is too painful.

## August 4, 2006
## Journal Entry

I have knots in my stomach the size of grapefruits. I have just looked up sinus fungus on the internet again and am horrified. We still haven't heard from the surgeon. Jack, my ex-husband, called this morning to suggest we go to the Mayo Clinic if we think that Redwan is not getting the attention he needs. I THINK THAT REDWAN IS NOT GETTING THE ATTEN-TION HE NEEDS! Early this morning he told me he had heartburn. That is the morphine. It may be contraindicated if it causes problems in the esophagus. Then what?

I am consumed with anxiety about Redwan. I don't want him to be a victim of a lousy medical system. I'm terrified to leave him this afternoon for a meeting I'm compelled to attend at Revenue Canada. I need to calm down, say some prayers, and call Negar. I also need to find someone to sit with Redwan while I'm gone in case the doctor calls.

**August 4, 2006**

**Email to David, Karen, Meim, Marlene, Brenda, Trudi, John, Sharon, Wendy, Jean, Kathie and Patrick, Pari, Stephanie**

**Subject: Brief update on Redwan**

Redwan was discharged from hospital yesterday after a ten-day stay. We hope to get the pathology report of a de-bulking he had of his sinuses by the end of the week. Though the surgeon thinks it is a tumour, Redwan still believes it could be a fungal infection because the Mayo Clinic says fungal infections are at the root of 30 per cent of all serious sinus conditions.

Redwan is on oral morphine and Tylenol. His pain is much worse at night and in the morning than from midday until evening. His spirits are great; he has handled this like a prince. Tonight our dear friends, Terri and Ted are coming for supper. Terri had major surgery for cancer while we were in Australia. She'll be a great source of moral support for Redwan, if that's what he has.

As for moi, I've been too busy running around trying to deal with everything to process this and, indeed, there may not be much to process, although I highly doubt that, given the destruction of the bones in Redwan's sinuses.

I managed to make it to Curves, today. As I exercised my way around the circuit I had a chance to reflect on what all this could mean. I almost wept. Then a new staff member, a kind Muslim woman, asked how my husband was doing and said she prays for him daily. I only met her once before. Honestly, we are surrounded by love and prayers. It is like being carried and buffered by a fluffy cloud. But back on the ground there's stuff to do, like preparing papers for Revenue Canada, which is chomping at the bit to audit us. I know there's always an upside to tests, especially horrendous ones, but I guess we'll have to wait to discover what that might be in this case.

So, my dears, much love to you all. I'll keep you posted.

Shar

P.S. Here it is Thursday and we've still not heard about the pathology so maybe I'll wait before sending this. Now I need to try to find my car keys that I lost this morning when I snuck off to exercise while Redwan was asleep.

P.P.S.  We just got the diagnosis. It is undifferentiated nasal cancer. Our phone is buzzing with medical people.

Love,

Shar

**August 4, 2006**
**Later Journal Entry**

Our life, as we've known it, is over. Redwan has a highly aggressive form of cancer. I can hardly type. My brain feels frozen. I'm so scared for him and what he will have to face; I'm scared that I will be on the street, my same old fear of destitution that shames me.

I need to take a little break before friends arrive with supper.

Redwan looks green. I just sent him to lie down. It broke his heart to tell Marianne he has cancer. I can't believe this, in a way. In another way, we both knew it was frigging cancer. I'm sick for him. If it takes him, this world will have lost one amazing man.

God willing, this is a fight he'll win! And I want to be by his side supporting him every way possible. I'm not going to cook for company anymore. I just can't. I'm too tired and my priority needs to be Redwan and putting our papers in order. Frigging papers. I hope the next world has nothing that resembles a scrap of paper.

I called Colby at work and put Redwan on the line because she'd left a message asking how Redwan was doing and wondering about his diagnosis. I heard her tell him she loves him very much.

**August 5, 2006**

**Email to Sarmad, Shatha, Sharaf, Aqeel, Ikbal, 'Abdu'l-Razak and families in Iraq**

**Subject: Our dear family**

Our sweet family, how difficult it must be for you to be so far away from Redwan at a time like this. My heart breaks for all of you. You already have so much suffering to bear. But, God willing, Redwan will win this battle. He is strong, has a great appetite and a very positive attitude. And, of course, he has profound and deep trust in God.

Fortunately, like your father, dearest Sharaf and Sarmad, he adores movies. When we bought a new bed a couple of years ago it came with a free television. We have it set up in a cupboard in our bedroom. In the midst of this drama, Redwan is watching a comedy and is entirely engaged in it.

Our phone rings constantly with calls from friends wanting to see Redwan or do something for us. Honestly, prayers, love and good food surround us. After we navigate through this long weekend, we have the promise of good medical support.

So that you know, Redwan's diagnosis came in yesterday. It is undifferentiated carcinoma. We should have a clear picture of the plan of attack once the medical team is assembled.

Redwan's good friend, Dr. Qutayba Hamid, has been consulting with Redwan about his health since mid-June when we were in California. When Redwan was in the hospital and stressed about his grant applications, which are due in September, Qutayba said, "Defer them. You're a perfectionist. Even if you get better soon it'll take you a month to get over being on morphine."

Redwan agreed and the university arranged for his grants to be deferred. Redwan was so relieved by this decision. I told him, "It is as if your mother is talking through Qutayba."

Qutayba is a busy doctor with a wife and four daughters. He works out of McGill University in Montreal but originally comes from Mosul and is

Muslim. He and his wife have family in Iraq. Qutayba and Redwan worked together at the National Heart and Lung Institute at the University of London from 1988 to 1993 when Qutayba moved to Canada. They've remained close. He told Redwan yesterday that it would be very important that he have strong faith through this period, which, of course, Redwan has.

Mujib Cadili (el Qadhili in Iraqi) also has been of great support. He came to the hospital twice to see Redwan, once with his wife, Sousan, and one of their daughters. Sousan is also from Baghdad.

So, the movie is over. Redwan is going to have a sleep but first he wants me to read him some of his emails. One is from Shahriar Razavi, his precious friend, who is currently travelling in Europe with his family.

We love you all very much and, as I said to Sarmad, we look forward to seeing you, perhaps in Turkey after our pilgrimage with Marianne and Sam. November 12-20, 2007.

Hugs and more hugs and prayers and more prayers,

Shar

The next email is from our friend Terri Flanagan about her bowel cancer. Somehow she managed to transform that ordeal into a blessing.

**August 6, 2006**
**Email from Terri to Shar**
**Subject: A thought to share**
I forgot this until this week, remembering my own experience through Redwan's, but one thing that came to me so clearly, and was a sustaining foundation almost for the whole experience…

When I got home from the colonoscopy that Wednesday night and I was telling the kids that the doctor had found something he didn't like the look of, and I was a bit numbed by even speaking such words, this realization came like a bolt, a host of something: God remembered me. He hadn't forgotten me. With all of my faults and weaknesses and childishness, He had remembered me and was calling me to come closer to Him. And in that self-same second, I was so grateful, overwhelmed with joy that lousy little me had been given this opportunity to draw closer. And that I was loved by Him.

It became like a spiritual fasting process over months, feeling awash in the process of being loved undeservedly by so many people, of appreciating every breath, and of learning to live life again step by baby step. It really was akin to fasting, and purifying, and cleansing.

I know that I was blessed by the test of cancer. And was so heartened that God hadn't forgotten me…that life was dependent upon Him…And that He wanted me close to Him, one way or another.

It was such a joy, Shar, and just made me cry. It was almost unbelievable to me.

I love this quote. It too gave me lots of solace and sustenance.

"O thou who art turning thy face towards God! Close thine eyes to all things else, and open them to the realm of the All-Glorious. Ask whatsoever thou wishest of Him alone; seek whatsoever thou wishest from Him alone. With a look He granteth a hundred thousand hopes, with a glance He healeth a hundred thousand incurable ills, with a nod He layeth balm on every wound, with a glimpse He freeth the hearts from the shackles of grief. He doeth as He doeth, and what recourse have we? He carrieth out His Will, He ordaineth what He pleaseth. Then better for thee to bow down thy head in submission and put thy trust in the All-Merciful Lord."[2]

Ted told me tonight not to be afraid or sad; Redwan has absolutely nothing to be afraid of; his life is one of complete service and it is totally in the Hands of God. What better place to be?

Lots of love and hugs,

Terri

---

2       'Abdu'l-Bahá, *Selections from the Writings of 'Abdu'l-Bahá* (Wilmette, Illinois: 1982), #22, 320.

**August 6, 2006**
**Journal Entry**

I'm stealing a moment before the Samaroos arrive with dinner. This weekend, a long weekend, has been interminable from the perspective of Redwan's health. Last night at midnight, as I was trying to go to sleep, I had a panic attack. Visions of the tumour the second surgeon saw when he scoped Redwan eating the bones in his face and mushrooming close to his brain, filled my head. He needs it stopped either by surgery or radiation. I don't know which. Please God make it stop growing.

I had an hour and a half walk with a friend last night. I really enjoyed that time. Pirooz insisted I take a break while he stayed with Redwan. But I am tired, tired and stressed. I unplugged the phone today at 4 p.m. and lay down with Redwan. He finally slept but I couldn't. I was too consumed with worry about our affairs not being in order should anything happen to him.

Redwan talked in Arabic to Sarmad yesterday before I talked to him.

I am freaking out and Negar knows it. She just called to read me something I gave her on a flight to Vancouver in 2004 where she was headed to write her medical qualification exams. We happened to be on the same flight. I took advantage of the fact that she hadn't seen me to play a trick on her. After the plane took off I shot up the aisle and slipped into the galley out of sight of the passengers where I conferred with a flight attendant. Soon thereafter a handsome young pilot entered the cabin and over the PA asked Negar to identify herself. Once he spotted her he wished her luck with her medical exams. She was gob smacked. She looked around to see who the culprit might be and found me. Before we landed I wrote out this quote from Bahá'u'lláh for her: "He who trusts in God, God will suffice him. He who fears God, God will send him relief."[3] Negar's call was to remind me of those words.

---

3    H.M. Balyuzi, *Bahá'u'lláh–The King of Glory* (Oxford: George Ronald Publisher, 1980) 138.

**August 7, 2006**

**Email to Negar**

Last night I tried again to sleep without a pill but gave up about 1:00 a.m. I was stressing about too many visitors. I have to find a way to say "no."

I am only searching anti-cancer diets this morning, teas, raw foods, etc. I'm not going to look at anything else related to Redwan's potential condition.

I am trying to focus on laying down Bahá'u'lláh's words in my head to replace my worries.

I can't tell you how much I appreciate your many kindnesses!

Much love,

Shar

**August 8, 2006**

**Email to family**

**Subject: Update on Redwan**

Redwan is asleep but I will wake him up shortly and take him to Emergency as his doctor advised.

Sharaf and Aqeel, we are investigating obtaining visas for you from the Canadian Embassy in Amman. I'll be in touch as soon as we hear back. It would be absolutely amazing and a dream come true to have you here with us.

Sam and Marianne, your dad loves you so much and longs to see you. We just need to make sure you are headed to the right destination before you book your flights. Right now we don't know if that is Edmonton or Rochester, Minnesota. We should know more within the next week to ten days and will keep you posted.

Much love,

Shar

**August 8, 2006**
**Email to family**
**Subject: Update on Redwan's readmission**

I'm happy to report that after a mere eight-hour wait in Emergency, Redwan has a bed in the hospital (University of Alberta). Thanks to morphine, today he was feeling pretty good so that wait wasn't too arduous. He told me he had such a sense of contentment. He really did. I am sure it is the prayers people are saying for him.

Hopefully, Redwan will have a CT head scan tomorrow. He has an appointment at the Cross Cancer Institute on Friday morning. An oncologist friend of ours told him the type of chemotherapy he will have doesn't cause hair loss.

Before I left him at the hospital tonight Redwan had received his medications and was happily preparing to retire for the night.

He was at home for ten long days after our return from California, in the hospital for ten days, home for another eight days, during which we had a flood of visitors. Yesterday I declined visitors because it was too taxing on him (and me, truthfully).

Unofficially, I've faxed his test results to his colleague, Dr. Qutayba Hamid, a molecular pathologist in Montreal and to another colleague at the Mayo Clinic in Rochester, Minnesota. The Mayo Clinic will provide a second opinion or perhaps treatment, depending upon the results.

So off to bed I go with a much lighter heart. I hope this report cheers you too. Redwan sends you all his love. He was so happy to have spoken to many of you over the weekend, especially the Baghdad family.

Much love and gratitude for all of your prayers,

Shar

**August 9, 2006**
**Email from Anonymous**
**Subject: Sweetheart**
Dear one,

I hope that Redwan's readmission went okay but I think the house must have been empty when you went back, and I hope that you just slept and slept and weren't too sad.

Huge love,

Anonymous

**August 9, 2006**
**Email to Anonymous**
**Subject: Sweetheart**
The house was empty but peaceful and I felt happy until I lay down. Then panic swallowed me up; panic that financially we are in a mess. I just need to attend to some details and then I'll be able to sleep better. If only I could wrestle our relevant papers back from The Canada Revenue Agency I could get on with it.

Much love,

Shar

P.S. I got a copy of Redwan's reports. They're a total disaster. How the first surgeon could turn his back on him and insist that he couldn't do anything until the end of August I don't know. Redwan has bilateral cancer in his sinuses, yet his MRI from May 11, 2006 in Australia showed no sign of cancer. Strange.

**August 9, 2006**
**Email from Anonymous**
**Subject: Going for it**
Dearest Shar,

I can't believe this but know it's a really good thing that there is a God factor in all of this because the surgeon would have his knees broken if there weren't. I am afraid to look on the Internet to see what bilateral cancer is, but I'm going to do it anyway.

**August 9, 2006**
**Email to Anonymous**
**Subject: Going for it**
My first laugh of the day. Broken knees! Good one.
Much love and hugs,
Shar

**August 11, 2006**
**Email to family**
**Subject: Redwan's Update**
Today we met with a team of doctors at the Cross Cancer Institute. If surgery is an option, and this is still uncertain, 36 radiation treatments will follow before chemotherapy.

We had just returned to Redwan's room at the hospital when Negar arrived. She'd come from dropping off her rent cheque at her landlord's but had no idea until then that he is the chief pathologist at the U of A. Not only that! He happened to have prepared Redwan's biopsy report! Can you imagine? He told her it was a difficult type of cancer to identify. She came with us to see Dr. Jeffrey Harris, who will operate on Redwan if surgery is possible, and was able to discuss with him the primary question at hand; Redwan's exact diagnosis.

The situation is as follows: the tumour is on both sides of Redwan's face and extends to the base of his brain. It is extremely aggressive and will require radical surgery. There is a slim chance it is a rare type of cancer called SNUC that has a poor prognosis. He wants a second opinion on the pathology before proceeding with surgery. Thank goodness we approached the Mayo Clinic. Hopefully we will hear from them before the end of the week.

If it is the more common undifferentiated sinus cancer, and not SNUC, the surgeon will try to operate in two weeks. He wants to move swiftly because this type of cancer is curable. Others have told us that his team is Canada's "dream team." Residents vie for positions with Dr. Harris. Redwan's surgical team will also include neurosurgeons. One happens to be Negar's fiancé.

Okay, here's the thing: the surgery will take 18 to 24 hours. They will try to save Redwan's left eye. Post-op recuperation will be arduous and long term. Even knowing this, his spirits remain high.

Colby has been such a help today cleaning our apartment, organizing, shopping, answering the phone, cooking, checking emails and creating an email distribution list for me for family, friends, colleagues, etc. I am so grateful for her assistance. She has also been trying to expedite paperwork to see if it is possible to get Sharaf and Aqeel here from Baghdad.

I am typing this at Redwan's bedside. Colby just passed me a note to remind me that Redwan's birthday is on Monday. She invites you to send messages to him from which she'll create something special for him.

It is 9 p.m. Colby and I are about to say goodnight to Redwan and trundle home in the rain.

With much love and appreciation for your thoughts and prayers,

Shar, Redwan and Colby

**August 12, 2006**

**Email from Shemma (a Bahá'í youth from Edmonton)**

**Subject: Birthday**

**Dear Aunty Shar,**

...I'm keeping you all in my thoughts and prayers every day. I'm sure you will all get through this and you won't have to "trundle home through the rain" again for a very long time.

I love and miss you Aunty Shar, and I was wondering if you could please read the following message to Uncle on his birthday.

Thank you Aunty :)

Hi Uncle Redwan! Happy birthday!! I don't know how old you're turning today but you don't look a day over 24! Personally, I think it is your smile.

I've missed you so much while you've been away and I really hope I get to see you sometime soon.

There are a few things I wanted to tell you in person, Uncle, but I don't know when I will be able to so let me just say this: I love you so much Uncle Redwan and I hate that you are sick. I don't understand yet why these things have to happen, but at the same time I know that you will get through this and pretty soon we'll be having our intense discussions on the meanings of convergence and divergence, which I've missed so much. You've taught me so much, Uncle. I don't know if I ever told you, but I've always wanted to make you proud and you've made me want to be a better person. I know that you would want me to be a better person for myself or for Bahá'u'lláh, but I just love you so much and want so badly to make you happy.

I wish I could come in and see you, even just to say hi, but please know that I'm keeping you in my thoughts and prayers and I hope that when this is all over you and I can have a nice chat and maybe some chai and catch up because I miss hearing your beautiful stories.

I love you Uncle, take care and have a wonderful birthday.

Your Shemma

**August 12, 2006**
**Email from Moqbel (Redwan's nephew in Baghdad)**
**Subject: Birthday**
Dear Aunt Shar and Colby,

I sent you two e-cards for my Uncle Redwan for his birthday, one from my mom and one from me and Sama. Really wishing to celebrate his birthday: all of us with him here in Baghdad. We are praying for him every day to get better soon and to see him walking with all those he loves here in Baghdad.

Yours,

Moqbel and Sama

**August 12, 2006**

**Email from Marlene**

**Subject: Your flight**

Dear Shar,

I wouldn't offer to come if I thought you'd pick up the tab. It is, indeed, our pleasure to offer my flight and moral support. What are friends for?

We've been there, done that! And, if I recall correctly, you were there beside us much of the time. I remember the days you'd rush into our Sharon Drive home [in Toronto] with your red coat flapping in the breeze. You'd empty the dishwasher, pick up toys, fold laundry, etc. etc., then use the telephone and toilet and hop in the station wagon again to head off on your next mission.

Colby has always been a good organizer and I'm so glad she's with you now. I remember the time when you were pregnant with Asher and Michael and I slept over so you and Jack could have a break. Do you remember me telling you how she woke up saying, "Bottle, bottle?" She knew the plan and was just making sure we knew what to do. I think she was 15 months old at the time. Give that girlie a big hug from me. I'm sorry that our paths won't be crossing on this occasion. If she'd ever like her home papered with Holly Hobby motif, I'm the person to call…

I want to write a birthday greeting for Redwan before my eyes close totally.

Love you and sending little snippets of my heart to you and Redwan,

Marlene

**August 12, 2006**

**Email from Muneer (Redwan's cousin Ikbal's son in Baghdad)**

Dear Uncle Ridhvan,

Although I haven't seen you, I have heard so much about you that I feel I have known you all my life, and I felt so sad that you are sick, but cheer up, everybody is praying for you day and night, and I have a special feeling that you will soon be alright, and you will have a new birthday… I am sending you my photo to show you how handsome I am!!!!!!

Muneer

**August 15, 2006**
**Email to Sharaf from Colby**
**Subject: Surgery**

Dear Sharaf,

I just forced my mom to go to sleep and she asked me to please email you tonight and let you know that they got the surgery date moved up to August 29 instead of September 7. Redwan and my mom are both so relieved about this.

Also, we sent all the papers to Jordan today and if all goes well, they will be there by Friday or Saturday. There is one set of original documents and then a full set of copies for you to keep. We also have a full set of copies here, just in case.

I hope that you get some rest and that your preparation for travel goes smoothly. You are in our thoughts and prayers, always.

With so much love and respect,

Colby

**August 16, 2006**
**Email to family**
**Subject: Update on 15 and 16 August re Redwan**

Colby and I are just back from the hospital where we spent the last two hours reading emails that have poured in to Redwan from all over the world with birthday and well wishes. We hardly made a dent in them but will keep reading them to him in the coming weeks. He is deeply touched by this outpouring of love and kindness and so are Colby and I. Colby used many of them to create a massive birthday card.

Redwan is in great spirits after hours of laughing with two dear friends,

Mojdeh and Shahram Mottahed, who flew in from Vancouver for the day to visit him. Some other Persian friends provided a wonderful Persian feast for us as well as a birthday supper last night, which we shared with Ailsa Hedley and Dale Leftwich and their newborn baby, Aleta. Their visit was particularly special for us because we match-made for them.

The next day

I was too tired to finish this email last night so while I wait for Redwan to complete his PET scan I'll update you on the latest developments.

Today has been wonderful for us because we spoke to both Sharaf and Sarmad within the same hour. This is almost history making given that for so many years they've been cut off from the rest of the world. But the gap is closing. I feel it more each day.

A kind gentleman, Hugh Locke, who lives in New York City, and his extensive network of friends and acquaintances, are working the phones to try to expedite visitor's visas from the Canadian Embassy in Jordan for Sharaf and Aqeel. God willing, all the effort that so many have made, especially Colby, will pay off.

Earlier today Redwan invited his colleagues to a devotional gathering at the hospital chapel. He had prepared the program from his sick bed. About 20 people attended. Colby facilitated the gathering, played the music and organized the readers. We were touched by the heartwarming comments Redwan's colleagues made about him.

When I heard that Redwan's surgery (if he is eligible for it) was scheduled for September 7, I left a message on Dr. Harris' voice mail in which I pleaded for an earlier date. But when he visited Redwan he stood firm on that date. Redwan accepted that decision but asked Dr. Harris to tell me because, he explained, "It will break my wife's heart." With that Dr. Harris pulled his phone out of his pocket, spun around on his heel and headed out of Redwan's room. "I'll be back," he called over his shoulder. Later he returned to report he had conferred with the neurosurgeon and they'd rescheduled the surgery for August 29. We took the date change as a victory. God willing Sharaf and Aqeel will arrive before then.

Redwan will be discharged from the hospital tonight. Tomorrow morning we will say goodbye to Colby. She has been a lifesaver for me with her clear thinking, loving heart and capable hands. She stepped in and organized what needed to be organized, cleaned what needed to be cleaned and calmed me down when I was freaking out.

Tomorrow we will bustle around to various medical appointments. Meanwhile, our young friend, Meead Asdaghi, Negar's cousin, will drive three hours to Calgary airport and back to pick up Redwan's children who live in the UK; Marianne, Sam, and Sam's girlfriend, Amy!

That's it for now, except to thank you for your love and prayers. Redwan has just returned to the waiting room where I sit. His test is finished. He has a big smile on this face and is ready to return to the U of A Hospital to be discharged and then EAT!

Much love,

Shar

**August 18, 2006**
**Email from Negar**
**Subject: Some good news**

Dearest Shar:

Good morning. The result of Redwan's CT scan of his chest is back and everything is clear. This is extremely relieving since I had nightmares about lung metastasis and so on.

I will let you know about any other results as soon as they show up on our system.

Thanks for dinner last night. Dave and I enjoyed it.

Talk soon,

Negar

**August 18, 2006**
**Email to Negar**
**Subject: Some good news**

Gari joon, this is wonderful news! Thank you so much.

I too had nightmares that included insects, you, Dave, lots of dogs and a polar bear that licked Redwan's entire head. At least there was no repeat of the baby that was crawling along an escalator grate in my dreams last week. I'm going to quit taking those sleeping pills. I don't know how you manage with so little sleep…

Love,

Shar

**August 19, 2006**

**Journal Entry**

Redwan slept and slept all day. Between naps he said, "I want to live to be with you."

"Who wouldn't?" I said, which made us both laugh.

**August 20, 2006**

**Email to family**

**Subject: Request for prayers**

We talked to Sharaf about noon today. She and Aqeel made it to Amman but not without significant challenges including an "almost encounter" with bus hijackers that hit on five buses ahead of their convoy. Sharaf told us that they prayed their way through that nightmarish ordeal. When they finally arrived at the Jordanian border their suitcases were the only ones that weren't searched.

Sharaf and Aqeel are staying with a wonderful woman named Muna Tehrani. She is committed to helping them achieve their hearts' desire: to arrive in Edmonton before Redwan's surgery.

The Canadian Embassy was closed today because it was a national holiday in Jordan. Sharaf asked for prayers for their visit to the embassy tomorrow with the package of material Colby prepared for them. They're aware that they may be turned down given that only a handful of applicants are allowed to visit Canada. Still, she believes that if they manage to get an interview anyone with compassion will grant them visas.

After an interminable weekend, tomorrow, finally, is Monday. We should hear the results of Redwan's metastatic workup, the staging of his cancer and whether or not he is eligible for surgery. In the meantime, Redwan is enjoying a happy day of visiting with his children and Amy. Earlier today an old university friend from Baghdad, who now lives in Australia, visited. Pierre-Yves and Gordon Naylor came to see him later too.

Thanks so much for your interest, support and prayers.

Much love,

Shar

**August 20, 2006**
**Email from Muna Tehrani (in Amman, Jordan)**
**Subject: Update**
Dear Shar,

Aqeel and Sharaf went to the Canadian Embassy; they were asked to fill in additional forms, plus CVS for both. They did that but were told later "their passport is NOT accepted," because it is an "M" series. In addition to that, they should have separate passports.

They both went to the embassy in Amman. It took them quite some time to convince the officials there but fortunately, they could meet the consul and after long hesitation he agreed to issue new passports for them by 8 a.m. tomorrow.

The Canadian Embassy opens for visa processing from 8:30 a.m. to 10:00 a.m. only. If we're lucky enough, they will make it and submit their applications within the working hours. I hope that they'll get an answer this afternoon. I contacted the visa section several times today asking lots of questions. They were very helpful.

According to the outcome of the Canadian Embassy, we'll process the UK visa. Taking all this into consideration, I wonder if they'll be able to take their flight on the 24th.

Will keep you posted.

Warm and loving greetings,

Muna

**August 21, 2006**

**Email to family**

**Subject: Redwan's surgery is a go!**

I'm so sorry to be late in sending this note. It has been such a busy day. The meeting with the surgeon, Dr. Harris was excellent. He is a lovely man. Sam, Marianne and our dear life-saving Negar came too. Dr. Harris answered all our questions, and we had a long list. We came out of there feeling very positive and confident, not only in him but also in the course of the treatment outlined.

Dr. Harris needs one more MRI to determine the degree of penetration of the cancer in Redwan's left orbit. He'll try to save Redwan's eye. Six weeks post op Redwan will begin six weeks of radiation followed by six weeks of chemotherapy. He shouldn't expect to return to work for a year. That was a shock!

We're still hopeful that Sharaf and Aqeel will make it here before the surgery...

It's late; the kids are heading to Melody (Negar's cousin) and Rubens' where they are bunking so I'll sign off too. Thank you for all of your prayers and best wishes.

Much love,

Shar, Redwan, Sam, Marianne and Amy

**August 23, 2006**

**Email from Muna Tehrani (in Amman, Jordan)**

**Subject: Ticket booking**

Dear Shar, Redwan, Arasteh and Hugh,

Aqeel and Sharaf went to the Canadian Embassy to collect their visas as they were told to do earlier this morning. The officials at the visa section told them that it is not issued yet, and that they need to wait for another two weeks at least. She further told them that this is the usual procedure with all Iraqis. (I personally do NOT think so, because if this were the case, they wouldn't have told them to come back the same afternoon to collect their visas.)

I have a feeling that their papers were admitted to the consulate only and were NOT referred to the ambassador. We are crippled here and cannot push the matter further. The ambassador did not answer my email, and nobody called us as a follow-up on all the contacts being made from outside. They insist that they are following the regulations. The officials we meet do not give answers; they say we refer your case to the concerned people.

Sharaf is asking if you think there is any hope, or even any use of following up on this. She just came back from the embassy and needs some time to adjust to all this frustration.

If we wait for another two weeks the situation will get more complicated. Aqeel and Sharaf, as you probably know, got new separate passports from the Iraqi Embassy in Amman. BUT, these passports bear (S) series, and the UK Embassy requires (G) series from September.

We'll keep praying and truly believe that God works in mysterious ways!

May God bless you all,

Muna

**August 23, 2006**

**Email to Muna Tehrani (in Amman, Jordan) and Hugh (in New York)**

**Subject: Ticket booking**

I'm so sorry that Sharaf and Aqeel hit a brick wall at the consulate. Is there something you can do Hugh? These people have already endured a lifetime of disappointment and waiting, not to mention what they went through to get to Jordan. They are extremely patient in their suffering but being held back because of red tape feels like it is entirely too much for them to endure.

Thank you for your loving concern. We too are very concerned.

Loving regards,

Shar

**August 23, 2006**

**Email to family**

The Canadian Embassy called Sharaf and Aqeel to go and pick up their travel visas! The next challenge is to obtain transit visas to and from England and airplane tickets and flights to Edmonton, hopefully before Redwan's surgery. Hugh and Muna have obviously been working behind the scenes to achieve this result but I am unaware of those details.

This morning we bid farewell to Marianne, Sam and Amy whose visit lifted our spirits. By now they will have returned safely to the UK.

My dear friend, Marlene Russell, from Ontario, who was about to come here to help out for a week, had to cancel her trip. Sadly, she was diagnosed with uterine cancer. Marlene and Redwan will undergo surgery on the same day. What an amazing coincidence: two positive and happy souls who will rely on your prayers, particularly on Tuesday, 29 August (only five days from now).

My youngest son, Asher, just called. He's flying here on Monday from Toronto, compliments of his dad. Asher is anxious to see Redwan before his surgery and to meet Sharaf and Aqeel. Sam, Marianne and Colby hope to return in September. Meanwhile, Gabriel, my eldest, successfully defended his PhD thesis today at Princeton. He and Erica are busy settling into their new home in Boston and Gabriel into his new job at MIT. They want to see Redwan and meet Sharaf and Aqeel as well.

More great news today! An MRI of Redwan's head appears to indicate cancer hasn't breached his left eye orbit. We hope this bears out in surgery.

Please forgive us for not responding to all your email messages and phone calls individually. Redwan's energy level is limited but we cherish all your messages.

With love and appreciation,

Shar and Redwan

### Reflection

Sharaf wasn't about to allow cancer, or diplomatic red tape, for that matter, to rob her of her reunion with her brother. After three and a half decades of pining for him, her love became the driving force that cracked open the exit door just wide enough for her and Aqeel to squeeze out of war-torn Iraq. Once outside, invisible hands collaborated with Hugh and others to pry open Canada and England's reluctant doors. For example, Hugh just happened to interview someone for a position in his company who happened to be the ambassador to Jordan's niece!

Instead of us meeting Sharaf and Aqeel in Turkey or Jordan, as we had imagined, they were headed to Canada. It was beyond surreal for me to write them the following:

**August 26, 2006**

**Email to Sharaf and Aqeel**

**Subject: Invitation to a devotional gathering, August 29**

It you are up to it, after travelling half way around the world, it would be wonderful if you could attend the devotional gathering described below.

Much love,

Shar

I'm organizing a devotional gathering at the 5th floor, U of A Hospital Chapel between 12:00 and 1:00 p.m. on Tuesday, August 29 during Redwan's surgery.

Redwan's sister and her husband, whom he hasn't seen for 34 years, may attend. They should arrive from Baghdad, via Amman, London and Vancouver, a few hours before Redwan's surgery.

### Reflection

Far from being a fearful or even gloomy atmosphere during Redwan's surgery, the mood was jubilant, even celebratory. It seemed to me that the spiritual forces, amassed by popular demand, hovered over Redwan in that operating room.

My intention with these missives was to focus on the confirmations, to help others to see what had become so obvious to us, that there was more at work than meets the eye. To quote Buffy Ste. Marie again: Magic is alive, God is afoot.

**August 29, 2006**
**Email to family, friends and colleagues**
**Subject: Wonderful news**

The August 29, and the events leading up to it, will stand out forever in our lives. In the early hours of the morning last night, when Sharaf and Aqeel stepped off the plane at London's Heathrow Airport, Sam's girlfriend's mother, Simone, who works for British Airways, was there to greet them. She conducted them to a special room where they met their nephew, Sam, for the first time, and fell in love with him and Amy.

From Vancouver International Airport, Mojdeh and Shahram Mottahed called to alert us to the fact that the BA flight would be two hours late arriving so Sharaf and Aqeel would miss their connection to Edmonton. Panic stricken, I called our travel agent, Arasteh, at home. She worked her magic again and cancelled those tickets and booked the two remaining seats in business class on the last Air Canada flight out of Vancouver that evening but we had no way to convey this change of plans to our intrepid travellers. As it turned out, however, although novice international travellers, Sharaf realized they would miss their connection. Being the proactive woman she is, Sharaf asked someone if there were other flight options. They pointed her to an Air Canada counter where Sharaf and Aqeel were amazed to be immediately issued boarding passes.

In the meantime, Shahram, Mojdeh and a friend, wandered around in vain in Vancouver Airport carrying large signs in search of them. Shahram called in desperation 25 minutes before the flight was to depart. I immediately called Air Canada and somehow managed to get the necessary information: Sharaf and Aqeel had already boarded.

At 1:15 a.m. they descended the escalator and walked into Redwan's arms. Asher, our cinematographer, captured this reunion through the eye of my video camera, which was hastily yanked out of mothballs thanks to Pirooz's suggestion that we capture that moment.

The previous day, Qutayba cautioned Redwan not to become too emotional pre-operatively. So, while Sharaf sobbed, and tears ran down Aqeel's face, Redwan kept his emotions in check. Later, when I asked him how he felt he had done with that advice, he replied, "I think I did pretty well. I was afraid if I started crying I'd never stop." This said by a man who has not had one second of "why me?" thinking.

A few short hours after the airport pickup, which included Pirooz, there was Pirooz again, this time dressed in OR greens waiting at the Operating Room door to greet a very surprised Redwan. Pirooz works as a medical technician at another hospital. Somehow he managed to wangle a favour from a colleague at the U of A Hospital and was able to slip in and out of the OR all day providing us with surgical updates. "They think I work here," Pirooz said grinning.

In fact, as I write this I'm strategically located in a hallway en route to the particular ICU where Redwan is headed post surgery. Pirooz suggested I wait here so I can see Redwan as he is wheeled by.

Earlier this afternoon a group of 30 to 35 of us gathered together in the hospital chapel to pray on Redwan's behalf. It was such an unbelievable thrill to have Sharaf and Aqeel there. Asher took over Colby's DJ role and, according to him, "totally left her in the dust with his smooth mixing," whatever that means.

The surgery, which might have taken up to 24 hours, miraculously lasted only 11.5 hours. Redwan's left eye was saved so he didn't need skin grafts from his arm or leg or a neck resection.

Negar's fiancé called from his cell phone while walking home to pack and head to the airport en route to T.O. for their wedding this weekend. He said Redwan was stable throughout the surgery, that things could not have gone more smoothly, and that they had successfully removed a large tumour and taken wide margins of tissue beyond the tumour's reach. "The bottom line is that he is doing great!" he concluded.

I just saw Redwan roll by on a full-sized hospital bed surrounded by an array of bags, bottles and tubes. I recognized his pronated left foot sticking out of the covers, pointing slightly to the left.

One of the doctors noticed me and stepped out of the procession to tell me how pleased the surgical teams were with the surgery. They used titanium mesh to reconstruct the bony areas of Redwan's face that the cancer destroyed. Then the anesthetist, who had been kind enough to allow Pirooz in and out of the OR, stopped to speak to me too. He explained that Redwan will be quite anemic. They didn't give him a blood transfusion lest it flush stray cancer cells throughout his body.

For the next few days we're all going to be focused on Redwan's recovery from this monumental surgery and the hectic preparations leading up to it, including the 37 phone calls that came in yesterday alone. Literally, we've had scores of wonderful emails, which will take us some time to read. We look forward to joining the human race in the near future.

In the meantime, Colby will return to Edmonton on Saturday. My brother Don, from Calgary, and his partner Dani arrive the same day. Then, amazingly, my brother Gerry and his wife, Ann, from Austrailia, arrive next week. All will get to know and love our dear Sharaf and Aqeel. BUT Sam wants everyone to know that he met them first!

Surely our cups runneth over. Saying thank you for your kind wishes and prayers hardly feels adequate.

I will write again soon.

With much love,

Shar, Asher, Sharaf and Aqeel

**August 30, 2006**
**Email to family, friends and Redwan's colleagues**
**Subject: Redwan's progress**

Redwan remains in intensive care with an assortment of drains attached. He is off the ventilator but is still breathing through his tracheotomy. They will unplug it tomorrow to see if the swelling has receded sufficiently for him to breathe out of his nose and mouth. Evidently he won't be able to speak for several more days.

Redwan's primary concern before surgery was that he would lose his faith and his ability to think. He thought about it for a while and then hit upon a scheme. As soon as he regained consciousness post surgery he would try to remember the words to a long prayer he had memorized. If he could recall it that would confirm for him that his brain was still functioning and he would signal a "V" with his index and middle finger to let me know. As soon as I saw him today, though he could scarcely open his eyes for the swelling, he made a V with his fingers and then squeezed my hand. My heart leapt into my throat, and my eyes welled with tears that Redwan had sought and found such confirmation. What a solace that must have been to him, buried as he is under a mound of dressings.

Only immediate family is allowed into ICU but a couple of doctor colleagues also dropped in to offer encouragement and support.

I took Sharaf and Aqeel with me to Redwan's beloved shopping destination, Costco, for a quick foray. Aqeel would love to have spent hours doing a price comparison on the warehouse contents. In the limited time I afforded him, he discovered that only bananas were priced on par in Baghdad. Sharaf and Aqeel are so good humoured, so kind and so loving that it is a treat to be in their presence. But thankfully, Asher has replaced me as a more hopeful Arabic student for Aqeel.

I am sorry not to be able to keep up with your many loving emails but as Redwan recovers I am sure there will be time to savour your words, though not likely enough time to respond individually. As Ezmina said this morning when she dropped off tonight's supper, which was delicious, "The emails will wait." She's right.

With loving gratitude,

Shar

**September 3, 2006**
**Email to Shahriar and Tiffani**
**Subject: Redwan post-op update**

Thank you for your note. I'm sorry I haven't been in touch. Many are wondering what is going on with Redwan. While he has made progress in certain areas he lags behind in others. I don't yet know how to put that in an email and make it sound positive.

Yesterday, Redwan, who can't speak because of his tracheotomy, whispered to me, "I've seen the Supreme Concourse." I couldn't make out what he was saying and handed him some paper and a pen. When I understood him I asked how he felt about that. Tears spilled from his eyes.

"Are you crying because it isn't time to go?" I asked. He thought about that for a moment and then shook his head no.

As for me, I feel fully supported and loved by family and friends and there have been so many bounties. I just pray that Redwan will turn the corner soon.

Loving regards to you and your precious family,

Shar

*Reflection*

Redwan also tearfully described being surrounded by sweet, tender and loving little children who tended to him.

**September 9, 2006**
**Email to family**

Last night after eating too much pizza, popcorn and slurping down a milkshake with my Aussie brother and sister-in-law, I had trouble sleeping. Little wonder. In an effort to put myself to sleep I began to count back to the first family member's visit and cycled forward as family arrived and departed. As I did, an image of a Ferris wheel came to mind as family members disembarked and re-embarked, with what became clear to me, amazing symmetry.

It began with Colby's weeklong visit. She climbed back onto it and the next day Marianne, Sam and Amy stepped off. Then, just before Sharaf and Aqeel's remarkable arrival, Asher disembarked. Five days later, my brother Don and his partner, Danielle, emerged, followed later that evening by Colby again. The next day, Asher climbed back on. Three days later Colby got back on the Ferris wheel, just two hours before her Uncle Gerry and Aunt Ann stepped off.

Gerry and Ann left this morning en route to Alaska. They will return to Vancouver via a cruise ship before returning to Australia.

I could never have imagined what would befall Redwan, nor could I have imagined the constant and encircling support we've had. And it continues with Gabriel and Erica's arrival on September 19 for five days. Sam and Marianne plan to return soon too. And from every part of the globe come kind words and news of prayers.

As well, the local Bahá'í community has made sure that we, Sharaf, Aqeel and I are extremely well fed. I may have forgotten how to cook or at least that will be my excuse for some time.

As I write, Redwan is asleep in the room he has shared with three different people since he was released from ICU last Sunday about midnight. The first one was the sweetest little lady. At 91, she was as bright as a daisy and still doing crossword puzzles. When I told Sarmad, Redwan's brother in Baghdad, that Redwan was sharing a room with a woman he said, "Are you sure she's an old lady? My brother is a very handsome guy."

Redwan has another challenging week. He is jittery and still trying to ward off disturbing dreams and images from his ICU experience. Part of that, I'm sure, is drug induced. His memory is intact but his mind is racing, thinking up things he wants to do to make a difference for future ICU patients or matchmaking, a favourite hobby of ours. I guess it will take some time for him to relax and stabilize emotionally.

Qutayba told me some patients that spend more than 48 hours in ICU develop "Post ICU Syndrome." He said it is important to minimize Redwan's external stimulation by restricting visitors and limiting their visits to 10 minutes. I haven't found time to look up this syndrome but would imagine those patients relive the waking/sleeping nightmares they experienced in ICU just like Redwan is.

Just after Colby left, and before Gerry and Ann arrived, Redwan had a number of tubes and drains removed. Yesterday, he had his tracheotomy out. Half the staples remain on the suture line that runs in front of each ear and over the top of his head. They are superficial and will be removed tomorrow. The underlying bones are wired together. He has a few stitches at the tracheotomy site and some in his lumbar region, where a drain was inserted. He also has an IV running for intravenous antibiotics.

Mercifully, Redwan's headaches are declining, though he still feels a great deal of pressure in his head. He has double vision, understandable given the swelling in that area plus the fact that his eye that has repositioned slightly. Then there are the titanium implants to adjust to as well.

Today, Redwan, the cleanest person I know, was allowed to have a shower, his first in 11 days. He was thrilled. Tonight, as the sun lingered in the evening sky, he enjoyed another first; a wonderful Persian meal prepared by some loving friends and served to us at a picnic table on the front lawn of the hospital.

As I left the hospital tonight, Sharaf and Aqeel had already been scooped up by one of a number of Edmontonians that have fallen in love with them. I thought about how each night when we leave the hospital early signs of fall greet us, though the weather is unseasonably warm. As we pass under the trees outside the front door of the hospital we see how the light shines through the increasingly yellow canopy of leaves. For the first time this season I heard one of my favourite sounds, crunching leaves under foot.

When I opened the front door of our apartment Sharaf and Aqeel were busy hunting for my cell number. They were concerned that it was late and I still wasn't home. This dear, sweet couple put their lives in danger in order to see Redwan and to support us. They are pure love. Had Redwan not become seriously ill they couldn't have come, nor would our family members have come from afar to visit. I'm so grateful they've all had the opportunity to meet Sharaf and Aqeel.

Thank you, once again, for your most loving support and encouragement. It will surely never be forgotten. "Prayers," said Redwan, who just woke up from a brief nap, "are the most beautiful thing when combined with skills and scientific knowledge."

Much love,

Shar

**September 11, 2006**
**Email to Sam (Redwan's son)**
**Subject: Please book the flight**

As of late this afternoon your dad is home. He is improving daily. He had a great sleep last night and that made a huge difference. He is still weepy, like very.

Wish me luck tonight. I'll be trying to sleep on the office floor but on either side of both walls will be 3 snoring bodies. Fortunately, I remembered to buy some batteries for my white noise machine.

Can't wait to see you and for you to have time with your aunt and uncle. They are truly amazing.

Much love,

Shar

**September 12, 2006**

**Email to family**

**Subject: Redwan at home**

Redwan spent his first night home from the hospital thrashing around in bed until 3 a.m. Then he slept until almost noon.

Providentially, I bumped into friends at the pharmacy this afternoon. One of them mentioned something about being a Canadian. I suddenly remembered that Redwan has a citizenship interview tomorrow morning as well as an ophthalmologist appointment, which he needs because of his double vision. We postponed the latter.

Redwan said he couldn't go to that interview with the hair beyond his ear-to-ear suture line sticking straight up like some kind of cartoon character. His barber was about to close his shop but when Redwan called he kindly agreed to cut his hair.

Hopefully Redwan will sleep better tonight as we've got an early start. We're trying a Middle Eastern sleep remedy that Sharaf told us about: yogurt!

Much love,

Shar

**September 17, 2006**

**Journal Entry, Edmonton**

To quote Dr. X. "I've neither the time nor the inclination…" to write, though periodically some thoughts worthy of capturing drift through my brain. I'm sitting in my home office trying to drown out Redwan's voice, as he talks on the phone, so I can think. Cranking up the volume on my CD player hasn't helped. I've shut myself in here because I don't want to talk to anyone, be nice to anyone, or have anyone in my space whatsoever. I need a break. That might mean leaving the building, which isn't so convenient. What is this Western thing of needing personal space? Apparently, it doesn't play a role in Eastern psyche. So I just have to push those thoughts down deep and escape into writing.

Here's something of note: Sharaf wears a pair of black pants from time to time. They're the first pair of pants she has ever owned. She finds them comfortable and "convenient" but says she couldn't wear them in Iraq, a country she describes as being in a "primitive condition." Yesterday I told her I'm thinking about taking a yoga class. Sharaf said Iraqis would consider it nonsense to consider one's body in that way, which makes sense given their struggle just to stay alive.

Because of my Iraqi in-law's presence I see our world through new eyes. Last night, after returning from supper at friends, I parked our car in our indoor lot. As we approached the elevators Aqeel noticed a wall-mounted doorstop behind the door. He and Sharaf conferred about it in Arabic. Then Sharaf turned to me and said, "That's to prevent the door from hitting the wall." She shook her head and added, "They think of everything here."

At supper last night, she showed us photographs of her mother, Hajer, and her fellow prisoners in Abu Ghraib Prison, which led to this story: Each Friday when Hajer was in prison, Sharaf and her family would take a picnic lunch to the prison grounds. One day when her daughter Carmel, then five years old, overheard some discussion about her grandmother being released from prison, dismay registered on her face before she blurted out, "But where will we go for our picnic if we can't come to the prison?" Sharaf laughed heartily as did we all.

Just before Sharaf and Aqeel arrived, after decades of association with Middle Easterners, I finally realized that they drink tea from glass and not porcelain cups. We have two sets of glass cups both with metal components. Redwan and I spotted one in the microwave and immediately turned it off. It was likely me that put it in there but it got me thinking that microwaves, or any other electric appliance for that matter, can't be terribly relevant in a city where residents are lucky to get more than an a half an hour of electricity a day.

Recently, water and electricity were cut off in Sharaf's neighbourhood for three days as a punishment for some infraction or another.

**September 18, 2006**
**Journal Entry, Edmonton**

I was beginning to feel sorry for myself when a care package arrived with a stuffed dog, several books, a cloth bookmark in the shape of a worm and some chocolate from my friend Meim. Much to my shame, I couldn't have felt more deserving and then humbled that, in the midst of the chaos my life has become, someone understood and had compassion for me.

**September 30, 2006**
**Email to family, friends and Redwan's colleagues**
**Subject: Update on Redwan**

As we crossed the University of Alberta foyer yesterday en route to Redwan's post-operative appointment with Dr. Harris, it occurred to me that we've been at war, a war that started inside Redwan's sinuses and over the following two months extended to the stage of that hospital and will, we hope, ultimately culminate in victory at the Cross Cancer Institute.

The surgeon remains pleased with how well the surgery went but is concerned because the postoperative pathology indicates "a couple of positive margins." Dr. Harris reiterated that despite some narrow margins the surgeons still believe they got all the cancer. But another concern is that the cancer is "poorly differentiated." Now here is the good news: while there is no scientific evidence that radiation and chemotherapy are effective in treating this type of cancer, Dr. Harris told Redwan, "We want to give you the benefit of the doubt with an aggressive regime of both chemotherapy and radiation."

When I briefed Sharaf later she said, "Well, the surgeons have done their job. We hope that the next part of the treatment will do its job. And we pray."

Today a friend reminded me of the body of work by a man who, over half a century, studied the impact of prayer on healing. He concluded that prayer was as effective a treatment as anything else and that patients that were prayed for, even if they didn't know anyone was praying for them, did better than those without prayers.

The worldwide groundswell of prayers for Redwan has carried us through this ordeal and will continue to do so. We know that. We also know that if it is God's will for Redwan to beat this sucker he will. Ezmina commented last night that the surgery went much better than the surgeons expected and so why shouldn't the rest of the treatment? Why indeed.

Redwan remains tired as his hemoglobin is still building. "Little by little," Sharaf says, "he's improving."

With his buzz cut Redwan could double for the Dalai Lama. With an orange robe he'd be a ringer for one of the Buddhist priests we saw in Cambodia. Long gone is his white turban from ICU when he resembled Marg Simpson from *The Simpsons*. Gone too is the Fu Man Choo look with Redwan's puffy eyes, shaved forelock, staple headband and shock of spiked hair, plus the charming mustache created by the blood-blackened strings extending from his nasal packs that were looped up and taped to his cheeks.

In addition to his headband scar, Redwan's incision line, which runs across the bridge of his nose, down the left side and under his left nostril, is healing beautifully. It is mostly disguised behind his glasses.

The surgeon was delighted to see how great the bridge of Redwan's nose looks. It is entirely constructed from titanium. Redwan has no feeling on the left side of his nose, has permanently lost his sense of smell and feels as if his forehead is being stretched over his head (could be a metaphor for childbirth). The titanium plates in his head are inert and won't pose a problem at airport security but it is going to take some time for him to adjust to the feeling of the structural changes in his head.

This morning we met with psychologist and head of the arts therapy program at the Cross Cancer Institute, Dr. Marilyn Hundleby. Terri Flanagan, our friend and fellow cancer survivor urged us to meet her. As a consequence of that meeting, Redwan (and I) will soon commence painting and sculpting sessions. Dr. Hundleby maintains that creativity is a powerful vehicle of healing. "We don't have the scientific proof yet," she said, "but I see it over and over again." I believe it and am thrilled. Redwan is sitting on a mine of untapped creative energy and it is going to be a treat to witness him unearth it.

We continue to enjoy our special Iraqi visitors who braved horrendous odds to support us. They have surely achieved their goal and inspire us by their supreme patience in the face of the severe tests they face back home. Today, I asked what it will be like for them to return to the impossible conditions they have described to us in Iraq and that we glimpse on the daily news. "Well," replied Aqeel through Sharaf, "it's our home. Plus, we have a purpose that will keep us busy. And we will get used to it."

We're having some fun with English. Aqeel, whose English improves daily, still gets caught on the words "kitchen" and "chicken," which he uses interchangeably. Sharaf has some cute words too, such as "pomegranades" (for pomegranates) She told me there is an Iraqi idiom that states, "You can't carry two pomegranades in one hand," kind of like you can't have your cake and eat it too. Given the current situation in Iraq, pomegranades is quite apt.

In the last few days we said goodbye to Gabriel, Erica and Sam. Marianne will arrive from Scotland on October 11. When she returns home on October 18 she'll escort her Aunt Sharaf and Uncle Aqeel, whom she has yet to meet, back to London via Vancouver, where they will explore the city for a few hours. They'll spend one night in London before returning to Amman en route to Baghdad.

And so, with your continued love and prayers, the battle continues.

With so much love and profound gratitude,

Shar

P.S. Next day: Though I tried to downplay our concern about the surgeon's news regarding the positive margins, our nerves were jangled. But, once again, fate intervened in our favour. Dr. Hundleby happened to have time to see us. She skillfully assisted Redwan to regroup and reframe his thinking around the uncertainty raised by the pathology report. To celebrate last night we took Sharaf and Aqeel to see "Superman Returns" on Asher's recommendation and now ours too.

**October 2, 2006**

**Email from Carmel and family (Redwan's niece in Iraq)**

Dear Aunt Shar,

I had read your last message and I saw my uncle's picture...are you sure they didn't forget anything when closing my uncle's head? I hope that your surgeons are not like our mechanics.

Carmel

**October 5, 2006**

**Email from Moqbel (Redwan's nephew in Iraq)**

**Subject: My uncle is so cool**

Dearest family,

We were so happy to see uncle in a soooo cool photo that you sent to us. Also, we were happy to see him full of joy as we always used to see him. You are handsome uncle. We are praying for you with our fingers crossed to pass the radiation and the chemotherapy successfully. UNCLE, you must be sure, as we are all sure, that you are going to make it and beat it, and that you will cross this hard river unimpaired, full of faith and healthy.

Dear father and mother, Aunt Shar and Uncle Redwan, we are missing you so much, especially as we are going to celebrate our second year of wedding [anniversary] next Friday. We wished to celebrate it with you all.

Dear mother, we emptied your refrigerator last week and now it is open because there is no electricity at all and the generator is not enough to operate it enough to freeze.

About us, we are all fine and yesterday we had lunch with Carmel at their house. We spent a nice afternoon with them. The weather is now fine and we can sleep inside the house.

Yours,

Moqbel and Sama

**October 6, 2006**

**Email to Moqbel and Sama (Redwan's nephew and his wife)**

**Subject: My uncle is so cool**

Please accept our best wishes for a wonderful second anniversary.

Your uncle had a great day, a day in which he did some sculpting, had two doctors' appointments and went for a long walk. Now it is almost 11:00 p.m. and he is on the phone catching up with a friend. Things are very good here. He is not only healing well but also coping with the stress associated with the uncertainty of his condition.

We can't begin to tell you how much we appreciate your loving concern.

Also, please accept our best wishes for a very Happy Birthday, Moqbel. Much love,

Shar

**October 8, 2006**

**Email to Meim and Marlene,**

A positive margin means that Redwan still has sinus cancer, as far as I know. Today, I'm worried because he has no energy at all but he did have a big day yesterday that included a fun evening out for supper with friends.

Sharaf and Aqeel have gone to Jasper with some amazing Bahá'ís. It is the first quiet day we've had in a long time. Maybe that's part of why Redwan is so flat, though he can't be for too long because my brother and his partner are arriving from Calgary in an hour. They're staying in a nearby hotel. We are supposed to go out with them to a neighbourhood pizza joint.

My Winnipeg visit was great! I got everything done for my parents in two days, which normally takes longer. Even though it was busy, it felt like a real break. I came back feeling much better and ready to face whatever. I'm grateful to Sharaf, Aqeel and Sam for covering for me.

I must return to sorting photos to send to Winnipeg. A social worker in Mom's nursing home is making a picture book for her. Mom is really confused. Colleen, one of her nurses, commented, "There are a lot of loose ends in there when you scratch the surface." But Mom isn't unhappy so I'm grateful for that.

Thanks again, for the care package, Meim.

So much love to you my faithful friends,

Shar

P.S. Last night at this Thanksgiving dinner, Marlene, I found my-self talking about you and how you rescued me, you and Michael, repeatedly during those busy years of raising little kids. I hope you too had a friend as good as Marlene when your boys were small, Meim. But then there aren't too many Marlenes out there.

# Dire Straits

### Reflection

After 51 days in Edmonton, Sharaf and Aqeel were heading back to Iraq. I arranged Marianne's return flight to coincide with theirs so she could accompany them as far as London.

It is almost impossible to imagine anyone courageous enough to return to the carnage in Iraq. But Sharaf and Aqeel completely eschewed "victim" mentality and didn't even entertain the notion of not returning. They trust in God implicitly, believe in the nobility of the Iraqi people, and are committed to playing a role in rebuilding that country.

For my part, I am worn to a frazzle. I long for time alone in which to rebuild my psyche. Why is it that at so many junctures in life when one has the least resources, the most is expected? After the death of a family member, for example, loved ones are expected to quickly pull together a befitting interment or cremation and funeral. If we live long enough we will see our abilities stripped away, one by one, as our daily challenges mount accordingly. Talk about learning detachment from the world.

As grateful as I was to Sharaf and Aqeel, uquestionably, there couldn't have been a worse time for me to host guests. This was a test made to measure for someone that craves solitude and strives to create order as a self-soothing strategy like I do. Though I aimed at "grace under fire," irritations I tried to hide left me far short of the mark.

And what about our truly gracious guests? They risked their lives fleeing their war torn country, leaving their family behind, to support us. And how convenient was it for them to host groups of families for years during that U.S.-led invasion of Iraq? often without water or electricity and in insufferable heat, sometimes up to 50°C. Imagine the body odour. Yet, I never detected the slightest hint of complaint from them about anything. They always maintained their good humour.

With the flow of family slowed, and Redwan now into the next stage of his ordeal, my full time work became managing his care, which included radiation and chemotherapy. Talk about fire and vengeance. And the wretched Canadian Revenue Agency audit continued.

Despite everything, the magnitude of support and prayers offered on our behalf buoyed me up, helped me to trust, and to let go. The only time I experienced pain was when I tried to remain in control of things that were obviously beyond my control.

**October 22, 2006**
**Email to family, friends and Redwan's colleagues**
**Subject: Update on citizen Moqbel and Sharaf and Aqeel**

Sharaf and Aqeel set off with Redwan's daughter, Marianne, on Wednesday, October 18. After a six-hour stopover in Vancouver, during which a dear friend, Mehran Kiai, took them on a tour of that fair city, the threesome flew to London where Marianne's Aunt Janet and Uncle Georges hosted them. Sam and Amy took them on a whirlwind tour of London that included visiting Shoghi Effendi's (Guardian of the Bahá'í Faith), resting place.

Sharaf and Aqeel arrived in Amman yesterday morning and left for Baghdad this morning. They will be delighted to see their family again but we can't begin to imagine what it will be like for them to return to the unspeakable horrors of daily life there. What courage and determination they have. Our prayers and thoughts are with them every moment of the day. We are so grateful to have had them with us. Thank you to all who helped to get them here, looked after them en route, and while they were with us in Edmonton.

Since I last wrote, Redwan has become a Canadian citizen, has undergone eight of his 27 radiation treatments and one of the three of his chemotherapy (cisplatin) treatments. It is an aggressive regime and he is certainly feeling the impact. He is fatigued and sometimes nauseated. Still, he remains positive and grateful for your love and support. He is happy to report that during a cancer retreat at the Cross Cancer Centre, with Marianne and me (I missed most of it due to back spasm caused by two sneezes), he carved "Arnold," a soapstone bear that, like The Terminator, "...will be back," to attack any remaining cancer cells. Marianne carved "Faith," a beautiful bear that represents her belief in her "Papa Bear's" recovery. Sweet.

Redwan still has double vision occasionally but is grateful, of course, to have both his eyes. The radiation treatment area is located between his eyes, a very narrow window, apparently. The radiologist worked diligently to design a treatment plan that hopefully won't compromise Redwan's vision.

With warm and loving regards,

Shar

**October 25, 2006**

**Email from Janet (Redwan's first wife's sister in England)**

**Subject: Update on citizen Moqbel, Sharaf and Aqeel**

Dear Shar and Redwan,

It was such a pleasure to receive Sharaf and Aqeel in London. They are such a lovely couple! Sharaf reminded me so much of Redwan it was uncanny, even the way she laughs! It was so funny because when we greeted them in Arabic, Lebanese dialect, which is the only one I really understand, poor Aqeel thought I was fluent and spoke to me most of the time in Arabic, Iraqi dialect, which I don't understand at all! Never mind, we all got on fine!

Our neighbours, Soraya and Ehsan, took them to a Bahá'í Feast at Layla and Sean's house where they met lots of local Bahá'ís, and although they must have been exhausted, I think they really enjoyed the evening.

Do hope that you are both resting now and taking it easy after all that has gone on. Hope Redwan continues to feel comfortable with this treatment, which must be difficult at times.

Much love to you both and prayers for Redwan's continued improvement!

Janet, Georges, Fiona and Ed XXXX

**October 25, 2006**

**Email to Janet**

**Subject: Thank you!**

Thank you and Georges so very much for hosting Sharaf, Aqeel, Marianne, Sam and Amy.

Redwan has "bitten the dust" in terms of side effects from his chemo and radiation. He is being blasted in a major way and is barely able to do a thing. He is too fatigued even to watch TV or talk on the phone. A radiation nurse told me today that Redwan will continue to feel this way and worse for the duration.

Hope that all is well with you and your family. Thanks so much, again.

Loving regards,

Shar

**October 26, 2006**

**Email from Sharaf (back in Iraq)**

**Subject: We are in Baghdad**

Dearest Shar and Redwan,

We miss you very much. How are you both? Our thoughts and prayers are with you all the time. Thank you sooo much for all that you have done for us.

Sorry to write this short email but they should go out to send it and the hour of the curfew is due.

All are well and send their love and greetings. Kisses and hugs and lots of love to you both and to all the friends there.

With warmest love and kisses,

Aqeel and Sharaf

**November 6, 2006**
**Email from Ann Boyles**
**Subject: A little message for Rizzy MacBell**

Dear Redwan,

Although I have so far resisted the temptation to clog up Shar's email with messages to you, today I am giving in! Dear friend and brother, you have been very much in my thoughts and prayers over the past months, and I have felt very closely connected to you. Let me tell you a little more about why.

On the day of your surgery, David and Ginny Rochester-Orr and their daughter, Caitlin were here visiting and we sat down shortly after the time your operation was supposed to start to say some healing prayers for you. While we were saying the long healing prayer, I became aware that somehow, on the spiritual plane, you were very much present "visiting" us, communing with us. It was a very real impression the likes of which I've never experienced before.

In reflecting on it later, I wondered if, while you were sedated and your body was undergoing all of those incredible medical procedures, your spirit just decided to soar a bit and to spend some time with all of the folks around the world who were so united with you in spirit during those hours, and continue to be with you in our daily prayers.

I often remember your story about being dubbed the honorary Scot and rechristened "Rizzy MacBell", but having seen the pictures that dear Shar (God bless you, Shar, for your wonderful emails!) forwarded awhile back of you wearing the dark glasses and black shirt, I wonder if perhaps you should now become known as "Rizzo Mocbelli." You were certainly looking Italian!

Rest assured that you will remain in my prayers, and I eagerly look forward to Shar's updates on how you are doing.

With much love,

Ann

**November 8, 2006**
**Email to family, friends and Redwan's colleagues**
**Subject: Picasso Drinks Green Smoothies**

When Redwan was diagnosed with sinus cancer I expected an extensive treatment regime but never "daycare." But that's where we are today as Redwan spends the next five or six hours receiving his second chemotherapy treatment. Redwan's oncologist just left his bedside. He said Redwan is only halfway through this ordeal of "short-term misery for long-term recovery."

He told us Redwan's nausea is due to chemoreceptive centres of his brain being radiated and not the chemotherapy. The effects of the radiation will reach a peak two weeks after his last treatment. Six weeks post radiation the surgeon will do a visual inspection of Redwan's sinus passages. Ideally, the oncologist says, PET and CT scans will be done three months post treatment. So, it will be a wait-and-see process to discover how the cancer has responded to this rigorous onslaught.

Redwan's hair is "falling off," as he says, in large clumps. When we leave the clinic today we'll stop by the barber to have the remainder lopped off. His hair was just beginning to grow in to cover his scar. Fortunately, as it turns out, Redwan is not vain.

An angry, dark red burn covers his forehead, cheeks and nose in a kind of inverted triangle that levels off just above his upper lip. The radiation is directed between his eyes and nose, which is the most deeply burned section of his face, rendering him a good candidate for upcoming Crescendo Rising Pizza commercials that featured people with mask-like burns from peering into the oven to ogle their pizza.

Redwan is on his fifth course of antibiotics to try to clear up a sinus infection he's had since the end of September. His eyes run most of the time and he still has double vision. This is partly due to the slight relocation of his left eye when his eye orbit was rebuilt during surgery, plus post-surgery and radiation inflammation. The good news is that he's had no pain for the last couple of months.

These days, Redwan is often too tired to even talk on the phone. At such times of intense fatigue he is barely able to make it to his daily radiation sessions, yet he remains in good spirits. He still says, and he means it, that he is the luckiest guy alive. He is profoundly grateful for the sustained waves of love and prayers that surround him, as well as for the wonderful people he continues to meet at the Cross Cancer Centre, including fellow patients. In fact, the other day when Redwan walked into our painting class late a collective cheer went up and a few people shouted, "Picasso's here!" They seem to take comfort and inspiration from his contributions to group discussions just as he does from theirs.

I'm spending way too many hours in the kitchen for my liking but for a good end. We've switched to a plant-based diet (at least when we are at home). Each day starts with a green smoothie that includes, apart from various fruit, hemp hearts, chlorophyll, sprouts, green leaves, Siberian ginseng, kemp, spirulina, flax oil, nuts and seeds in a base of green tea. Our juicer, which had been stored in a distant cupboard, grinds away almost daily. Seeds sprout in trays on our counters. This is all thanks to Victoria Laine, a holistic nutritionist and generous and loving friend who arrived one day loaded down with books on cancer and nutrition plus food she'd prepared for her photo shoot for her new cookbook. Each dish tasted even more amazing than it looked, and they all looked great; not something I can say for all vegan fare.

One of the books she lent us, *The China Study*,[1] provides evidence that lower protein levels, especially plant-based, dramatically decrease cancer cell advancement. It is a most interesting book that blows holes through Western society's beliefs about protein requirement. Diet is one thing we can control in our efforts to make Redwan one of the 50 percent of people that overcome cancer.

While hordes of people flood out of Iraq, Sharaf and Aqeel are, indeed, back there in the midst of an increasingly terrible situation. They have asked us to convey their best regards to one and all. They report that people in

---

1    Written by T. Colin Campbell, published by BenBella Books, Inc. in 2005.

Baghdad are bracing for something terrible to happen in the wake of Saddam Hussein's trial.

Today was a very proud day for us. It started with listening to "So She Dances," from Josh Groban's new CD *Awake*. The CD was released yesterday to much acclaim. According to AOL's website, "So She Dances" is the best song on the CD. We agree strongly, not just because my youngest son, Asher Lenz, co-wrote it with his writing partner, Adam Crossley, but also because it is a beautiful piece. It brought Redwan to tears in the car this morning on our way to the Cross Cancer Centre. I took an extra bit of time to park the car because I was listening to it for the fourth time in a row. We'll be having withdrawals from that song until we return to our mobile audio booth later today.

We are really excited that Colby is returning next Monday for a few days. Her dad is paying for her Edmonton stop over en route home to San Francisco from New York.

Ten years ago tonight we were shopping for shoes for Colby (who had the flu) and a suit for Sam at West Edmonton Mall. Ten years ago tomorrow, in an effort to be helpful, but with an iron that was too hot, Redwan seared a triangular hole through the white blouse Marianne intended to wear to our wedding that afternoon. Ten years ago tomorrow, it started to snow for the first time that winter and didn't let up for four days. In the midst of that blizzard, Redwan and I were married. The snow turned out not to be a bad omen. We are grateful to have enjoyed 10 richly rewarding years filled with travel, friends and learning. We'll celebrate our anniversary later, once Redwan feels better and I finally wrap up an extensive Canadian Revenue Agency audit!

With love and gratitude,

Shar and Redwan

P.S. We're home now. Redwan's hair is clipped close to his head. He's back to his Buddhist monk look with the addition of a red raccoon facemask.

**November 22, 2006**
**Email to family, friends and Redwan's colleagues**
**Subject: Last radiation and second last Arabic tea bag**

This frosty -17C morning I am sitting at my computer with a cup of hot Alwazah (the swan) tea, Aqeel's favourite tea. This is the first day in weeks that we've been spared any kind of medical appointment. Great timing in terms of the frigid weather.

I wanted to share two milestones with you: First, Redwan had his 27th and final radiation treatment yesterday. Second, his surgeon scoped his sinuses and was happy to report that the surgical cavity appeared "very clean" and advanced in its healing. Negar Asdaghi, our dear advocate and ally, joined us for that visit.

Trials are indeed followed by victories. The day before, when Redwan reported for his second last radiation treatment, he was ushered into a private waiting room. Some time later a gloved and masked doctor appeared. The week before, this particular doctor had swabbed Redwan's inflamed eye. We were deeply saddened to learn that he "is MRSA" (multiple resistant Staph aureus bacteria) as they say in medicalese. This is a serious bug that is sweeping through hospitals, often with dire results for infected patients.

I had to meet our dear friend Jean Hedley, who had spent the day riding the Greyhound bus from High River specifically to visit with us, at the bus station to tell her that because she is older it is too risky for her to stay with us in light of the MRSA. This is her second trip to Edmonton to see Redwan. Once again she'll return home with her mission unaccomplished.

We're not worried about two new inhabitants of our condo catching MRSA, however. They're framed creations from our art class at the Cross Cancer Centre, a striking zebra head that Redwan painted, and a mother and baby leopard I painted with a great deal of assistance from our teacher.

Since Monday, Redwan has been swallowing his way through 14 days of antibiotics ($2,200 for 24 tablets), his sixth in a series of antibiotics (plus one anti-fungal) that he has taken since late September. If his WBC (White

Blood Count) is satisfactory he will have his third and final chemo treatment on Tuesday, 28 November.

Hopefully, by mid December his raccoon-like burn will fade, his hair will grow back (apparently it fell out where the radiation exited the back of his head) and, most importantly, he will begin to feel better. He'll have a baseline CT and MRI done in a month or so.

We loved having Colby here last week. Aside from keeping me company and cheering up Redwan, who was totally drained in the aftermath of the chemotherapy, she also seemed to animate a stuffed dog that Meim sent me. He gave up being a couch potato and began to strike jaunty poses, with his long legs crossed, in various locations around the room. That's what we need around here in the absence of all our dear family members; a humourous point of interest.

While Redwan watched hockey on TV, I got a ton of laughs with Jean at a play called, "Erros and the Itchy Ant," which a friend of Jean's wrote and directed. I'm going to see if I can take Redwan to see it on Saturday afternoon. He'll wear a mask and we'll sit in a corner.

Now, oh joy! back to the Canadian Revenue Agency audit, which is finally starting to come together thanks to the help of a friend.

As for Redwan, well I think it may be time to get out the paintbrush and paints I gave him on our honeymoon in Greece 10 years ago this month. Maybe he will start to build his own art collection. Who knows, maybe he will even begin to carve with the gear Marianne and I bought for him for his birthday nine years ago!

As always, we send our love, very best wishes and profound gratitude for your loving encouragement.

Shar and Redwan

**Undated, circa December 6, 2006**
**Email to family, friends and Redwan's colleagues,**
**Subject: Out of the other end of treatment with a little drama**
As I write, Redwan, whose radiation "tan" is beginning to recede into patches, is sitting in his bed at the Cross Cancer Centre waiting for a nurse

to remove his IV. He is dressed and ready to go home! His voice, which for the past two weeks has been barely a whisper, has returned. This morning his MRSA test results returned negative (the second negative in a row). In the last two days his WBC count and platelets have made a dramatic recovery.

After Redwan's last chemotherapy, though he opted for 75 percent of the regular dose, he sank into unbearable nausea and fatigue. As he languished in bed I, having finally completed the first and hopefully last round of that wretched Canadian Revenue Agency audit, began to catch up on matters pending since our return in July after an absence of almost a year. But as it turned out, Redwan was not to pass through the loathsome climax of his radiation and chemo without drama. Last Sunday morning he bottomed out. Lack of food and drink set his head spinning as he retched up what little he'd taken in that morning. He almost passed out, wedged between the bathroom wall and the toilet as he was. His pulse was weak and his blood pressure alarming. The nursing supervisor at the Cross Cancer Centre advised me to call an ambulance. Within minutes the paramedics arrived. A young but resourceful visitor, Meead Asdaghi, solved the conundrum of how to transport Redwan from the bed through the narrow passageways to the stretcher using one of our rolling office chairs.

Once inside the ambulance the paramedics started an IV. After seven hours in emergency, Redwan was admitted to the Cross Cancer Centre where he has been in isolation all week. After he was settled into bed that first night the head nurse appeared. "I wanted to meet you," she said, "because I've heard so much about you and all that you've done to help others." Perfect timing for such encouragement. Redwan's tears began to flow. Evidently, her family knew Redwan.

Then the resident oncologist paid a visit. As he surveyed the back of Redwan's head and the horizontal three-inch bald landing strip that starts on the right side, then takes a sharp right turn into a parking lot of baldness, save for a tufty oasis in the middle, he commented, "Oh, that usually grows back in six to eight months." Redwan and I exchanged shocked glances.

On Monday morning I was delighted to see Redwan looking and feeling better. The IV rehydrated him and the anti-nausea drugs worked. On Tuesday, however, his WBC count and platelets took a nosedive. That night he received the first of three infusions of GCSF (Granulocyte colony-stimulating factor) to stimulate his bone marrow. (He found it ironic that his lab uses GCSF in their research.) That day he ate for the first time in ages but with his eyes closed; he was just too tired to keep them open.

Yesterday Redwan had to cope with the news that he has to go on another round of antibiotics, this time for a bladder infection. But again, victory follows crisis. His MRSA is gone! This means he doesn't have to feel like a pariah anymore.

While Redwan has learned even more about patience and resignation this week, I mastered typing while wearing rubber gloves all day and all evening thus proving that prunes, which is what my fingers look like by nightfall, can type. I also mastered breathing through a mask for hours on end without fogging up my glasses. But today I don't have to wear that get-up!

Now that Redwan's illness and treatment is behind us, I look forward to a more normal life. Over these stressful months I've done some strange things. Apart from locking myself out of our car and apartment more than once, dropping and forgetting things, I grossed myself out by mistakenly brushing my teeth with foot cream that listed ureic acid (animal urine!) as a second ingredient. Just this week I almost scared myself to death. I arrived home from the hospital late one night to find our door unlocked. I opened it gingerly and was alarmed to see large gritty footprints heading down the white-carpeted hallway. Heart racing, I crept into our apartment and forced myself to search for an intruder in every potential hiding place. Finally, it dawned on me that those footprints were mine. In my haste to get to the hospital that morning I'd left my boots on as I charged down the hall in search of something I thought I'd forgotten, but hadn't, only to forget to lock the door on my way out.

And speaking of hallways and forgetfulness, off we go home (where the only remnant of the six foot, four-inch paramedic are her footprints down that same white-carpeted hallway, across our bedroom floor and over to Red-wan's side of the bed)—that is if Redwan manages to squeeze his feet into his shoes with his thick bed socks because I forgot to bring regular socks.

With loving regards,

Shar

P.S. Back at home now, Redwan has returned to his Buddhist monk look after a quick stop at the barber's. And it's back to the kitchen for me after a week's break from grinding and juicing.

P.P.S. Josh Groban will perform Asher and Adam's song, "So She Dances," on Oprah on December 11!

**December 11, 2006**
**Journal Entry**

Tonight marks five months since we returned from California in or-der to attend to Redwan's ailing sinuses, headaches and the pain in his face. Though we suspected cancer, we had no understanding of the path that diag-nosis would dictate.

After his mammoth surgery, we met a couple our age at a "head and neck cancer" retreat. The man had been down a similar road. To my horror his wife commented off-handedly to me, "Oh, you aren't even half way yet." She spoke the truth. We weren't half way there by a long shot.

I hope never ever to see Redwan undergo surgery or chemotherapy again. He has received his life's quota of radiation to his head so that will never be an option.

Though he bore it all with grace, dignity and courage, it was a nightmare.

Yesterday morning Redwan apologized for being short with me the night before when he thought I was getting, or trying to fend off, another cold. He explained that he is obsessed about not catching a cold. "It isn't as if this area," he said, pointing to his sinuses, "wouldn't be affected by a cold." I agreed with him. "What can I do?" he asked. In addition to mentioning that he needed to make sure he is well rested and that his nutrition is good,

I suggested he wear a mask when he feels the need to. Then I hesitated a moment before mentioning that some of his obsession might be the result of the frontal lobe retraction during his surgery and radiation to that area of his brain. The day before I watched a documentary in which a young man became obsessive following frontal lobe surgery.

Finally, finally the Canadian Revenue Agency audit is done. The agent told me they failed to find any discrepancies. Well, thank you so much!

**December 12, 2006**
**Journal Entry, Edmonton**

As I type, Redwan is flying somewhere over the Atlantic en route home from Qatar where he was invited by one of the wives of the Amir to attend a meeting on medical research. The fact he was so intrigued by the invitation helped him to rally his physical resources in order to make the trip. There he was delighted to meet up with Karim, his old buddy from first year zoology in the late 1960's at the University of Baghdad. After the professor announced to his class of 100 that Redwan had achieved the distinction of scoring the lowest grade ever in that class, Karim, who was a visiting student from Africa, offered to study with him. It was the beginning of a wonderful friendship. Karim had to repeat that class for some reason. At the end of that school year, Karim stood first in class and Redwan stood second.

**December 31, 2006**
**Email to Marianne (Redwan's daughter and my stepdaughter in Stornoway, Isle of Lewis, Scotland)**
**Subject: I sent you an e-card**

Thank you so much for your loving thoughtfulness, as always. This is a beautiful birthday card and I am most grateful. Thank you for the anniversary card you sent us last month as well. So sweet.

Your dad isn't feeling great today. There's a virus going around that I wrestled with for a couple of weeks. He is tired and head achy. I gave him some ibuprofen and made chicken soap (oops, that would be soup). That was his 1:30 p.m. breakfast followed by, I might add, one of my sacrificially donated chocolate-dipped coffee shortbread cookies Terri and Ted sent. (I'd already eaten three of them for my birthday breakfast.)

Tonight we are invited to Ezmina and Vernon's for supper. So, although I wouldn't mind polishing off the remaining two cookies I'll try to restrain myself.

So happy old world New Year to you and your mom. And thanks, again.

Much love and appreciation,

Shar


**January 4, 2007**
**Email from Gabriel [my eldest son, in Boston]**
**Subject: Thanks for a wonderful visit!**
Hi Mom,

Erica and I just got home. We sure had a great time. I'm so glad we could be there for your birthday! I'll never forget the look on your face when you first saw us.

Thanks for everything.

Love,

Gabriel


**January 4, 2007**
**Email to Gabriel (in Boston)**
**Subject: Thanks for a wonderful visit!**
Thank you!!! for taking the time and making the huge sacrifice to be here for my birthday. Such a show of love and support gobsmacked me. I just got off the phone with Ezmina. She was delighted to have been able to host our reunion.

Thanks again, honey.

So much love to you both,

Mom

**January 9, 2007**
**Email from Ikbal (Redwan's cousin in Iraq)**
**Subject: Our visit to Dehok**

My dear Shar,

Allah'u'abha![2]

So many thanks for your nice email, which I got while in Dehok. On Wednesday, December 27, we left Baghdad for Dehok: Sharaf and Aqeel, 'Abdu'l-Razak and I and Quddus. We had spent a whole week there and we have returned to Baghdad since Saturday. It was a very nice week.

Our journey from Baghdad took the whole day. We left home at half past eight in the morning and it was so nice and sunny. After about two and a half-hours car drive, dust started, to be followed by a very heavy sand storm. Sharaf said it was not sand; it was soil. The storm was so strong one could not see farther than one to two metres and you can imagine how nice it was driving in such weather! The speedometer was pointing at 10 to 15 km/hr. and at times, we had to stop for some minutes, but not longer because we were in a rather dangerous part of the way.

After some 200 kilometers the weather cleared and then it began to rain, and again, it was such a heavy rain the wipers had to work hard to keep the front glasses rather clear. We arrived in Mosul at around 6 p.m. and it was so dark from the cloudy, rainy weather on the one side, and no electricity on the other, we took the wrong path in two or three instances, but finally were on our way.

The road to Dehok, even when dark at night, is quite safe so we had nothing to worry about.

At about a quarter to eight we were finally safe at home. The journey took nearly 12 hours while under normal conditions it should have taken seven to eight hours!!!!! But we were all happy and enjoying ourselves in spite of everything!! Muneer was at home to welcome us but it seems he thought we wouldn't come so he didn't even prepare for us hot tea!!! But never mind,

---

2    Arabic for "God is Most Glorious." Used as a greeting among Bahá'ís.

we made tea, warmed ourselves, and were ready for supper: kebab, bread and salad, and then to wake up to see it snowing. Just imagine, four types of weather in 24 hours!!!!

Dehok is in the very north of Iraq and is in a mountainous area so, compared to Baghdad, it is very cold, but not compared to Canada. We have rented a house there and Muneer is staying there and going to the engineering college, computer and electricity, and we have arranged for Quddus to go to secondary school there after he finishes his mid-year exam in Baghdad. Soon all our family will settle there; only Tahireh will stay in Baghdad because she has to finish her medical studies there.

During this week, we went to some mountain areas where we enjoyed seeing the area covered with snow and took some photographs. We went to Zakho, which is the most northern area of Iraq, just at the Turkish border, and again all the mountaintops and sides of the road and trees were covered with snow. (As you know, snow is something strange and thrilling for us because in Baghdad there is no snow. I personally have seen it snowing just once, about 15 years ago, again in the north!!)

We really enjoyed ourselves; we wished you were with us. As we say in Arabic "Mekanekum Khali" (your place is empty).

We are very glad Dear Ridhwan is doing well. We hope he will be better and better and all after effects of treatment disappear, and we are looking forward to meeting both of you, we hope, if we can make it next November in Turkey. It would be a very thrilling family reunion, but we hope and pray that our looked-for reunion will be in Baghdad, when we will welcome you in our homes and in our hearts.

In coming letters I will try to write to you about Aunt Hajer. Actually, I had a special relationship with her, not of aunt and niece, nor of mother and daughter, but something special; we spent six years together, day and night [in prison], while happy and sad, relaxed and frustrated, calm and angry... and this relationship continued even after we were home again, each living her life!

For me, she was a special person, and I am sure you would have loved her very much if you had seen her! Never mind, you have her son, and you met her daughter!

Here, all the family is in the best of health. Today we had a lot of bombarding, but, thank God, all are well and safe. Sharaf and Aqeel send you their love and best wishes, as do Moqbel and Sama, Sarmad and his family, Carmel and her family.

'Abdu'l-Razak sends his special love and greetings to Ridhwan, and his greetings and best wishes to you, as do Tahireh, Muneer and Quddus.

My love and kisses to you, my dearest sister, and goodbye for now,

Ikbal

**January 14, 2007**
**Email to Ikbal**
**Subject: Your visit to Dehok and ours to Lumby, B.C.**

What a wonderful surprise to find your email and to be able to bask in so much detail about your challenging trip to Dehok. Thank you so much for taking the time and going to whatever length it took to be able to email us. We really appreciate hearing from you. We think of and pray for our family in Baghdad every day.

I know that God is the All Wise so there must be a mysterious wisdom in your suffering over all these decades, but I pray that you will soon know peace and tranquility.

I am writing to you from the Edmonton International Airport. Redwan and I are flying to Kelowna, British Columbia, which is only an hour's flight from Edmonton. I wanted to write to you before we left home but didn't have time, or so I thought. We got to the airport early only to find that our flight had been cancelled due to yesterday's blizzard. Today it is −30C but the snow has stopped blowing. Anyhow, here we sit waiting for a later flight. Redwan is wearing his striped toque (a tightly knit hat), and his parka, and is reading a magazine I just bought. It was expensive but I thought that we could give it to our hosts in Vernon, Ted and Terri, whom Sharaf and Aqeel met. They pioneered to a small town called Lumby, which is just outside Vernon about a 45-minute drive from Kelowna.

This week Redwan found out that as of December 18 he has MRSA, again. He was doubly disappointed because the nurse that delivered that bad news also said he would have it for life. Our family doctor referred Redwan to an infectious disease specialist. This doc was much more encouraging and is going to commence a three-pronged treatment approach after we return from B.C. It will consist of two types of antibiotics, a nasal bath and a cream (not ointment) for his sinus passages. God willing, this will clear up his congestion and puffy eyes.

We hope it will be possible to meet you and all the family soon, maybe in Turkey. What a thrill that would be!

Please tell Aqeel that, despite the fact we have 24-hour-a-day electricity, no one has even plugged in the iron since he left. Also, please tell Sharaf I plan to wear her dress when I perform in the women's drum group I joined a few months ago.

Also, please give everyone our deepest love and assurance of regular prayers for their well being in the face of your daily calamities. May God bless your move to Dehok and protect your beloved daughter in Baghdad.

With so much love,

Shar

## January 26, 2007
## Journal Entry

I have been procrastinating about writing this because I don't like to spill my guts anymore than I like vomiting. Yesterday marked a potential turning point in Redwan's demise. Some random doctor from the U of A called to say there may be a tumour in the operative site. Negar indicated as much to me yesterday. I was hoping that the reason the site lit up was because it has only been two months since Redwan's last radiation treatment. Dr. Harris had mentioned this often happens.

As I type, Redwan is sound asleep. He's afraid to be alone because he's had two dreadful panic attacks in the last week. The last one, three days ago, left him shaking. I wonder if it is frontal lobe involvement. I'm going to look on the Internet to see.

I just did a search and found some symptoms that seem to relate to Redwan's condition of late. He has lethargy, short-term memory problems, trouble thinking clearly sometimes and changes in sensations in his head, perhaps because he is mostly bald, but he also feels it in his body. For example, recently I had my arm slung across his back. My touch bothered him, whereas it never would have before. He had difficulty (as would I), counting backwards from 100 by sevens when another doctor tested him. The doctor seemed to think this was a problem and raised his eyebrows at me conspiratorially over Redwan's head.

How do I feel? Absolutely sick! I feel as if Redwan is dying and that it is going to be a short journey at that. It's hard to imagine life without him. Though he doesn't see it this way, from my perspective I've been living entirely in Redwan's world for the past ten and a half years in that our lives revolve primarily around his work and commitments and in the last half of a year, his illness. We've only been apart briefly a few times in the last year and a half. Redwan wanted me to sit with him when I returned home from my meeting this morning. He said, "If I go, will you stay in Edmonton?" I said I didn't know, that I couldn't see leaving Canada while my parents were alive so maybe I would move to Winnipeg. I'm just not sure. It will take me a year, at least, to get through all of our papers.

But I decided today that Redwan comes first; my tasks must come second to his needs, otherwise I will regret sacrificing his needs for my elusive quest for order. It took a great deal of inner stamina for me to sit with him while the kitchen counters were yelling at me, "Come here! Clean me! Can't you hear me? Get in here right now! Come on. I know you are out there!" I resisted until Redwan got up to go to the bathroom and then I jumped up and cleaned them.

In the early 70s, Mark Starowicz, my boss at CBC Radio in Toronto, pegged my need for order. Pausing beside my tidy desk one day he said, "Shar, could your extreme need for order indicate some internal disorder?" The solitary pursuit of order has always calmed me down but it is ridiculous that it renders relaxing at home a challenge. I feel badly that during Sharaf and Aqeel's 51 days with us I seldom stopped working long enough to sit down with them. There were always so many appointments to arrange and get to, so many meals to deal with, though Sharaf and Aqeel certainly did their share of cooking, so much laundry and recycling to attend to, and such a magnitude of correspondence in so many forms to deal with. And, of course there was the ongoing Canadian Revenue Agency audit. It was all too much.

Part of me is afraid to let too many people know about Redwan's current health developments if they continue in this downward trend, for fear of replicating that overwhelmingly stressful situation I experienced between July and December of last year where I almost went under because of communication overload.

Well, now I've done my duty: I've duly described my sorry state. Now I must get on with sorting and reducing Redwan's medical papers into some kind of order.

**March 6, 2007**
**Email to family, friends and Redwan's colleagues**
**Subject: Update on the Trumper**
Three days from now Redwan will see his surgeon, Dr. Harris, who will give us the results of Redwan's CT from yesterday. He will also scope Redwan's nose with his video camera to confirm, we hope, that the cancer has been arrested.

Since my last group email he has experienced some ups and downs, to say the least, but as of three weeks ago, when his son Sam gave him a pep talk, Redwan is much improved.

His big slump came after my kids and daughter-in-law left here on January 4. Despite appalling fatigue, Redwan had worked behind the scenes, to conspire with them to surprise me on my birthday, which was on New Year's Eve (thereby trumping me, according to Terri Flanagan). We were invited to the Samaroos for supper that evening. As the evening wore on it seemed strange that, according to Ezmina, the lamb refused to cook. I detected an odd conspiratory moment between Redwan and our hosts but it wasn't until another friend physically barred me from exiting the living room to take a call from Redwan's brother in Iraq that I knew for sure something was up.

Redwan quickly grabbed a wooden tray and thrust it into my hands telling me to hold it in front of my face. When he allowed me to drop my guard, there before me stood Gabriel, Erica, Colby and Asher. Each wore a bandana onto which Colby had ironed cloth letters that spelled, "H-A-P-P-Y B-I-R-T-H-D-A-Y M-O-M." I was stunned. Earlier that day each of them had called to wish me a Happy Birthday and to share their plans for New Year's Eve, fictitious, as they were. None included flights to Edmonton (though two had called from airports hoping no loud speaker announcements would give them away). We enjoyed five wonderful days together.

After the kids left, Redwan's emotions flattened like a punctured tire. News that his MRSA had returned shackled him. We took a short trip to Lumby, B.C. to visit Terri, Ted and Emily. Being in a lively environment with three-year-old Emily provided Redwan with the perspective necessary to realize he was depressed.

Upon our return to Edmonton, he experienced some scary anxiety attacks that woke him from a dead sleep, his heart racing and in a panic. During those times he couldn't bear to be in a room alone.

Then a well meaning, but misinformed, doctor read him the results of a PET CT that indicated cancer re-growth in the surgical site. For the next four days, Redwan felt like he was waiting a stay of execution until Dr. Harris arranged a second reading by an oncology radiologist. Dr. Harris, this saint-like surgeon, took time out of the operating room to call and explain to Redwan that ALL of the changes were attributed to postoperative repair and NOT to cancer.

During those stressful days, if I had to go out, a whole roster of friends either stood by or stepped in to companion Redwan. How could we have managed without their devoted assistance? We are moved beyond words by such love and support.

Redwan is rapidly recovering from this deep, dark funk with the help of a variety of mainstream and alternative doctors. As well, I heard the energy level in his voice rise while he was talking to Sam on the phone one day. It was like watching a thermometer gauge shoot up. Since then, Redwan has been working on a proposal for a two-volume textbook for medical students on inflammation, an ambitious project that may take up to three years to complete. Such thoughts keep him happy and engaged. He is also looking forward to spring so that he can learn to golf. Good work, Sam!

Our Iraqi family is doing its best to endure an intolerable situation in Baghdad. Our hearts go out to them. Their moral strength and courage is beyond our comprehension.

I started to write this email three days ago. Right now we are sitting in Dr. Harris' office, which is MRSA-proofed. Everything is draped with white sheets. Redwan is cracking his knuckles (something he normally only does in movie theatres much to my chagrin). Here comes the doctor, gowned, gloved and masked. Wonderful news! The MRI looks great and so does the surgical site. Redwan is good to go! He'll see Dr. Harris again in three months, before which he will have another MRI. He is also to have a PET scan every six months.

We are profoundly grateful for Redwan's state of health. Now he is keen to recovery fully (and hopefully permanently from the wretched MRSA) before he returns to work on June 1.

Thank you all for your most loving concern, inquiries and prayers.

With deep and abiding love and gratitude to each and every one of you, Shar

And profound gratitude to my daughter, Colby, who graced us with another visit!

**April 10, 2007**
**Journal Entry**
Tonight we took one last drive in our red BMW, the car that brought

Redwan so much joy but opened a deep well of ongoing complaints about it from me: the ride was "sporty" meaning driving in it felt like riding on a stage coach over corduroy roads; the heater fogged up the windows; the radio didn't work properly, something to do with the wiring in the back window, and it was absolutely useless on snow more than 5 mm deep, let alone ice. Still, Redwan loved it and was sad to give it up. He asked me to honour the car for keeping us safe over the past four years. I refused, stubborn person that I am. I am just relieved to get rid of it.

**April 19, 2007**
**Journal Entry**

Last night Gabriel told me that the Irish writer, Anthony Trollope, used to write each morning for two hours before mounting his horse and going about his duties as postmaster. Gabriel was encouraging me to get down to the writing work I maintain I want to do.

Each day I feel a bit sicker about the situation for our family and all Iraqis. The news there couldn't be bleaker. I have absolutely no idea how they cope. I tried to call Sarmad on his cell today but it was turned off. I didn't try his other number or call Sharaf.

Okay, here's the rub: It is 2:00 p.m. Redwan is out having lunch with a friend. He left two messages for Dr. Harris but is still waiting to hear back from him about the results of the PET scan he had on April 11.

This morning Redwan called out to me from the bathroom. My heart sank. Bloody nasal discharge! I thought: the cancer is back! Thankfully it was something else. But his call made me realize that for the rest of Redwan's life that fear will haunt us.

Later in real time, Redwan answers the phone: "Oh hi Jeff," (Harris) I recognize the forced casualness in Redwan's voice as he speaks into the phone. He stands with his back to me, his nose almost touching the glass door to our balcony, his form a dark silhouette against the leaden winter sky. I approach him quietly from behind. He is listening too long for this to be good news. My stomach knots. I draw close to the receiver he holds to his ear. He swallows several times. I faintly hear the surgeon say, "I wish it could have been all good news but…" his voice trails off. Then he adds with more energy, "But I don't think you should worry about this too much; it's probably another false negative like you had with the MRI in January."

After he hangs up Redwan tells me a spot behind his left eye lit up. He is to have another PET scan in six weeks. I give him a pep talk and a hug and ask how he feels. Then I perch on the arm of his chair and begin to recite a prayer. By mistake, I say a prayer for the departed. After I finish Redwan asks, "Who was that for?" Both prayers begin the same way and I often mix them up. Not a good time to do that though. Fortunately, Redwan doesn't take offence.

Before I leave him to watch Dr. Phil he says, "Don't worry about me. I'm going to be fine. I've decided not to stress about this." What a relief!

But later, Redwan tells me he's going to keep this news to himself. That means I must keep this scary news under wrap too, which is a bit of a bitter pill for me as I glean immeasurable comfort from consultation with friends.

**April 20, 2007**
**Journal Entry**

We are on the eve of the most holy Bahá'í Festival, the Festival of Ridvan. It marks the anniversary of Bahá'u'lláh's declaration of His mission in the Ridvan Garden in Baghdad but that aside, I am about as bummed out as I have ever been. My head feels like it is full of cotton batting and my nose is stuffy. I slept poorly partly because Redwan and I are sleeping in the same bed again and he was restless too. Despite his best efforts, he is worried about whether or not his cancer has returned and how things will play out if it has.

Last night, as we were returning from a medical Qi Gong breathing class, on the elevator on our way up to our apartment, Redwan asked, "What should I do if it has come back?"

I looked into his eyes, one normal and the other slightly misshapen from the radical surgery that saved it, and the thickened and crinkly tissue that surrounds it. "You'll have that little surgery and have it taken out," I said without missing a beat." Then I added, "If you want to."

I found it easy to suggest more surgery because Redwan seems so well these days. His strength has almost fully returned and he has more energy than I do. But when I considered all the trauma associated with such surgery, I found it unbearable to imagine him enduring that again. Unbearable! He would do it for my sake, his kids and mine, but how could I live with that? I don't want him to make that sacrifice for me, but I certainly don't want him to die.

For now I need to focus on his health and the belief that, as the surgeon said, this is likely a false alarm. Everything has worked in his favour thus far so I should maintain a positive perspective and say to people that ask about him, "Redwan is great!" just like I have been over the past three weeks. How quickly I adjusted to that happy thought when we seemed to have returned to the normal status quo. Every minute of our lives is precious. There is no time for despair.

**April 23, 2007**
**Journal Entry**

This morning I replied to an email from a friend, Pat Verge. She spent 10 years researching and writing a book about a man she barely knew. As I flipped through her book again last night it struck me how important it will be for future historians. I thanked Pat in my email for bringing that book into existence. That may sound odd but not to someone who hasn't been on the receiving and acting end of such inspiration. Pat's inspiration to write that book came, I believe, because that book needed to be written; she was willing and capable of doing it. Certainly it required an enormous sacrifice of time, energy and money on her part, as well as that of her family, without which that history would probably be lost.

Maybe the story I have to tell is similar. Whatever the case, there is no doubt that I feel driven to push on, though I can make no sense as to where this is all going. Somehow it feels right to be doing this work in this humble room I've rented in a local church off Whyte Avenue.

Recently, I happened upon this email from June 2004 from Pat Verge:

Dear Shar,

Don't give up! I know the feeling of being part way through and not knowing if you will ever finish. Believe me. I know that feeling!!!

When I told her I was so afraid to fail, a dear friend of mine told me that the only failure would be if I failed to finish it. And that was right. We just do the best we can with whatever project we are doing, but the important thing is to finish it!!

And I know you will. Your book becomes daily more relevant, with all the happenings in that part of the world, and the sacrifices the Bahá'ís are making to show a completely different and better way of life.

As Bahá'ís, interruptions are inevitable, with all the travelling, serving, and in yours and Redwan's case, the illness. So it is easy to lose the thread. But you will get it back. I know you will!!

Much love and best wishes for your writing, one line, and one paragraph at a time!

Pat

xoxoxo

### April 27, 2007
### Journal Entry

Things have settled down here. Redwan does not seem to be too worried about the potential of the return of cancer. Twice when I was complaining (who me?) about something he retorted with a kindly smile, "Oh, you think you've got something to complain about? I'm facing potential death." The second time he said that I retorted, "Well, about now I'd welcome that," meaning dying. He laughed.

Actually, we are grateful that he was the one that got sick and I was the one to look after him. Things wouldn't have worked out so well had it been the other way around.

I called Sharaf early this afternoon. Right off the top she asked for our prayers so they "can keep surviving." She asked about our kids and said how much they miss them. Moqbel is back at his government job and Sama has returned to college.

"Our normal life is explosions going off and killing people every day," she said. A car recently exploded three cars ahead of them. Their windshield protected them from the flying debris that hit their car. Recently, a sniper shot at Shatha and Nibras while they were driving but the bullet hit the windshield wiper and penetrated the dashboard. That must have been terrifying. Sharaf told me also that one of her friends was hit by mortar.

When I asked Sharaf if they had enough food she said they did but they only have a half an hour a day of electricity. Fortunately, they can use their generator. Once again, she commented on the never-ending storms that cloak them in dust. Just surviving there is an achievement I don't think I could accomplish.

**April 30, 2007**
**Journal Entry**
I find myself admiring red cars, especially a certain red Lexus I see from time to time. I never liked red cars and didn't appreciate our orangey-red BMW. Now that we have a non-descript, mud-coloured Honda, I miss the distinctive appearance of our old car. Contrary I am.

# Light and Mercy

June 10, 2007
**Email to family and friends**
**Subject: Changes and Chances**

When Redwan returned to work June 1st he could barely squeeze into his office crammed as it was with helium balloons. That day he attended a welcome back lunch at the Faculty Club and partook of a cake his Moldavian student baked for his group's celebration of his return to work after almost two years away: a sabbatical year and a sick year.

But his first foray back to the University of Alberta was actually May 1st when the Faculty of Medicine and Dentistry presented him with a "Spotlight on Achievement Award." Earlier that week Redwan joked with his surgeon that the faculty probably gave it to him because they thought he was dying.

"Well, you fooled them, then," said Dr. Harris, "because you're not!" They both laughed.

Before returning to work, Redwan travelled to Scotland to see his daughter, Marianne, and her mom, Ann, in Stornoway in the Outer Hebrides. He also visited his son, Sam, Sam's girlfriend, Amy, and her parents in London.

Four days back to work and Redwan is already putting in overtime and is stressed. If he doesn't soon learn to detach from the more taxing aspects of his work I'll be encouraging him to find a job selling shoes, or maybe linens, even better; books!

Best wishes and gratitude for your kind and deeply appreciated support over the past year,

Shar

P.S. You might recall that my friend Marlene, from Ontario, planned to come to Edmonton last August to help me but had surgery for cancer the same day Redwan did. I'm delighted to report that she is doing extremely well. In fact, she and her husband, Michael, drove all the way to Edmonton so that she could give her "cancer buddy" a hug.

P.P. S. We just talked to Redwan's sister, Sharaf, and her husband, Aqeel. He described things as "180 degrees worse" in Baghdad than when they returned eight months ago. Their daughter, Carmel, and family, received a death threat. They have to vacate their home immediately. As always, Sharaf asks for prayers for Iraqis and sends her fondest regards to everyone they met in Edmonton.

### July 11, 2007
### Journal Entry

Four days from now will mark the one-year anniversary of our return to Edmonton from our Australian sabbatical. I've been thinking of this year as the July 11th sandwich. Stuffed between July 11, 2006 and July 11, 2007 were challenges of just about every sort. Redwan's tests encompassed physical, emotional, mental and spiritual arenas. Given my craving for solitude, one of my biggest tests was losing control over my time and space. Raising three children certainly acquainted me with having to put others first but that went with the territory. I tried to give unconditionally to Redwan because I wanted to but sometimes dreaded resentment crept in at the associated demands of our lives.

### September 26, 2007
### Email to family and friends
### Subject: Great news re Redwan's health

Redwan's PET scan was clear, 100 percent! Dr. Harris told him that if it remains that way at 18 months he will likely have overcome any danger of cancer recurrence in his sinuses. Statistically, if Redwan makes it to two years without a reoccurrence it will be as if he's made it to five years. So, we rejoice in this news and thank all of you for your heartfelt loving concern and prayers.

Warmest love,

Shar

**September 30, 2007**

**Journal Entry**

Though it is mid-day I am writing from my bed.

Today is Sharaf's daughter Carmel's birthday. She emailed me from Dehok (in Kurdistan) where she and her family fled after a death threat. Carmel was responding to my email of September 26 (my dad's 87th birthday).

Redwan had been preoccupied about the results of his PET scan from September 11. He must learn to live with one of the few certainties of life, uncertainty. When he went for the results, Dr. Harris strode into the waiting room, greeted Redwan with a smile and said, "Come with me. This won't take long."

Immediately, Redwan understood that it was good news. How compassionate of Dr. Harris. It brings tears to my eyes to think of it.

Recently, I dreamt he was going to operate on me too. After my surgery I kept trying to shake his hand to thank him but couldn't get a grip on it because it was shaped like a chicken claw. Weird.

In reality, while Redwan had his PET scan I had my uterus and ovaries removed. Mercifully, there was no cancer. Pre-surgery I surprised myself by going into mourning over losing my children's first home. I asked the surgeon if I could see my eviscerated uterus. Instead, one of the residents photographed it for me. I was surprised to see that it looked like a small pink urn. I pondered that picture and the mysteries of that vessel for a long time before filing it.

I regret losing my ovaries. The doctors I consulted, including three gynecology residents, were of one voice: ovaries can be silent killers. Given my age they strongly suggested yanking them out. So, although evidently they looked healthy, they are gone.

Soon, Redwan will pick me up to take me to a friend's house for supper. An hour and a half ago he came home to check on me. He'd been making a presentation at a Campus Association for Bahá'í Studies conference at the University of Alberta about the denial of access for Bahá'ís in Iran to post secondary education because of religious persecution. I woke up as Redwan approached the bed and saw him through fresh eyes. Today he is wearing a white shirt with a stand up collar, a brown plaid sports jacket and brown pants. He looks the absolute picture of health.

Yesterday, I had an email from Redwan's cousin Ikbal. She asked us to pray that she and her husband, 'Abdu'l-Razak, obtain passports so they can meet us in Turkey when we're en route to Haifa, Israel in November…tada!

That's in five weeks! I can hardly believe it. Redwan and I will arrive in Istanbul on November 5. Marianne will join us a few days later. We hope Redwan's brother, Sarmad, and perhaps his wife, Shatha, Sharaf and Aqeel, and now maybe Ikbal and her husband will meet us there. On November 11, we will fly to Israel for our nine-day pilgrimage to the Bahá'í World Centre. I'm not sure when or where Sam will catch up to us but hopefully he'll be able to spend a few days in Turkey too. Like me, Sam and Marianne have never met Sarmad. Redwan's life imprisonment sentence, levied against him after he escaped from Iraq in 1972 and returned to England to study, precluded him seeing his brother for 35 years.

**November 1, 2007**
**Journal Entry**

When I lay down this afternoon I turned off the ringer on our phone so I could sleep for a bit; I'm struggling to throw off a bug I picked up in San Francisco while visiting Colby last week. When I checked for phone messages an hour and a half later I realized I'd missed a call from Sarmad. I was disappointed not to talk to him but didn't return his call because it was 3:00 a.m. his time. Sarmad's message delighted me.

"Thank you, Sheeyar. Hello, Sheeyar, Allah'u'abha. I am Sarmad. I just want to tell you that Nibras [his eldest son] had his passport today and from now on, I and Nibras, we are working to try to reach Istanbul maybe the eight or the ninth, or maybe the seventh or eighth or ninth of this month. We hope we can see you there. Much, much love and greetings. Thank you. Sarmad."

**November 4, 2007**

**Journal Entry written on board a Boeing 767 (business class! Yay, travel points!)**

When the Báb[1] prayed in the mid 19th century for travel to become less arduous, I'm sure He envisioned such transport vehicles as this; it is unbelievable! Right now I am snuggled under a royal blue airline quilt with my feet elevated on a footrest that will soon recline into my in-flight bed.

Redwan is sitting across the aisle on my right. He is busy exploring all of the nooks and crannies of his console that includes a telephone, an illuminated keypad for various reclining positions, a pop-out television screen, a dinner tray, and a storage shelf for books and papers.

The flight attendant just handed me a large turquoise toiletry bag with an assortment of items including hand cream that will replace mine that security confiscated.

We're headed to Turkey en route to Israel. We are travelling through Turkey in the hope of seeing some of Redwan's family from Iraq. For various reasons Sharaf and Aqeel and Ikbal and 'Abdu'l-Razak can't join us. Sharaf told me recently in a phone call that it would break Sarmad's heart if he can't make it.

After his message last month we called Sarmad on November 2. He said, "Sheeyar, I never ask for anything. It is dangerous to want anything but now I am in trouble because I am starting to want this [reunion] very much." He is anxious to meet Sam and Marianne, whom he claims he already loves as if they were his own children. He says that about my children too and I believe him.

Sarmad and Nibras have tickets on a Jupiter Airlines flight scheduled to leave Baghdad at 10:00 a.m. on Wednesday, November 7. Jupiter Airlines is rather an appropriate name given that until recently the odds of flying out of Baghdad would have been about as good as going to Jupiter.

Our plane is in the air now. One year ago, Redwan was desperately ill and in the maelstrom of radiation and chemotherapy. Last winter, when he thought his cancer had re-occurred, he made me promise to keep our

---

1    The forerunner of Bahá'u'lláh is titled "The Báb", Arabic for "The Gate."

pilgrimage date with Sam and Marianne if he was too sick to travel or dead. Well, well, well, what a difference a year makes!

Tomorrow I will be eight weeks post op. I cried during my post surgical check up. I was so upset that I agreed to have my ovaries removed. I wish I'd followed my intuition and kept them. Now I have constant hot flashes that are difficult to bear. Despite being postmenopausal, my ovaries were obviously keeping my inner thermostat in check. Now it has gone haywire. But, apart from constantly running hot and cold, and acquiring a Buddha-like belly with a concave middle section, I'm happy, excited and grateful to be alive and undertaking this trip with Redwan. Though this is very tough: sipping cranberry juice cut with mineral water and munching my way through a bowl of warmed mixed nuts!

### November 7, 2007
### Journal Entry

10:30 a.m. (from the Hotel Nazar in Istanbul)

Nurullah, Redwan's cousin, who lives in Istanbul, just called to say that Sarmad and Nibras are at the airport in Baghdad waiting for their plane. They will call him before they board. Time for us to pray that they are able to make it safely to Turkey.

12:15 p.m. from a call centre in Istanbul

Redwan is trying to call Sarmad in Baghdad to see what is happening because he hasn't heard back from Nurullah. It is coolish and drizzling outside, though the sun shone briefly a little earlier.

Redwan is extremely irritable. Even his bargain purchase of four pairs of socks for five lire didn't improve his mood.

Breakfast at our hotel was great. It included white cheese that looked like feta but was softer and less salty, cucumber, tomatoes, yogurt and rose petal jam.

Redwan just talked to Nurullah. He left us a message at the hotel but it was indecipherable. Nurullah says that Sarmad and Nibras are in the air!

Their plane will land at 2:30. It is 1:00 p.m. now. Nurullah will pick us up at 1:30. The countdown is on!

Redwan apologized for being irritable. He says he is either worried about Sarmad and Nibras or just plain messed up.

I slipped on a banana peel, literally, beside a banana vendor and almost wiped out. You've got to keep your eyes on the ground around here. Uneven and broken sidewalks abound, not to mention the four-foot drops off those sidewalks to lower levels. I wonder how many tourists break their legs here each day. I don't aspire to be one of them.

2:20 p.m. from the backseat of Sarcan's car

Sarcan is somehow related to Nurullah who got stuck in traffic on a bridge. He called Sarcan to pick us up and take us to the airport to meet him. Sarcan is handsome and perhaps in his 30s. He is friendly and sweet but doesn't speak a word of English, Arabic or French.

From the front seat Redwan says to me, "This is another miracle!" I think he means Sarcan locating us and taking us to the airport but Redwan clarifies, "Sarmad arriving."

Someone told me that between 12 and 24 million people live in Istanbul and that it is 200 km wide. Can that be right?

We're speeding by zillions of large apartment buildings. Red flags, with a quarter moon inverted over a star, are draped everywhere. The streets have no painted lane dividers. Traffic just merges. Cars nudge around in search of a bit of open pavement.

Sarcan is talking on his cell phone to Nurullah. I think Nurullah is at the airport. Soon we will meet him. Nurullah, or Nur, as Redwan calls him, told me on the phone this morning that he's still in pain from a tooth extraction yesterday. He has really put out for us. Yesterday, when we arrived he sent someone to meet us on his behalf because he was in a meeting.

2:50 p.m. Istanbul Ataturk Airport at Gloria Jean's (of all places! We frequented this coffee shop chain while in Australia).

Nurullah brought us here because the plane is delayed and not due to arrive until 3:00 p.m. I'm watching the clock and thoroughly enjoying a first rate latté.

Nur is friendly and, judging from the twinkle in his eyes, fun-loving. His hair is thinning, he's a tad chubby and maybe in his late 40s. His phone rings every few minutes. He owns a business, something to do with telecommunications.

Redwan and Nur are talking in Arabic. The fact that I'm writing helps them to feel more comfortable to speak in their native tongue.

Nur has an office here and one in Cypress. He travels there twice a month.

It is 2:55. Five minutes until the plane arrives.

Nur's wife's name is Samra. Their young daughter is called Nil, pronounced Nile.

Nurullah tells Redwan that his family in Saudi Arabia prayed for Redwan when he was sick.

Nur hasn't seen Sarmad for 32 years and is visibly excited. "Sarmad was very special," Nurullah says. "He was an extremely good example for young people. He was always talking. Everybody followed Sarmad. God was protecting him."

3:00 p.m.

Nur fights for the bill and wins. My latté cost US $7.00. I feel badly.

We approach the gate. I can hardly believe the moment has arrived. I can't begin to imagine what is going on inside Redwan's head and he is not saying. We position ourselves in front of electronically operated doors and stand, mostly in silence, for the next three hours! I catch my breath each time the door slides open. We scrutinize every man that walks through it. As time passes we become increasingly concerned that Sarmad and Nibras have been denied entry. Given the current turbulent political situation between Turkey and Iraq, that is entirely possible.

The last time Redwan saw his brother, Sarmad was a slim, dark-haired second year engineering student. Now wait? Who is this? A portly, graying mustached man advances towards us accompanied by a tall, thin young man. "That's them!" says Redwan as he rushes towards his brother and nephew. I stand back ready to capture the reunion I've dreamt of for the past 11 years but am unfamiliar with Redwan's camera and botch it. I stuff the camera into my bag.

As brothers, involuntarily separated for 35 years by religious persecution, embrace, I watch. Sarmad is crying. When they pull apart Sarmad turns to hug Nur. Redwan wraps his arms around Nibras. Then it is my turn to greet the travellers. Any shyness I might have felt melts into ease. Hugging Sarmad is as comforting as hugging a giant teddy bear. Nibras, whose name means "lamp" or "light," is handsome, soft spoken and quiet, but alert.

We follow Nur out of the terminal into the dark evening. As Nibras and I trail behind Redwan and Sarmad, I notice the sweetest thing: my husband is holding hands with his brother. Now there, I think, is a captivating window into Iraqi culture I hadn't anticipated; men, for whom it is not taboo to show love and affection in public. Never in a million years would that happen in my culture. Redwan tells me later that his heart stopped when he first caught sight of Sarmad for it was as if he was looking at his father in his later years; certainly he did not look like the Sarmad he remembered. "When our hands touched," he said, "it brought back memories of holding hands with my dad. Both had unusually soft hands."

I chat with Nibras in the car en route to a restaurant. He recently graduated from medical school. His wife, Hoda, is expecting their first child. Nibras explains that his family always told him he looked exactly like his uncle, Redwan. In fact, he does, based on photographs I've seen of Redwan as a young man. If Nibras fails to see himself in his 60-year old uncle he politely refrains from comment.

In a vast upscale roadside restaurant Nur orders a multiple course supper of mostly unfamiliar but delicious dishes. We learn that until the day before Sarmad and Nibras didn't know if they would make it to Turkey because their travel agent had called to say their reservations had fallen through. Their seats were swiftly restored, however, after Sarmad's friend, a man that happened to have booked 12 seats on an international flight the following week, threatened to cancel that reservation if Sarmad and Nibras' seats weren't reinstated.

### Reflection

The next day Sam and Marianne arrive from the UK. Their uncle greets them in tears in the hotel room he shares with Nibras. Then Sarmad props himself up on one of the beds and elevates his chronically aching feet. We gather around as he and Nibras distribute gifts they brought from Baghdad. Presents include a Bahá'í ring for Sam, a Bahá'í symbol that Nibras painted in black on tan coloured paper with the edges burned to make it look antique, a bright pink children's wallet, some prayer beads and a leather pillow cover.

Over the next five days we soak up each other's company visiting constantly as we take in the local sites including the old Sultanahmet district. There, in the massive Grand Bazar Sam purchases an engagement ring for Amy at half the price of a similar ring he'd set his heart on in London. For her part, Marianne surreptitiously texts a certain drummer in Stornoway.

Nibras quietly looks out for me as we accompany each other on errands in this unfamiliar city. When I ask about his work he says, "I'm not sure how I can explain it so that you will understand." He knows I come from another world and tries to frame things so I can grasp them. I come to think of Nibras and his dad as angels. Redwan agrees. For him, despite all of their years apart, being with his brother feels like reconnecting with his twin. "We are the same," he explains to me. "It just feels right and normal to be with him again." Our time together is an enveloping peaceful interlude.

Despite the fact that we're staying in a hotel, Nur manages to host us like royalty. We enjoy a wonderful lunch at his home where we meet Samra and Nil. They present us with beautifully wrapped gifts. For me, a necklace and red and black patterned scarf. For Redwan, a smart shirt and tie. We dine on November 10, Sam's 30th birthday, at Nur's mother and sister's apartment, along with a host of their relatives. Somehow we manage to buy a chocolate cake and sneak it in as a surprise for Sam.

On our second last day in Turkey, Nur rents a van and takes us to

Edirne, formerly Adrianople. This is a pilgrimage site for Bahá'ís, and one I never dreamed I would be able to visit. Bahá'u'lláh was incarcerated there as part of a series of exiles by the Persian and Ottoman Empires. From Edirne, in 1867, and continuing after His exile to Akká [Acre, modern 'Akó], in what is now Israel, Bahá'u'lláh wrote to the kings and rulers of the time. In those letters He proclaimed His station as a Manifestation of God, urged those rulers to pursue social justice and disarmament, and to band together to form a commonwealth of nations. He also warned them of the dire consequences facing them if they failed to establish peace.

Nur conducts our tour to the mosque where Bahá'u'lláh prayed and the house where He lived. In the back garden the custodians treat us to honey-soaked sweets and tea. I wander around the garden aware of the fact that, unlike the rest of us, Sarmad and Nibras have never had the freedom of movement to visit that Bahá'í World Centre in Haifa despite their proximity. This afternoon in Edirne is their first and only pilgrimage to holy places associated with Bahá'u'lláh outside of Iraq.

In a heartbeat our five days are up. Sam, Marianne, Redwan and I depart for Israel on the pilgrimage we booked from Australia in 2005 before we knew Redwan had cancer. As that destination had provided spiritual and emotional solace after his mother's death, once again, the Bahá'í World Centre buffered another separation, this time from Sarmad and Nibras. Had our destination been anywhere else, leaving our freshly discovered relatives, two men so pure-hearted the thought of them could make me weep; Sarmad with his endearing fluent but broken English and his tender heart and lovely (his favourite word) sense of humour; and Nibras, a bright, sincere and thoughtful soul, would have been unbearable. It was also a great comfort to leave them in the loving care of Nurullah and his family for their final day in Istanbul.

Once in Bahji, Israel, as I lay my head on the crimson petals on that sacred threshold in the Shrine of Bahá'u'lláh, I recall the words I heard in my head a decade earlier admonishing me to pray to become worthy of my association with Redwan's family, and I realize that the circle is complete. God willing, my humble efforts to learn about his family constitute something like a prayer.

I no longer harbour any doubt that there has been a master plan all along. I believe it began with Kaykhosrow's encounter with that thief in the night. Then another thief, cancer, threatened to rob Redwan of his life but it also impelled an unexpected and poignant reunion with Sharaf and Aqeel hours before the mammoth surgery that could have marked the end of Redwan's normal cognitive abilities.

I raise my head and inhale the fragrance of the roses arranged on that hallowed altar at Bahá'u'lláh's resting place. A nearby nightingale warbles its melody. My heart fills to overflowing with gratitude as these words from Bahá'u'lláh come to mind:

> ...Lo, the Nightingale of Paradise singeth upon the twigs of the Tree of Eternity, with holy and sweet melodies, proclaiming to the sincere ones the glad tidings of the nearness of God...[2]

I thank God for bringing those "sweet melodies" to my attention and enabling me to find the faith I'd longed for when I was young. I thank God for giving me the sacred trust of my children, for filling my life with meaning and purpose, and for leading me to Redwan and his children, and ultimately to his family in Baghdad, so long forbidden us.

As I bring my puny efforts to learn about Redwan's family history in the Bahá'í Faith to a close, I remain profoundly grateful for the impetus that set me on this path of learning and sharing. Though unworthy, I sincerely hope to meet Redwan's family in the mysterious spiritual realms beyond. Should I be granted that honour, the first thing I'll ask my father-in-law is if he planted that story about his encounter with the robber in my mind in order to guide me to his son, and if so, why; just curious.

To my family in Baghdad, robbed of religious freedom for generations, surely Bahá'u'lláh revealed this prayer for people like you:

---

2       Bahá'u'lláh, "The Tablet of Ahmad," in *Bahá'í Prayers* (Wilmette, Illinois: United States Bahá'í Publishing Trust, 1991), 208.

Methinks, the lamp of Thy love is burning in their hearts, and the light of Thy tenderness is lit within their breasts. Adversities are incapable of estranging them from Thy Cause, and the vicissitudes of fortune can never cause them to stray from Thy pleasure.

I beseech Thee, O my God, by them and by thy sighs which their hearts utter in their separation from Thee, to keep them safe from the mischief of Thine adversaries, and to nourish their souls with what Thou has ordained for Thy loved ones on whom shall come no fear and who shall not be put to grief. [3]

---

3        Bahá'u'lláh, Prayers and Meditations by Bahá'u'lláh (Wilmette, Illinois: United States Bahá'í Publishing Trust, 1987), 3.

# Epilogue

**Printed in the *Winnipeg Free Press* and the *Globe and Mail***

With grieved hearts we announce the passing of our dearly loved Redwan (Ridvan) Moqbel on 9 October 2013 in Winnipeg after a protracted battle with cancer.

Born in a border town on the Iraq/Iran border (14 August 1947), Redwan's family history is linked with the earliest days of the Bahá'í Faith. Redwan served the Bahá'í community in the UK and Canada in volunteer capacities, including as a member of the national governing council of the Bahá'í community of the United Kingdom for 13 years.

Redwan was a speaker of rare eloquence, clarity and depth whose spiritual beliefs were firmly anchored in Bahá'u'lláh's writings and whose abundant humour was never at the expense of others. His life long focus was on creating unity. He loved everyone but particularly youth whom he mentored on three continents. In confirmation of his efforts, Redwan received the Lieutenant Governor of Manitoba's Award for the Advancement of Interreligous Understanding in January 2013.

In 1976, Redwan obtained his PhD at the University of London, UK (LSH & TM). He became a faculty member there at the National Heart and Lung Institute in 1980. He was among the first to identify the immunological cell types that regulate asthma and allergy.

Recruited to the Department of Medicine, University of Alberta as a Professor in 1995, he served as the Director of the Pulmonary Research Group. There he received such prestigious awards as Alberta Heritage Medical Senior Scholar, Heritage Scientist and Heritage Senior Investigator.

In 2008, Redwan became Professor and Head of the Department of

Immunology at the University of Manitoba, and Professor Emeritus at the University of Alberta. He was well recognized for his mentorship of young biomedical scientists, whom he encouraged to adopt "a noble goal."

An international authority on the immuno molecular basis of asthmatic inflammation, in particular the role of eosinophils, Redwan's research garnered him numerous distinctions and awards. The International Eosinophil Society, of which he was a founding member, awarded him their highest honour, The Paul Ehrlich Award, named a mentoring award after him, and further honoured him with the prestigious Service Award in recognition of his "cardinal leadership" and innovative research.

A recent example of his work as a champion reconciler was in March 2012 in his role in organizing a scientific conference in which protagonists in the controversy over Lyme Disease came together in an atmosphere of mutual respect.

Aggressive treatment for sinus cancer in 2006 resulted in a cure for Redwan, but from 2009 he suffered recurrences with metastatic lung and chest wall cancer. He accepted his ordeals with gratitude, grace and fortitude.

Left to cherish his memory are his wife, Shar Mitchell, Redwan's son, Sam Moqbel, (Amy and grandsons, Thomas and Evan), Redwan's daughter, Marianne Greenhowe, (Gordon and grandson, Oliver), Shar's father, Jack Mitchell, Shar's children, Gabriel Lenz, (Erica Carlisle), Colby Lenz, Asher Lenz, (Emily Dragoman), Redwan's brother, Sarmad, his sister, Sharaf, their families in Iraq, and hundreds of friends worldwide.

∾

The summer before Redwan died he made me promise to go to Hawaii with a friend for a month, "after all was said and done." As challenging as that directive turned out to be in the wake of his death, and the ensuing avalanche of paperwork, there Karen McKye and I sat enjoying coffee and fresh papaya on the patio of a condo in Maui. Seventeen years previous, she had held my hand as I took the scary plunge into my second marriage. Now, once again, she was holding my hand, this time as I mourned Redwan's death.

Karen, a poet at heart, sensitive and acutely insightful, began to read me a passage from a book I'd never heard of, *The Great Divorce* by C.S. Lewis.[1] The selection centered on a conversation between a gatekeeper and a man seeking admittance into heaven. The man had a lizard on his shoulder that represented an addiction. Although often annoyed by that lizard, the man found comfort in its familiarity. Despite his persistent begging, the gatekeeper insisted he get rid of it. The moment the man gave up the lizard it transformed into a magnificent white stallion upon which he rode into heaven.

As I listened to Karen, heartbreaking images of Redwan's physical demise rose before my eyes but like a gigantic wave that story washed them away. Instead, a fine white steed appeared in my mind's eye and carried my beloved away, trouble and pain free. My relief was profound. His suffering had not been in vain.

Karen had more to offer by way of "bibliotherapy." Online she managed to find her favourite, if obscure, movie, "Off the Map." It centres around twelve-year-old Bo who lives with her eccentric parents in a remote area of New Mexico. She puzzles over what the edge of the world looks like. She asks an IRS agent who tracks down her tax delinquent parents, to paint it for her. He produces a 41-foot masterpiece that depicts the ocean, the horizon and the sky. In the last scene in the film, Bo, now an adult, says she has come to think of the ocean as the past, the horizon as the present and the sky as the future.

Seated there in Hawaii in front of the computer screen, my eyes filled with tears because I realized that nestled in the narrow band of the horizon between the ocean that represented "the known," my life with Redwan, and the sky, my unknown future, I was safe and secure. I needn't fear what lay ahead. When I was ready it would be waiting.

∾

It is almost a year since Redwan died. In a recent coaching session, Dr. Jen Sulymka reminded me of Joseph Campbell's *The Hero's Journey*.[2] As I thought about it, I realized that Redwan's journey was exactly that: a

---

1    C. S. Lewis, *The Great Divorce* (London: Geoffrey Bles, 1945).
2    Joseph Campbell, *The Hero's Journey: Joseph Campbell on His Life and Work*. Edited by Phil Cousineau. New York: Harper & Row, 1990.

hero's journey. From his humble beginnings in a dusty little town on the Iraq/ Iran border he fought this way through 67 years of personal challenges and disappointments, frequently caused by the lack of love he witnessed around him, to becoming a renowned medical scientist and a deeply caring person with hundreds and hundreds of friends who sincerely loved him. His two regrets were having to leave his family and not writing a book on the harmony of science and religion and the role of inspiration. Months before his death, Karen eased his sadness over the latter by reminding him that, according to the teachings of the Bahá'í Faith, from the next world, souls such as his are the inspiration behind advances in the sciences and the arts.

Redwan spent his last 172 days in the palliative unit at Riverview Health Centre in Winnipeg. Once again, Karen happened to be visiting from Toronto at the critical juncture when I was forced to make the painful decision to abort Redwan's palliative home care. Her support through that trauma was vital to me as was that of my step-children, Sam and Marianne from the UK.

Colby, my daughter, returned to Winnipeg the same day Karen departed. I lost track of the number of times Colby came to our rescue. She said she was a stand in for Sam and Marianne who spent as much time as they could with us given their young families and busy lives, as did my boys and their wives. From his little room in a Winnipeg nursing home, where he has lived for 12 years, my 93-year-old dad dedicated his pension money to Colby's travel to Winnipeg and to paying her enormous medical bills. He says he is grateful he was wounded in the war because it has meant he could be generous with others and he is!

In the years since we moved to Winnipeg, Colby had suffered the impact of late-stage persistent Lyme Disease. She endured three years bedridden with debilitating pain. Her suffering, and her loving and supportive nature, rendered her an ideal companion for Redwan. Not only did they adore each other but they "got" each other's suffering.

Colby spent so much time with us that staff at Riverview were shocked to learn she actually lived in California. During that transitional time, when Colby couldn't be with me, she ensured someone else was. She couldn't bear the thought of me returning alone to an empty home late at night.

Grieving is said to have several stages. I believe Redwan and I worked through each of them as they came up. By July 2013 we arrived at the last one, acceptance. By that point, one by one Redwan had sewn all the seams in the spectacular virtual robe that represented his life's work. Now his robe was complete. He was ready to go and we both knew it, but it was a long and exhausting journey to October 9 for us, even with the phenomenal support we had.

Each day I woke Redwan up about noon and stayed with him until the drugs knocked him out at night. If I had to leave to visit my dad, or go to a medical appointment, one of several friends came to sit with him. I hated to leave Redwan at night, but as a light sleeper I knew if I was going to support him to the end I needed to go home to bed. On the 170th day it was clear that Redwan was approaching the end. I couldn't bear to leave him for fear that he wouldn't have sufficient pain coverage, so I slept in his room.

The night before Redwan died our dear young friends Anis Sabet and Natasha Mohebi came to say prayers with us. Redwan was barely conscious but when I told him they were there to say some prayers he smiled his last smile. Early the next morning, from my mat on the floor beside his bed, I heard him cough quietly once. I thought, if he coughs again I'll get up and check on him as I had the night before. But Redwan didn't cough again and I fell asleep. About an hour later the night nurse came in and told me he'd gone. I wish he'd died in my arms but physical contact was painful for him. Redwan knew I loved him and he knew I was there. I take comfort from that as well as from knowing that to the best of my ability I danced him to the edge of death. He took the final steps on his own.

After Redwan died, my father, who had been an amazing cheerleader for both of us said, "Well, there will be some relief but it is a hell of a loss."

He was right on both counts. Part of me was hugely relieved for I was worn out, exhausted, stressed to the max and badly shaken. In short: I was a wreck. My doctor, Brian Sharkey, who provided wise counsel to me throughout this ordeal, told me it would have been impossible for me not to sustain some physical impact. But I am on the mend now; my body is healing. Although the baby and ring fingers of my left hand still tremor (which is symbolically interesting now that I think of it), especially when I am nervous, I have more range of movement in my shoulders, which took the brunt of six months of pulling Redwan into a sitting position. Pins and needles still run in rivers up and down my neck and shoulders but maybe slightly less often. My memory is somewhat better despite often sleeping poorly and my blood pressure has returned to normal.

Emotionally, I am much less fragile and less easily overwhelmed. At the outset of the year I couldn't take too much activity or too much talking. Finding the balance between too little and too much company was a daily challenge. Even walking and talking with friends was too much so Dr. Sharkey encouraged me to walk alone. I found comfort in my nightly solo walks until the dead of winter deterred me. One night I returned home with a gift: I remembered that I had adjusted to living alone after my first marriage broke up so many years before. That realization gave me hope that over time I could do so again.

As my dad said, losing Redwan was a massive loss for all of us who loved him. I found comfort, and still do, in a photograph of him that friends selected, cropped, blew up, framed and ultimately delivered to me after his memorial. I hung it on the wall at the foot of my bed. Suddenly I could talk to my dearly beloved in a way I hadn't been able to since he died. I started to greet him each morning and review my day with him each evening. I keep tabs on his help during the day and thank him. No matter what I say he smiles at me with love and acceptance. I believe that picture reflects his present happiness in the spiritual realms because I understand that realm is all about love, which was always paramount to him in all his relationships no matter how incidental. I've come to believe that whatever makes me happy here on earth makes him happy there.

Sometimes when I came home during the first few months after Redwan's death our apartment felt so empty that I would call out, "Hey Honey, I'm home." I just needed to say those words out loud to feel somewhat normal. And it has taken months to allow myself to sit down in the living room. For two years I almost never went in there. There was no time to sit down, not an extra second.

After Redwan's passing I would rail when people asked me if I was lonely. I thought, I could fill up every waking moment of my life or get a dog but what would the point be? Had our relationship been only so I wouldn't be lonely? Even though I knew their question came from a place of love and concern it confounded and irritated me. Then on July 11th (remember my July 11th sandwich? July 11, 2006 marked our return from sabbatical in Australia and the beginning of one year of treatment and recovery from sinus cancer for Redwan) I had a dream that reminded me how wonderful a safe, happy and committed relationship can be. I finally got it: yes, I am lonely for a true partner. A true partner is a gift from God and Redwan surely was a true partner. In addition to all he was for me, he was a committed father to my children and a devoted son to my parents.

Early spring brought with it sad memories of Redwan's hospitalization. Those depressing thoughts didn't linger but I still find it challenging to approach the neighbourhood of that hospital.

Redwan always worried that I didn't cry enough. The truth is I hate crying, as much as I hate vomiting, and try to avoid both although lately I have cried more. Redwan would be pleased, not that I am unhappy but that I am more in touch with my feelings.

For the first 10 months after Redwan's death I avoided listening to music. Instead, while driving I sought emotional relief by escaping into talking books. Of late, however, I mostly prefer to sing along to my favourite songs, not well but with gusto. 'Abdu'l-Bahá described music as a ladder for the soul and that's exactly how it feels. I am reclaiming joy and that feels wonderful.

I consider myself the most fortunate person in the world to have such a wealth of wonderful family and friends, and of course, the teachings of my faith to help me deal with Redwan's death. I believe my healing process was hastened by the fact that there was no element of betrayal involved. Redwan didn't choose to have cancer and die.

In late spring I was perplexed as to why family and friends seemed to seldom talk about Redwan. I mentioned this to my daughter-in-law, Emily. "Have you told people that you want them to talk about him?" she asked. "Maybe they aren't saying anything because they don't want to upset you." She was right. So, I asked a few people what they liked about Redwan. Their comments felt something like manna for my soul. Here is an eloquent and insightful response from a new and wonderfully insightful friend, Denise Ommanney:

> What did I like about Redwan you ask?
>
> For starters, I would say that Redwan lifted me up. He was high minded and large of spirit and in his company, I found myself challenged to consider big, complex questions. He was awake to the problems in the world but seemed to have optimism about humanity's capacity and desire for improvement. He spoke from a lofty moral and intellectual plane but without a trace of conceit or condescension.
>
> And he had a gift for intimacy, for connection. The way he would hold eye contact, so attentive and interested. The twinkle in his eye revealed a gentle humour and a benign disposition to human frailties and imperfections. He was loveable and loving.

Another dear friend, Kathie Neufeld said,

> I liked Redwan's humour. You had to go to the bathroom one day when I was visiting at the hospital and said you'd

be back soon. Redwan replied, "Well, considering the situation, you'd better not be too long!"

You were the tightest couple I'd ever seen. He depended upon you totally.

∽

I miss being able to share details of my life with my husband. Apart from my dad, who else would have the time to listen? I also miss not being able to turn to Redwan for advice, especially when I am anxious or fearful. His life experience and sensibilities rendered him a brilliant in-house consultant.

In a recent therapy session I had a vision of our union as a tree that produced a juicy purple plum, a metaphor for the fruit of our marriage. I don't want to give the impression that our marriage was perfect. What would we have learned had it been so? But our love and commitment to our union was solid as was Redwan's unfailing responsiveness to me. Without responsiveness there is nothing to work with. Remember Glory, the virtual baby that represented our marriage? We were determined to keep Glory alive and thriving. We consulted about everything but when we hit an impasse, rather than allow resentment to build up and issues to go unresolved, we marched ourselves into a therapist and submitted to a sound pruning. I will always admire Redwan for the courage it took to be so emotionally honest.

Kathie was right. We were a tight team. I was the stage manager and Redwan was the show, and what a magnificent show he was. It was my great honour to have been his partner on this earthly plane for 17 years. I gained from him insights into Iraqi and Persian culture. By his example I learned so much about living a life of faith, reverence and complete trust in God. Especially as his days were drawing to a close Redwan would say, "We have to trust in God one hundred percent; it can't be 99 percent." He surrendered to his Maker, albeit sometimes with a tinge of sadness but, as was the case with his father before him, never with complaint.

∽

Recently, I came upon Redwan's spiritual will and testament. As a Bahá'í he considered this non-material aspect of his will the most important one. He wrote one by hand before his major surgery in 2006. I recalled a day in the winter of 2013 when Redwan was well enough for me to leave him in bed for a few hours while I ran some errands. When I returned he was delighted to report he'd finished updating his will and testament. Other than asking him if he'd like me to type it, to which he responded, "No, that's not necessary. It is done," I hadn't thought about it much again. When I finally pulled the notebook out of his drawer it opened to a section he'd written about Colby. Tears sprang to my eyes as I read his words of love and admiration for her. As I flipped through the pages I was shocked by how much he'd written. In addition to testifying to his faith, he lavished love and praise on each family member, especially our five children and grandchildren. I've included brief excerpts below that speak to his faith, his thoughts about me, and his family in Iraq because, as Dr. Jen said, during my Skype session with her minutes after finding this epistle, "It shows the quality of man he was, his strength, courage, love and vulnerability and what he must have been through that he could say those things so freely and articulately."

> Before all else I bow my head, temple and countenance before the eternal Face of my Lord, the Incomparable, the Mighty, the Loving. I confess at this time to my utter and complete nothingness before the splendor of His infinite and glorious creation. All have emerged from Him and all will return unto Him.
>
> Beloved Lord, please accept my ardent love and most sincere expression of gratitude for permitting the consortship and marriage to Shar Mitchell, my dearly loved, adorable and uniquely spiritually equipped partner and wife. My life has been so enriched by her kind, pure and radiant heart, which she possesses, rendering everything that she does, all for the sake of others and for the love of God.

To my family back in Iraq, that remarkable congrega-
tion of souls every minute of whose lives are examples of sacrifice, love and trust in God. I love you and pride myself in being
permitted to belong to such an illustrious and remarkable family.
May Bahá'u'lláh, through His loving grace and bounty, allow
me to consort with you forever more…
    Signed: R Moqbel
    Edmonton, Aug. 11 2006

**—Written in the City of Winnipeg, MB, February 2013**

In the name of God, the Most Loving, the Compassionate, the Ever Bounteous, the Omnipotent!…

The last six and a half years have been a most precious
gift and bounty from my beloved Lord. Undeserved and unworthy as I am, He, through His potent decree bestowed health
and a few tests to this servant to remind him that our beloved
Lord would not cause anything to befall us except to allow us
chances of growth, refinement and certitude. "I swear by My
Name! Nothing save that which profiteth them, can befall my
loved ones."…

These tests and physical challenges are His candy and
reward for what He sees to fit the souls of His Creation. Whatever He ordaineth, that is my beloved. I am grateful for all of the
pain, difficulty in breathing and the effect of the poisonous chemotherapy, as they have given me an infinitesimal glimpse of the
suffering of the Lord of the Age, the Blessed Beauty, as He was
afflicted by the ungodly with the most excruciating pain and suffering, whether when He was burdened with the heaviest chains
around His blessed neck, whether the pain and suffering of the
travel and exile over the harsh and inhospitable terrains sepa-
rating His land of birth from the land where He declared His
Mission, or the pain and suffering of His days in the mountains

of Kurdistan, in Sargalu and Sulaymaniyeh, or the cruel and wicked deeds of His unfaithful half brother in Edirné, including the effect of the poisoning of that Divine Being's physical and blessed body, the tortuous and difficult sea journey towards His Divine Destiny to fulfill all the prophecies, arriving in the Holy Land as an exile and a prisoner, to outward eyes, when He arrived with Divine Sovereignty and Lordship. I can't even assume that the pains I experience are anything but a flimsy scratch on the surface of what He suffered. I am elated and ecstatic to experience a drop of that pain...

I guess my vocabulary will find the appropriate words to express my gratitude to the Lord of Hosts for having blessed my life and my path since 1996 with my angel and saint, my lover and beloved, my wife and partner, my rock and pillar of support in this world (and I look forward to that gift of reunion we are promised) in all the worlds of God. My love for you, Shar cannot be described by words and my complete and total appreciation of all, everything you have done, do and will do as I prepare to exit from this material world and transition to where God has destined for my soul. Wherever that may be, my love in my inner core of my being will seek you out to rejoice in your companionship, perhaps dressed in Royal Robes forever and ever. I love you so much and beg you to forgive any shortcomings and failures I demonstrated while in this world. There is nothing in my heart but love for you. Until we meet again, I need to exercise patience. I love you.

∽

Such a uniquely wonderful man was my bridegroom from Baghdad.

Now sometimes sad, sometimes lonely and sometimes scared, but with a heart filled with love and gratitude, I prepare to venture into that far-reaching sky; my unknown future with the reassurance from my beloved that he will always be with me.

# Moqbel-Wakil-Mitchell Timeline

**1853-1863**  At an unknown date, Mirza Mohammad Wakil (also known as Vakil), a Bábí, becomes a Bahá'í, and is exiled to Mosul twice.

**1869**  Zarbanoo is born to Khosrow Mehraban and an unknown mother.

**1870's**  Zarbanoo's father, Khosrow Mehraban, sends greetings to Bahá'u'lláh through his friend, Manoki Sahib, and receives a Tablet from Bahá'u'lláh in response.

**1881-2**  Zarbanoo, while living in Amiriyeh district, learns about the Bahá'í Faith from a neighbour her age. Thereafter, she secretly listens in on Mirza Abu'l-Fadl's talks, sometimes from a rooftop or tree.

Zarbanoo and husband Khoda Morad's children include: son Gooshtasb; daughter Sarvar (died of illness aged 6-7), daughter Golbanu (died of poisoning), youngest daughter Homayoon was severely burned at age 7 while playing with candles and died before she could be taken to the hospital.

**1906**  Fereidun Moqbel born to Zarbanoo and Khoda Morad.

**1909**  Khaykhosrow Moqbel born to Zarbanoo and Khoda Morad (date according to Hand of the Cause Mr. Faizi in *Bahá'í World* vol. 15).

**c. 1916**  Golbanu born to Zarbanoo and Khoda Morad.

**1917**  Hajer Wakil born to Melka Shoja'a and Husayn Wakil, Persians originally from Isfahan. They had 4 daughters: Shoughia, Munira, Munawar and Hajer; and 2 sons: Shoghi and Munir.

**1920's**  King Faisal I gives Bahá'u'lláh's house in Baghdad to the government.

**c. 1922** Zarbanoo declares her faith in Bahá'u'lláh after studying the Faith for two years with travelling teacher, Fereidun Khoosh-nu-Din.

**1932** November 11. Son Iradj is born to Golbanu and her husband Farrokh Tehrani.

**1933** Son Hooshmand born to Fereidun and Gohar Moghbelin.

**1937** Farahmand Moghbelin born at home on Vestahel Lane off Moiriye Street in Tehran.

**1940** Golbanu dies at the age of 21 or 22. According to Sharaf Moqbel, who has a clear memory of her father, Kaykhosrow Moqbel telling her this, she was poisoned by a neighbour who opposed her faith. However, Sharaf's cousin, Farahand Moghbelin, believes that she died of malaria. Golbanu's husband, Farrokh Tehrani sends their 7 or 8 year old son, Iradj Farrokh Tehrani, to a French boarding school in Tehran.

**1940-1941** Kaykhosrow Moqbel lives with his brother Fereidun's family for 8 months at their home on Vestahel Lane off Moiriye Street in Tehran. During his stay, while the Moghbelins are away in Bahman Abad so that Farahmand can recuperate from whooping cough, he has an encounter with a robber.

**1942** Kaykhosrow Moqbel; Fereidun, Gohar, Faramand and Houshmand Moghbelin; Masih Faranghi, his wife, daughter, Feri and another child; plus Mr. Faizi, pioneer to Kirkuk.

**1943** The above band of pioneers forced to leave Kirkuk.

**1944** January. Kaykhosrow Moqbel and Hajer Wakil marry in Baghdad and move to Khanagin.

November 23. Sharaf Moqbel born in Khanagin.

**1947** August 14. Redwan (Rithwan, Ridvan) Moqbel born in Khanagin.

**1948** December 31. Shar (Sharon Gail Mitchell) born in Edmonton at Royal Alexandra Hospital to Donna Catherine Mitchell (née Morrison) and John Mitchell.

**1950** Sharaf, Redwan, and Hajer visit family in Iran.

**1952** March 9. Sarmad Moqbel born in Khanagin.

**1953** July. Hajer Wakil, Khaykhosrow Moqbel, and their three children move back to Baghdad.

Munir Wakil becomes Knight of Bahá'u'lláh for Kura Muria Islands after Asian Intercontinental Teaching Conference in New Delhi.

**1954-1964** Shar Mitchell attends Sir John Franklin and J. B. Mitchell public schools in Winnipeg.

**1955** Melka Wakil (Hajer's mother) dies in Baghdad

**1956** Munir Wakil, his wife, Bahiya, his sisters, Munira, Shoughia, and Munawar, with their daughter, Ikbal, pioneer to the Seychelles.

**1962** Munir Wakil and family return from the Seychelles having established a Bahá'í community as well as a Bahá'í Centre there.

**1963** Munir Wakil elected to the National Spiritual Assembly of the Bahá'ís of Iraq.

**1964** Munir Wakil suffers a cardiac infarction.

**1964** Shar Mitchell is confirmed at Westworth United Church in Winnipeg.

**1967** Shar graduates from Kelvin High School. Enters nursing at Misericordia Hospital in Winnipeg.

**1969** January.  Farahmand Moghbelin visits Kaykhosrow Moqbel and family i⃞ Baghdad en route to London, England.

April 15. 2:35 a.m. Kaykhosrow Moqbel dies at home from adenocarcinom⃞ of the lung.

**1970** Bill 105 outlaws all Bahá'í activities in Iraq.

**1970** January.  Shar Graduates as a registered nurse.

Works as a nurse at Sherritt Gorden Mines in Lynn Lake, Manitoba.

**1971** January.  Shar sails on the SS *Columbo* to Malaga, Spain and travels through Europe. Works in Chelmsford, England for the last two months.

August.  Shar returns to Canada via a charter flight from Stanstead Airport, England.

September.  Redwan Moqbel leaves Iraq to pursue his MSc at the London School of Hygiene and Tropical Medicine in London, England.

**1972** March 26.  Shar becomes a Bahá'í in Cornerbrook, Newfoundland.

Shar attends Bahá'i National Convention in Edmonton and meets Jack Lenz.

November.  Redwan Moqbel returns to Baghdad to attend his sister Sharaf's wedding to Aqeel Wahid on 6 November.

Zarbanoo dies at the age of 105 in Iran. Redwan only met her once when he was three years old.

November.  Redwan escapes from Iraq.

**1973** April. Redwan marries Ann MacLeod (née MacLeod) in London, England.

June 16. Shar and Jack Lenz marry.

December. Hajer Wakil taken to the Security Police Office for questioning and is released on bail the same day.

Munir Wakil suffers from a CVA and becomes bedridden with hemiplegia.

**1974** February 25. Hajer Wakil and Ikbal Wakil taken into custody after their first day of trial and retained there until their final court hearing.

April 24. Hajer Wakil and Ikbal Wakil are charged with breach of Law 105 along with nine other women and fifteen men and are transferred to Abu Ghraib Prison.

Redwan Moqbel charged with breaching Law 105 that came into effect in 1970 and is sentenced to life imprisonment in absentia by the Government of Iraq.

**1976** February 2. Munir Wakil dies in Baghdad.

**1975** January 21. Gabriel Salman Lenz born in Granada Hills, California.

**1976** October 24. Colby Roxanna Lenz born at Mount Sinai Hospital in Toronto, Ontario.

**1977** Feridoon Moghbelin, who was suffering from dementia, dies in Tehran at the age of 84.

November 10. Samim Alastair Munir Moqbel born to Ann MacLeod Moqbel and Redwan Moqbel at Queen Mother's Hospital in Glasgow.

**1978** March 2. Asher John Lenz born at North York General Hospital in North York, Ontario.

**1979** August 19. Hajer Wakil and other Bahá'ís and remaining living Bahá'ís (two died in prison) are released from prison.

Iradj Farrokh Tehrani moves to Germany. He and his wife, Maheendokht, have two daughters and in time two grandsons and four granddaughters.

**1980** July to August 5. Hajer Wakil travels from Baghdad to Scotland to visit her son Redwan Moqbel, his wife Ann, and their son Samim.

26 August. Marianne Hajer Moqbel is born to Ann and Redwan Moqbel at Queen Mother's Hospital in Glasgow.

**1992** December. Shar and Jack divorce.

**1996** April 26. Redwan and Shar meet at Bahá'í National Convention in Toronto.

November 9. Shar and Redwan marry outside of Edmonton, Alberta.

**1998** September. Redwan, Shar, and Marianne visit Bahá'í World Centre in Haifa, Israel.

**2001** January 1. Hajer Wakil dies in her sleep of natural causes at her son Sarmad's home in Baghdad after having spent New Year's Eve with her family.

**2005-2006** Redwan and Shar travel back and forth to Australia three times.

July 11. Redwan and Shar return to Edmonton.

August 29. Redwan has 11½-hour surgery for sinus cancer.

**2007** November. Shar, Sam and Marianne meet Sarmad and Nibras in Istanbul, Turkey. Then Redwan, Shar, Sam and Marianne travel to Haifa for Bahá'í pilgrimage.

**2012** October. Redwan goes into palliative care at home.

**2013** April 20. Redwan hospitalized in Riverview Health Care Centre.

October 9. Redwan dies in Riverview Health Care Centre in Winnipeg.

# *Acknowledgements*

Before all else, I want to acknowledge my family in Iraq. I made a decision not to share any stories related to their present day Bahá'í activities, all of which are aimed at spiritualizing their society. That is their story when it is timely for them to tell it. But I'll give you a hint: in the wake of the US led invasion Sarmad said, "You know Shar, the Bahá'ís here are like ducks on a pond. You see them floating in the water but what you can't see is how fast their feet are paddling." I love and admire these people and am so grateful and proud to be counted as part of their family.

Born of an inner longing to get to know my new Iraqi family, *The Bridegroom from Baghdad* overwhelmed me for many years, whether I was actively working on it or not. Always there to encourage my every step was my daughter, Colby Lenz. Of course Redwan offered as much support and information as he could as did Sharaf, Sarmad and Ikbal from Iraq.

Early mentors at the Banff Centre for the Arts included the late Gloria Sawai, Eunice Scarfe and Dave Margoshes. Dave further mentored me through Sage Hill, in Saskatchewan. Thanks to an Anne Szumigalski Memorial Scholarship in 2010, again through Sage Hill, Ted Barris helped me reshape the first part of my manuscript.

My praise and gratitude goes to the small legion of family and friends who proofread all or parts of my manuscript. They include: Redwan Moqbel, Colby Lenz, Keith Bloodworth, Stephanie Bloodworth, my father Jack Mitchell, Norm Donogh, Sheila Pinkerton, Hamideh Towfigh, Sharni Ketter, Nancy Minden, Karen McKye, Nancy O'Brien, Meim Smith and my sister-inaw, Ann Mitchell. Thank you also to Melanie Tait and Murray Oliver for their ble assistance with word crafting. And much gratitude to Corinne Randall www.corinnerandall.co.uk) for her stunning cover art and Reza Mostmand mostmand.com) for his exceptional book cover design. Professional editorial assistance came from Rick Johnson of Final Copy and later Laura Burkhart. My son, Asher Lenz helped me whittle down the mountain of photographs had to choose from. To one and all, and anyone I may have neglected to mention, my profound gratitude.

Finally, in May 2014, my dear brother Gerry Mitchell issued me a challenge that worked so well it felt inspired, maybe by Redwan. If I agreed to finish this manuscript by December 13, 2014, Gerry would lose 20 kilos by the same date. We both succeeded. Thank you Gerry for lightening our loads.